Hawthorne's Shyness

Hawthorne's Shyness

Ethics, Politics, and the
Question of Engagement

Clark Davis

The Johns Hopkins University Press
Baltimore and London

© 2005 The Johns Hopkins University Press
All rights reserved. Published 2005
Printed in the United States of America on acid-free paper
9 8 7 6 5 4 3 2 1

The Johns Hopkins University Press
2715 North Charles Street
Baltimore, Maryland 21218-4363
www.press.jhu.edu

Library of Congress Cataloging-in-Publication Data
Davis, Clark.
    Hawthorne's shyness : ethics, politics, and the question of
engagement / Clark Davis.
        p. cm.
Includes bibliographical references and index.
    ISBN 0-8018-8098-x (hardcover : alk. paper)
    1. Hawthorne, Nathaniel, 1804–1864 — Ethics. 2. Hawthorne,
Nathaniel, 1804–1864 — Political and social views. 3. Hawthorne,
Nathaniel, 1804–1864 — Criticism and interpretation. 4. Politics and
literature — United States — History — 19th century. 5. Romanticism —
United States. 6. Ethics in literature. I. Title.
PS1892.E8D388 2005
813'.3 — dc22   2004019608

A catalog record for this book is available from the British Library.

Frontispiece: 1840 portrait of Nathaniel Hawthorne (1804–64), by
Charles Osgood. Photograph courtesy Peabody Essex Museum.

For Ethan
"a spell of infinite variety"

Contents

Acknowledgments

Hawthorne's Shyness was written at Northeast Louisiana University (now the University of Louisiana at Monroe) and the University of Denver. I wish to thank Gene Eller, Lea Olsan, Ed Brinson, Susan Eller, Mona Oliver, and John Smyth, all of whom took time from very busy teaching schedules to read philosophy and theory in a small study room in Sandel Library. Those meetings were crucial to the development of this work. At the University of Denver, Scott Howard read portions of the manuscript and offered his always careful and precise suggestions. Both institutions provided time and funding for research, the first through an endowed professorship from 1998 to 2000 and the second through a quarter's leave from teaching in the autumn of 2002. My thanks to John Smyth and Eric Gould for their support of those applications.

I owe a special gratitude to Kenneth Dauber, both for the inspiration of his work on Hawthorne and literary theory and for his consistent encouragement while this book was being written.

My deepest debt is to my family: my wife, Hillary, who remains the warmest, funniest, best person I know; and my son, Ethan, whose first seven years have coincided with the writing of this book. They have taught me more about love and responsibility, this study's true subjects, than I ever imagined possible.

Portions of this book have appeared in an earlier form: "Hawthorne's Shyness: Romance and the Forms of Truth," *ESQ: A Journal of the American Renaissance* 45, no. 1 (1999): 33–65; and "Facing the Veil: Hawthorne, Hooper, and Ethics," *Arizona Quarterly* 55, no. 4 (Winter 1999): 1–19. My thanks to the editors of these journals for permission to reprint this material.

Note to the Reader:

The following abbreviations are used in this book: *C*, Herman Melville, *Correspondence*, vol. 14, *The Writings of Herman Melville*, ed. Harrison Hayford, Herschel Parker, and G. Thomas Tanselle (Evanston, IL: Northwestern University Press;

Chicago: Newberry Library), 1993; *CE*, Nathaniel Hawthorne, *The Centenary Edition of the Works of Nathaniel Hawthorne*, ed. William Charvat, Roy Harvey Pearce, and Claude M. Simpson (Columbus: Ohio State University Press), 1962–. 23 vols.

Hawthorne's Shyness

The Whipple Daguerreotype, 1848

I don't much like pictures of that sort, — they are so hard and stern; besides dodging away from the eye, and trying to escape altogether. They are conscious of looking very unamiable, I suppose, and therefore hate to be seen.
— HAWTHORNE, *The House of the Seven Gables*

The fact should show that a strange repulsion — as well as a strong attraction — exists among human beings.
— HAWTHORNE, *The American Claimant Manuscripts*

If you have seen an image of Nathaniel Hawthorne, it is most likely the boyish beauty of the Osgood portrait (see frontispiece): the face, not merely fresh but serenely charged, elegantly featured, proportional, with a gaze both outward and inward. Notice the head, richly poised atop a mountain of cloak, the sable bow so large it seems a buttress for all: sensitive mouth, expanding brow, soft circumference of delicate hair. Its attractiveness is beyond dispute, though to readers of Hawthorne's fiction it can come to seem inadequate, even deceptive. Not that the young man was unhandsome, not that his blue eyes were less than blue. After all, we have Lawrence and his "blue-eyed Nathaniel," America's "darling," though even here (especially here) the blue eyes raise suspicions. What are they hiding? What are their secrets? We would not ask, of course, were it not for the fictions, the masks, were it not for the reluctant exposures, the shy man's games.

This is not the only portrait of Hawthorne. Rita K. Gollin's fascinating volume, *Portraits of Nathaniel Hawthorne: An Iconography*, records more than a hundred images made between 1825 and 1956: paintings, wood engravings, crayon drawings, etchings, pencil sketches, miniatures, daguerreotypes, busts, photographs, lithographs, line engravings, a photogravure, a statue, a white-line en-

Whipple daguerreotype, reversed, of Nathaniel Hawthorne. Library of Congress.

graving, and even a postage stamp. But the Osgood portrait is the most familiar, the face readers of the last half-century would be most likely to come across on a paperback collection of short stories or at the top of a Hawthorne Web site.

They would be less likely to encounter the only surviving daguerreotype of Hawthorne, made, it is thought, by John Adams Whipple in 1848. And for good reason: the Hawthornes disliked it. Sophia thought the paintings gave the "true likeness," and she apparently kept the Whipple image tucked away, lest the "haunted eye" and "protruding lip" give anyone the wrong impression.[1] The version Gollin prints is haunting enough in its damaged state: the eyes are gone mostly, except for recessive glints; the rest is mouth (horizontal, set), nose, and chin. The hair looms even wider, cloudlike, the forehead is exposed.

In the restored (and unreversed) version from the Peabody Essex Museum, the ghostly effect is gone, as though reabsorbed by the image itself, clearer now but no less recalcitrant. In both, there is a look, a disturbance in the eyes, in the fixity of the chin that bears no relationship to the Osgood face. Caught. This is the first thought, almost of surprise, despite the careful pose. He "had the look all

Whipple daguerreotype of Nathaniel Hawthorne, restored, not reversed. Courtesy Peabody Essex Museum.

the time, to one who didn't know him, of a rogue who suddenly finds himself in the company of detectives."[2] Thus Henry James, Sr. Of course, "rogue" may not be correct or palatable (certainly not to the Hawthorne family), but there is no denying the mixture of fear and defiance, of genuine dislike (distaste?) blended with the desire to be somewhere else, to vanish from his own attempt to present himself.

What else should we expect from the man who concerned himself with veils? And yet the image is more disturbing than that, more revealing too, fragmentary though it is. There is, of course, the phantom of the dark Nathaniel, a dream of sorts born in the dark-enough brain of Herman Melville. But the Whipple image speaks less of the heroic tragedian than it does of the resistant man. Whatever Hawthorne's preference for stories of secrecy, it is less the corrosiveness of guilt than the seriousness of personality that impresses here — a gravity over distance, over the self, and its boundaries and commitments, over the rights of the person to be seen or to see others, over human interaction. This may be nothing more than a sort of attention, but if so, it is a strikingly high level of attention, a visceral concentration born of a native shyness but matured into sustained inquiry.

No other picture so closely reflects the image of the fictional voice, of its style: meticulous, bourgeois, graceful yet malicious enough to look sharply, to hover between malice and an emerging, though ambiguous, smile. He is not so much "our Hawthorne" as his own — nervously fashioned, publicly private. We can approach him, of course, but only with the sort of caution caught in this glance, with the reserve that is more than simple reticence — more thoughtful and, in its way, systematic — but emotional all the same.

CHAPTER ONE

The Ethical Subject

We can therefore insist on good faith having priority over bad faith, good will over a will to power, only if we insist on an ethics of interpretation in which because authors are persons, they must be respected in the way persons in general must be respected.

— DASENBROCK, *Truth and Consequences*

For stories cultivate our ability to see and care for particulars, not as representatives of a law, but as what they themselves are: to respond vigorously with senses and emotions before the new; to care deeply about chance happenings in the world, rather than to fortify ourselves against them; to wait for the outcome, and to be bewildered — to wait and float and be actively passive.

— NUSSBAUM, *Love's Knowledge*

This in turn means, for me, defending the process of criticism, so far as criticism is thought of, as I think of it, as a natural extension of conversation.

— CAVELL, *Pursuits of Happiness*

In his memoir, *Writing Was Everything*, the late Alfred Kazin describes what he subsequently came to see as the formative moment in his life as a reader and critic:

My pivotal experience of the raw hurting power that a book could have over me came when I first read *Oliver Twist*. I was twelve years old, sick with a fever in my narrow little bedroom, and frightened of the book as soon as Oliver fell into the hands of Fagin and his gang. . . . There was nothing to look at from my bed but a thin strip of wall next to the window, which opened on a fire escape. I was so shaken and seized by *Oliver Twist* that even when I put the book down I could see it going on, figure by figure, line by line, on the wall itself. Confined as I felt by my narrow room, by my bed, by fever, I felt a strange if awful happiness. *Oliver Twist* was all around me and in me. I wanted never to get away from its effect. There was something in this I had to track down: why was Dickens compelled to write like that, and why did it work on me like a drug? Since that was the literary problem I represented to myself, I had to figure it out for myself. That was how I started as a critic.[1]

This may well be a bit of personal mythogenesis, but like all such foundational stories it has its purpose: to declare values, to state preferences. For Kazin the preference is for the personal, the unique connection between book and reader, reader and writer. It is, first of all, an *experience* and, second, an experience of strangeness — of a character and of the creator of that character as other beings, other minds. It is as though the young reader has seen a face and fallen for its beauty. Caught off guard, he is moved to question, to the analysis of two forces: the writer's need to write and the reader's obligation to respond. Everything else, all other reasons for criticism, Kazin implies, are secondary. Historical understanding, political analysis, philosophical or psychological extrapolation — all serve this one, overwhelming demand to understand why another person has written a book that has affected him so powerfully, so personally.

This declaration of purpose may seem odd coming from the author of *On Native Grounds*. Kazin made his reputation as a contextual critic interested in politics at a time when the prevailing critical approach was increasingly textual and apolitical. He distrusted the New Critics for their willful dissociation of all but the text and often prided himself on the rich social and political milieus he was able to conjure around the books he found compelling. But even as a politically attuned historicist he never lost his preference for the lone but impassioned reader:

> It is all rather funny in a way. I have lived through the Marxist thirties, when Proust was consigned to the dustbin of history; and the New Criticism forties and fifties, when hungry sheep looking up to be fed found no Donne-like tension, paradox, or ambiguity in poor simple Walt Whitman; and the angry sixties, when I heard that William Faulkner contributed nothing to the civil-rights struggle; and the unfocused seventies and eighties and nineties, when the tides of ideology washed over me without mercy. Living through all of this I have to say that, between racial-sexual-political partisanship and the devaluation of individual authorship by deconstructionists, criticism has become a threat to what my dear old teacher Mark Van Doren gallantly held up as the Private Reader.[2]

And what is the private reader, exactly? Kazin, to take him as an example, was the child of immigrants, "the first native son after so many generations of mudflat Russian Jews who never saw the United States."[3] He was in love with America as perhaps only a first-generation American could be, and his entire critical approach and output depended upon his status as "newly arrived" outsider. He was a part of a generation of American literature scholars who came from similar backgrounds and who exemplified the Jewish adoption of American ideas in the generations that followed immigration. So when he tells us in his published journals of his "passionate and even technical interest in images of the American past," of "the excitement [he gets] from 'Americana,' from Constance Rourke's saying, 'the poet of American nationality' — from the very names Cope, James, Peirce, Dickinson, and Roebling in Lewis Mumford's *The Brown Decades*," we can attribute his enthusiasm to his background, his environment, his cultural identity. We know where he comes from, and yet understanding the cultural sources of his work does not (and certainly should not) reduce the intensity of his interest or the potential validity of his insights. He speaks as an individual to individuals, to us, who may or may not be convinced by his contentions. Nevertheless, he assumes in us the decency to meet him as equals, to treat him like another human being, to listen and contend before we reach conclusions or pass judgment. He believes, in other words — and it is a belief — in responsibility. Though as interested in culture as any critic could be, Kazin begins with a faith in the writer's need to write, the critic's to respond, and in the burden of the choices each of us inevitably makes.

The Limits of "Ideology"

The contemporary world, scientific, technical, and sensualist, sees itself without exit — that is, without God — not because everything there is permitted and, by way of technology, possible, but because everything there is equal. The unknown is immediately made familiar and the new customary. Nothing is new under the sun. The crisis inscribed in Ecclesiastes is not found in sin but in boredom. Everything is absorbed, sucked down and walled up in the Same. The enchantment of sites, hyperbole of metaphysical concepts, the artifice of art, exaltation of ceremonies, the magic of solemnities — everywhere is suspected and denounced a theatrical apparatus, a purely rhetorical transcendence, the game. Vanity of vanities: the echo of our own voices, taken for a response to the few prayers that still remain to us; everywhere we have fallen back upon our own feet, as after the ecstasies of a drug. Except the other whom, in all this boredom, we cannot let go.

— LEVINAS, "Ideology and Idealism"

I invoke Alfred Kazin at the beginning of this book not only because I admire his passion but because his concern for the "Private Reader" — a phrase so quaintly historical and out of fashion that it startles — seems particularly appropriate at this moment in the history of criticism. It is not simply that we no longer believe in the personal as such; in fact, most of us do believe in it, if the shelves of major bookstores are any indication. But in an era sometimes designated as "post-human," the forces Kazin describes continue to argue that such categories as "personal," "private," "human," and "individual" cannot be used without an awareness of their ideological status. Kazin himself, in the mode typical of such criticism, seems to cry out for ideological placement — as a New Yorker, a Jew, the child of immigrants, as a product of the thirties and forties, of the radical Left, or of some other identifying context. His preference for the personal is to be ascribed to his infatuation with American individualism, an ideology with which he is complicit because of his background and his obvious liberalism. Kazin's ideas, in other words, cannot be strictly personal, nor can they simply issue from him as *his*. Instead, they are the markers of his generation, signs of his times and of his membership in various groups bound to history in ways beyond their own ability to understand.

What is wrong with this kind of reading? The assumptions that support it are very likely true, at least in general. Common sense would certainly approve the contention that all individuals exist in contexts, that ideas do not arise in a social vacuum, that relationships of power play a significant role in virtually all aspects of life. But given these general truths (which I assume no one disputes), we are still left to wonder how a particular individual relates to a particular context. Are we, for instance, to see the individual as participating in the culture, as a product of the culture, as a producer of the culture, or as a sometime independent agent within various cultural situations? And if, as I assume, the best answer is likely to be all of the above, how do we clarify this complex relationship when, according to many commentators, the individual is often unaware of his or her placement within these multiple, shifting scenes and when our own knowledge is often confined to a sampling of surviving documents?

We are limited, in other words, as are our subjects, and it is the awareness (or intentional ignorance) of these limits that is crucial. For the best historicist or culturally minded critics (both old and new), a careful intelligence wedded to a healthy suspicion of their own methods has always had the potential to produce exciting and illuminating results.[4] In many of their more recent colleagues, how-ever (and here I would include the large number of graduate students being trained to these assumptions), the so-called cultural turn has tended to foster an atmosphere of unconscious hypocrisy that encourages readers to recognize ev-eryone's contingency but their own, even while claiming a heightened awareness of their own motives.[5] Often ignoring the considerable complications of their own ideas, many of these critics continue to treat authors as little more than symptoms of contexts crudely analyzed in terms of one or more types of power. Individuality is conveniently ignored or taken up zestfully as yet another ideology. "Art," when thought of at all, is reduced to its lowest commercial or ideological denominator. And opposing arguments, too often minimized as the products of the past, are attacked, along with their proponents, as unconscious propaganda from one or more easily tagged "eras."[6] In its most unfortunate incarnation, this ideologically based criticism privileges only the ideological critic, who, despite occasional protests to the contrary, proceeds as if a political truth is the only truth while all else, no matter how appealing, amounts to a false consciousness.[7] As Morris Dickstein pointed out in a recent issue of the *Chronicle of Higher Education*, it can be difficult to accept so thorough an emphasis on ideological formation when "these theorists deliberately take no account of the extraliterary influences that may have shaped them."[8]

The logical flaws of this type of analysis are surprisingly obvious. They have been the subject of debate in ideological theory for some time but can be approached via the following basic question: Either we believe that ideological analysis is itself immune from its own procedures or we believe that it, too, is an expression of ideology, just as compromised by context as any other analytic mode. The first of these positions seems ludicrous at best. It is the legacy of Louis Althusser, chiefly, who attempted to label ideological analysis as "scientific" rather than ideological: "But to recognize that we are subjects and that we function in the practical rituals of the most elementary everyday life . . . — this recognition only gives us the 'consciousness' of our incessant (eternal) practice of ideological recognition — its consciousness, i.e., its *recognition* — but in no sense does it give us the (scientific) *knowledge* of the mechanism of this recognition. Now it is this knowledge that we have to reach, if you will, while speaking in ideology, and from within ideology we have to outline a discourse which tries to break with ideology, in order to dare to be the beginning of a scientific (i.e., subjectless) discourse on ideology."[9]

The difficulty with such a distinction, clearly, is that it violates its own basic principles, a point not lost upon Althusser's critics. As Jacques Rancière has argued, this division of knowledge merely recovers the metaphysical space previously rejected by materialistic analysis: "The functioning of the 'Science/Ideology' opposition depends on the re-establishment of a space homologous to that of the whole metaphysical tradition: it supposes the closure of a universe of discourse, divided into the realms of the true and the false, into the world of

Science and that of its Other (opinion, error, illusion, etc.)"[10] Raymond Williams makes a similar point in *Marxism and Literature*, with the added note that such a maneuver is not only contradictory but is itself a tactic for consolidating political opinion: "But it is just this kind of analysis which is prevented by the *a priori* assumption of a 'positive' method which is not subject to such scrutiny: an assumption based in fact on the received (and unexamined) assumptions of 'positive, scientific knowledge,' freed of the 'ideological bias' of all other observers. This position, which has been often repeated in orthodox Marxism, is either a circular demonstration or a familiar partisan claim (of the kind made by almost all parties) that others are biased but that, by definition, we are not."[11]

Williams's slightly more pungent critique is especially applicable to ideological criticism of the last twenty-five years, for though virtually all present-day critics might be willing to admit that their own analyses are contingent, such admissions seem to have little effect on the claims made for the truth value of their readings. Consider, for example, the influential collection *Ideology and Classic American Literature*, edited by Myra Jehlen and Sacvan Bercovitch and published in 1986. Jehlen's introduction includes a survey of the various conceptions of ideology at work in the essays collected in the volume. At its conclusion, she offers the following summation: "Previous studies have treated ideology as an aspect of the literature, but not usually of the criticism. In this respect, the new ideological approach is very much of its time, for current criticism in general, whether deconstructive, psychoanalytic, or focused on the reader's reception of the work, is marked by such self-scrutiny, expressed as a continuing interrogation of the analytical terms themselves. But when the terms are those of ideology, self-scrutiny has an additional social dimension or a dynamic that engages the critic in the history examined not as a separate object but as part of her or his identity."[12] Considering the potential impasse of what Clifford Geertz dubbed "Manheim's paradox" ("if all knowledge is ideological, no analysis can rise above the level of its own ideology"), Jehlen also claims that the contributors to her volume "seem to value an ideological approach precisely for the complications that trouble Geertz — its explicit political engagement and its aesthetic relativism. . . . Most of the essays gathered here . . . return to such considerations as the social or ethical value of a work in its time and the nature of the critic's own involvement in that judgment. For these critics, the attraction of an ideological analysis is precisely that it permits interested study of what has reemerged as interested art" (ibid., 12, 13). In other words — and this seems less and less plausible as time goes on — ideological critics circa 1986 were more aware than their predecessors of the contingency of all arguments, both their own and those of previous generations of critics. What these ideologists do is "interested," and from this interested perspective they critique the equally interested criticism of other critics and authors. There is thus no need for a realm of judgment that cannot be ideologically labeled because this critical dialogue is made up of nothing more than modestly competing, "interested" visions: "By extension, moreover, this tradition provides the individual critic with an opportunity for a particularly vivid refraction of his or her own problematical situation — as a person of particular race, class, and gender who also tries, as reader, to transcend the bias this entails — against the same paradox embedded in all literature. Each contributor to this anthology defines ideology somewhat differently, but they all share an ambition to illuminate the ideological dimension not only of the literature but of their own criticism as well" (14–15).

We might begin by asking how these critics hope to "transcend" bias if the fundamental tenet of their approach is that all arguments are inevitably contingent. What sort of transcendence is this, even if it is only a distant goal? Is it the aspiration to a truth that supercedes "interest"? And if so, what is its relationship to "interestedness" or ideology? It might be possible that consciousness of one's own interests clears the way, in a sense, for a partial transcendence of those limitations, but the criticism Jehlen presents seems to have little interest in acknowledging a space where claims to truth can compete free of ideological tags. Even so, these critics seem to hope that *their own* arguments will rise above the situation of their production to some higher realm of truth, even though the work of previous critics — and of the authors under examination — is rarely given the same opportunity.

In fact, with a few notable exceptions, it is difficult to find a critic in this volume willing to do what Jehlen claims: to examine "the ideological dimension" of "their own criticism."[13] What we do find is a heightened consciousness of the interestedness of past critics, particularly those who can be associated with specific schools and eras. This is certainly true of Donald Pease in his essay "Melville and Cultural Persuasion." After opening with a close reading of Ahab's famous quarterdeck speech, Pease soon confesses to other aims:

> Now, although I began by claiming the broad topic for this discussion would be the scene of cultural persuasion at the time of *Moby-Dick*, I must confess to a more personal motive — a failure to remain persuaded by the reading of *Moby-Dick* that has become canonical, the one in which Ishmael proves his freedom by opposing

Ahab's totalitarian will. In this chapter I do not wish merely to prove the superiority of an alternative reading but to argue that the reading to which I was not persuaded appropriated *Moby-Dick* to quite a different scene of cultural persuasion, the global scenario popularly designated as the "Cold War." The Cold War may initially seem an unfit context for a discussion of *Moby-Dick*, but I shall argue that the Cold War is crucial both for a canonical reading of that narrative and for its ongoing placement within the rationalist context F. O. Matthiessen called the "American Renaissance."[14]

It soon emerges, given this shift of target, that Matthiessen's reading — whatever may have been its own pretensions to transcend bias — is quickly explained by its entrapment in what Pease calls "the Cold War frame." This all-consuming context, in Pease's analysis, apparently converts all (even remotely political) positions taken during the Cold War to the terms of its simplistic structure: "With an even greater display of efficiency, the Cold War scene can displace any opposition against the scene itself into one of the agencies of the opposition. So when a political analyst as astute as, say, Noam Chomsky writes about the distortions of the Cold War frame, he can find himself pictured, in the reviews of his work, as the dupe of a totalitarian power. In short, the Cold War scenario manages to control, in advance, all the positions the opposition can occupy" (ibid., 390). Thus Matthiessen, whose earlier "anticapitalist" politics seem to Pease to contradict his role as canon-maker, must, like Chomsky, be a victim of sorts. Or, if not a victim, then a deeply divided individual whose anticapitalist side is being repressed by a desire to play an important role in the emerging Cold War structure: "Perhaps this recognition [that self-reliance enables national compulsion] will have its greatest value if we imagine it stated by the F. O. Matthiessen who led us to it: not the one who used Emerson's doctrine of self-reliance to form the consensus he called the *American Renaissance*, but the one whose dissenting political opinions were silenced by *Art and Expression in the Age of Emerson and Whitman*" (409). Certainly there is support in Matthiessen's biography for seeing him as deeply conflicted. Pease makes little attempt, however, to draw distinct lines between what we know of Matthiessen's life and what we find in his criticism. Aside from the reference to Matthiessen's earlier politics, Pease is content to let Matthiessen's homosexuality and suicide stay quietly in the background. Instead of constructing an argument to support his sense of Matthiessen as a conflicted cold warrior, Pease simply assumes that his own academic audience will accept both his analysis of the Cold War "frame" and his placement of Matthiessen in it.

He then treats Matthiessen as a symptom or victim of the frame. The result is that *American Renaissance*, and by extension the traditional canon, is presented as the product of Cold War politics. Given that the academic audience of the mid-eighties was almost exclusively opposed to the neo–Cold War policies of Ronald Reagan, it therefore follows that the canon established by Matthiessen is both out of date and politically unacceptable.

This line of argument is a familiar one, so familiar that it has become a simple reflex among many academic critics. It is the easiest way to settle the intended audience, to assure them both of the propriety of the critic's own politics and of his solidarity with academic readers. The method is basic: associate your target, however tenuously, with the New Criticism; remind your audience, as if they needed reminding, of the conservatism of the early fifties; and then contrast your own work with that of the discredited era. It must follow, therefore, that Pease's interpretive position (in 1986?) is somewhere outside this Cold War mentality, regardless of the ease with which he has implicated both F. O Matthiessen and Noam Chomsky in his all-consuming model.

These maneuvers are to be expected, and yet, after reading Jehlen's introduction, we might have waited for Pease to "illuminate the ideological dimension" of his own criticism. He does not. For all the attention he is willing to pay to Matthiessen's entanglement in mid-century politics, Pease seems uninterested in his own potential biases, political opinions, or his relationship to the era in which he is writing. Perhaps such a consciousness is implied by his arguments, but if so, how can he expect to remain immune from the sort of analysis he employs? What is to keep a subsequent critic from claiming that Pease's analysis is so compromised by its mid-eighties anti-Reagan biases (note his favorable opinion of Chomsky's politics) that we no longer need to take his actual arguments seriously? that his very analysis is not an argument at all but the expression of a political language of which he himself seems unaware, a "frame" of its own, equally dominant and rapacious. Despite Jehlen's claim for heightened self-consciousness, the practical reality of Pease's reading amounts to little more than Williams's description of the partisan argument. Despite such claims to self-awareness, many of the critics in Jehlen's volume operate on the assumption that while the arguments of earlier critics are the expressions of ideology, the analyses that demonstrate their biases are not.[15]

This is particularly true of Pease's defense of the so-called New Americanists in the special issue of *boundary* 2 published in 1990. Pitting himself against Frederick Crews's 1988 critique of the then-emerging New Historicism, Pease casts

Crews as the last defender of an outmoded Americanist "liberal imagination." This "ideological construction" — an anti-Communist individualism that suppressed the political reality of canonical American texts — is the product of the same "Cold War frame" he describes in the Melville essay. Embodied in Lionel Trilling's *The Liberal Imagination*, the post–World War II consensus produced "an *imaginary separation* between the culture and the public sphere" that enabled "liberal subjects to experience the otherwise threatening cultural contradictions released by the cold war consensus as the negative capability of a whole self."[16] Therefore, Crews's complaints that the New Americanists carry out politically reductive readings in the name of social activism are merely the enactment of his liberal ideology and need not be addressed in their substance: "Throughout the remainder of his 1988 review, Crews repeats the terms Trilling provided in 1946 for both critical blame ('reductionism,' 'partisan myopia,' 'sermonizing,' 'eagerness for moral certainties about the relationship between the books and their politics') and critical praise ('irresoluteness,' 'irony,' 'concentrated suggestiveness derived from the fusing and decontextualizing of many rhetorical strategies'). When deployed as a means of assessing the New Americanists, these terms of critical praise and blame reconstitute Frederick Crews's critical subjectivity within the realm of *The Liberal Imagination*" (ibid., 9). In other words, Crews cannot charge the New Americanists with bad critical faith because he is simply repeating the ideology of the liberal consensus. There is no argument here, only ideology, and because ideology can easily be assigned to a political scene no longer operative, Pease has no need to deal with the actual charge. He simply claims that Crews's distinctions are based upon a false separation, that all texts are ideological and therefore equally liable to political attack. There can be no such thing as "partisan myopia" because all texts are partisan to some degree and therefore limited by their historical placement and relevance.

And yet, Pease manages to find a place for the New Americanists to recover precisely the nonideological critical force he denies Crews: "The political unconscious of the primal scene of their New Historicist readings embodies *both* the *repressed relationship between* the literary and the political and the *disenfranchised groups previously unrepresentable in this relationship.* And as conduits for the return of figures and material repressed through the denial of the relationship of the field to the public world, New Americanists occupy a double relation. For as *liaisons between* cultural and public realms, they are at once within the field yet external to it" (ibid., 31, original emphases). This externality mimics the Althusserian "scientific discourse" by elevating the political to the realm of the real, recovering a space beyond ideology from which to clarify the blindnesses of the past. Indeed, it is arguable that Pease is simply fetishizing the political as an imaginary realm of materialistic truth which is, literally, the last word on all arguments. The alternative would be to invite analysis of his own position as a Marxist-inspired anti-individualism (itself a product of the local politics of the academy) that merely extends the "Cold War frame" into the 1990s. Such an admission would at least explain the metaphors of conflict that work their way into his argument, from describing American studies as "an appropriate battle-field to fight for the return" of repressed politics to troping his argument with Crews as a "war of paradigms" (19, 15). It would appear, in other words, that "power politics" is precisely what the New Americanists are about, and anyone who has followed American studies since Pease's article can attest to the unex-amined ideological line evident in their readings.

In his survey of current critical practice, *Truth and Consequences: Intentions, Conventions, and the New Thematics,* Reed Way Dasenbrock argues that a com-bination of Althusserian influence and philosophical "conventionalism" explains the contradictory position taken up by Pease and those of like mind. First, recent ideological critics have tended to focus more and more heavily on groups and group identity, using the "community" to identify a writer or to test an individ-ual's complicity or resistance to a dominant mind-set. Second, the critics so writing have little methodological requirement to communicate beyond the bounds of their own audience of like-minded academics: "If the truth about the nature of Elinor's and Marianne's relationship [in *Sense and Sensibility*] is available only to critics of a certain theoretical perspective, then we are talking not about truth, but about the views of a certain community, and this community, no matter how defined, cannot claim that its views are the truth, but only the beliefs of that community, what-is-true-for-that-community. In that case, there is again noth-ing to talk about in public, or, to put it another way, there is no public space in which to talk."[17] Indeed, the logical end of such a position is not dialogue but open conflict. For if such communities are isolated by context and ideology, if some standard of truth cannot exist across communal boundaries, then there seems to be little point in argument other than political recruitment: "If we believe that our beliefs create the evidence for them *and* that there is no escape from this vicious cycle because knowledge as separate from opinion is simply not a possibility, then both evidential procedures and the practice of argument come to have just one purpose, which is to persuade others that they should share our beliefs, that they should join our community" (ibid., 189).

Though some might favor such an all-out battle of ideological positions (or the corresponding chill of groups that refuse to talk to one another), I suspect that most "private" readers find this prospect both predictable and disappointing: predictable because the results of such analyses are fundamentally predetermined; disappointing because this mode of criticism gives individuals so little credit and treats them with such general contempt.[18] How predictable are ideological readings? Within the structure most commonly employed by contemporary critics, there are three basic conclusions we see time and again: (1) that the author, whose ideas are the product of a particular context or culture, is complicit with the dominant ideology of that culture (as identified by the critic); (2) that the author heroically resists this dominant ideology; or (3) that the author appears to resist but is unconsciously complicit. (The corollary to this last maneuver is an attack on previous critics for having mistaken the author's complicity for rebellion because they themselves were ideologically motivated.)[19]

The question clearly begged by such analyses is the extent to which an individual can be said to be a product of a culture. And, even if a product, how transparent or available for analysis is the relationship between the singular self and its social context? Gerald Graff has posed the question this way: "If I adopt a less than reverent tone toward the current reassertion of the politics of criticism, it is merely to underscore that its key proposition, that criticism has ideological motives and effects, is no more than a starting point, that *what* those ideological motives and effects *may be* is something we shouldn't assume we easily know. Motives and effects are disputable things, open as they are to the vicissitudes of inadequate evidence or interpretive bias. Even if the analyst of ideology were himself above suspicions of political bias, the fact would remain that the connections between ideas and their social uses are elusive."[20] Graff goes on to give a nuanced account of some of these difficulties, including a fairly early critique of the Foucaultian analytic that came to dominate the late eighties and early nineties and that has now vaguely merged with Althusserian ideas under the general rubric of "cultural" reading. Discussing Mark Selzer's depiction of Henry James as complicit with the "panopticism" of police surveillance, Graff asks the obvious, but generally ignored, question: "Of course, 'seeing' has often been used for politically sinister purposes, but it is also obviously indispensable to anyone who opposed those purposes. One could use the same tactics with a similarly accusatory tone to 'show' how Foucaultian investigations of specular imagery in fiction are just as deeply in complicity with disciplinary panopticism as any realistic novel is — perhaps some super-Foucaultian has already written the essay. One could perform such an exercise, but it is not clear what it would prove except that 'power' loses its value as a term of analysis once it is stretched to cover everything" (ibid., 115).

It is this overextension of the term, whether *power* or *ideology*, that is often the heart of the problem. Terry Eagleton, for one, has made it clear that as an analytic tool "ideology" functions only when it is given a clear set of limitations or specific applications:

> Many theories of ideology regard it as a kind of screen or blockage which intervenes between us and the real world. . . . But this is surely to widen the term to the point of uselessness. Any term which tries to cover too much threatens to cancel all the way through and end up signifying nothing. "Ideological" is not synonymous with "cultural": it denotes, more precisely, the points at which our cultural practices are interwoven with political power. Whether this is always a *dominant* power, or whether it always and everywhere involves naturalising, falsity, mystification, the masking or rationalising of injustice or the spurious resolution of social contradictions, are controversial issues in the theory of ideology; but if ideology just means something like "a specific way of seeing," or even "a set of doctrinal beliefs" then it rapidly dwindles in interest.[21]

If ideology is conceived as a sort of consciousness, then not only is there no escape for the ideological critic but the term itself becomes meaningless, simply another word for reality. The same can be said of the term *politics*. The mantra "Everything is political" — common both as an assumption and a weapon in graduate schools for many years — has served to place "politics" at the center of discussion while making distinctions between overt political activity and ideas with political effects or applications largely meaningless. As a consequence, it has become increasingly common to see explorations of "the politics" of everything but politics itself. And as for the writer or artist who deliberately stands apart from partisanship, the all-consuming category of the "political" will have no trouble reining in what its proponents consider to be nothing more than a sophisticated, political disguise.

What ideological criticism has brought us, in its more judicious moments, is a heightened awareness of the ways ideas can intersect with power and political activity.[22] What it has too often discarded in the process is nothing less than the complexity and strangeness of humanity and of art. In perhaps the deepest contradiction of all, ideological critics have often styled themselves — as have most members of their academic communities — as political activists, in Jehlen's phrase, as "interested" participants in a political struggle against such opponents as intolerance, racism, gender discrimination, and nationalism. Since locating another person within a particular ideology implies a critique of that position, critics of this persuasion have conducted a sort of moral campaign, praising writers whose ideas can be presented as aiding in the critic's own struggle or attacking those who appear to fall outside the lines of acceptable thought or behavior.

This argument in favor of the critic's values is certainly not new; criticism has never been, and never will be, scientific or objective, and the best readers have always been passionate advocates for their own moral vision. And yet the tools with which ideological critics assign praise or blame — ideological analysis inherited from Marxism, cultural criticism in general — make little room for individual human choice. Overwhelmingly deterministic, the assumptions that underlie these approaches posit culture as so powerful a creative force that it is often difficult to know what these critics mean when they speak of "individuals."[23] And though most might generally assent to the proposition that individuals are to an important extent the "products" of their surroundings, it is difficult to see how we can hold specific human beings responsible for ideas and actions that they themselves cannot possibly understand. In other words, without some concept of individuality and some allowance for choice (no matter how provisional), the very moral categories critics attempt to employ cease to exist: "For if the essence of men is that they are autonomous beings — authors of values, of ends in themselves, the ultimate authority of which consists precisely in the fact that they are willed freely — then nothing is worse than to treat them as if they were not autonomous, but natural objects, played on by causal influences, creatures at the mercy of external stimuli, whose choices can be manipulated by their rulers, whether by threats of force or offers of rewards."[24] It may not be necessary to quote Isaiah Berlin to remind ourselves that responsibility and freedom are necessarily interdependent. Nor is it required to recall that Marxist-inspired determinism makes little allowance for individuality. It may well be that in the twenty-first century we now find little use for such hoary subjects as "free will." We may not even believe in it, in any real sense. But if we wish to assign responsibility, if we wish to carry out an "interested" critique of another's ideas, to assert moral values or make claims for the greater value of a certain political position, if we wish to be "activists" of any sort, we must treat other individuals as if their choices are their own and not simply the product of their surroundings.[25] We must construct a model of culture that is as much the product as the producer of individuals. And we must pay attention, in a way that ideological criticism rarely allows, to the choices writers make.

Ethics and Intention

One way to attend to authorial choice, and the method generally followed in this study, is to return to the idea of intention. Intentional criticism is of course nothing new. Though theoretical schools — in particular, the New Criticism and almost all of the various poststructuralist theories — have been consistently suspicious of the usefulness or availability of authorial intention, practical critics have almost always worked with some understanding or hypothesis of an author's potential goals. Ideological criticism, as I have tried to show above, necessarily discounts intention by placing greater emphasis on the often unconscious influences of context. Since in this view writers are more the results of their surroundings than agents within them, intention as a workable concept ceases to have much meaning. We can speak, perhaps, of misguided or false intentions, of the failure of authors to understand their own contingency, but to suggest that a "proper" reading of a text might hinge upon the author's stated goals has come to seem naive at best.

Nevertheless, recent commentators have begun to refine and broaden our sense of what intention might include. Dasenbrock, for instance, sees intention less as a royal road to a "correct" interpretation than as a negative critical tool:

> The role I see intention playing in interpretation is parallel to the role I see for truth: largely a critical or in a sense negative role. Against the positive intentionalism of E. D. Hirsch who finds intentions useful in establishing the validity of hypotheses and against the universal intentionalism of Stanley Fish who finds no methodological use for intentions, the intentionalism I advocate can be called negative or disconfirmationalist because the primary use for intentions in my thinking is to question or challenge or disprove hypotheses about meaning. We add little if anything to an interpretive claim when we claim to have found the author's intentions; on this point, Fish and I are in agreement. But faced with an interpretive claim we find unpersuasive, the counterclaim that the claim could not possibly be what the author meant has considerably more power and bite. One could retort that it has this bite only for those who accept the author's intentions as relevant to interpretive claims and therefore that my claim is valid only for members of the intentionalist interpretive community. But as I have argued . . . , I have not encountered anyone

who is consistently not a member of this community; we are all intentionalists on some occasions and for some texts.[26]

Arguing that most human communication involves a measuring of intentions against potential interpretations, Dasenbrock imagines a sort of hermeneutic space in which interpretive theories can be developed and tested. This is the type of test posited by Donald Davidson, what he calls a "passing theory," "a provisional understanding of what the speaker or writer means by his or her words" (ibid., 74): "Intention is crucial here because we assume that the speaker is trying to make sense, that he or she is engaged in an intelligible action, and that what the speaker is saying makes sense by the light of the prior theory he or she holds. This does not give us a magic formula for how to figure out what the speaker means by the words being uttered; there is no formalizable set of rules for how we in Davidson's terms converge on a passing theory that enables us to make sense of the anomalous. Davidson cannot give us such a formula precisely because the construction of passing theories is unsystematic, not rule- or convention-governed in the way so many theorists have assumed it to be" (172). In this sense, Dasenbrock's intentionalism sets up a goal of intelligibility without a practical faith that the goal is attainable. Indeed, Dasenbrock insists that intentionalism as understood by Davidson allows for the sort of plurality of meaning we have come to expect from all texts, but a plurality governed by the basic assumptions of intended meaningfulness: "Nothing I have said here should be taken as suggesting that the process of interpretation stops when we have found the truth of an author's intentions any more than a scientist's search stops when he or she has found the truth. Neither truth nor intention gives us a stopping place, and we can never claim to be certain that we have found a match between interpreter and author. There is, I think Davidson would hold, no relation of perfect correspondence between a text and the passing theory an interpreter develops in response to it, no one indisputably 'correct' interpretation. Prior theories and passing theories are both irreducibly plural, and this is an accord with our actual experience of interpretation" (172–73).

The model that Dasenbrock sets up is precisely one of engagement, of interaction between the reader and the text as well as between the reader and the author as the object of intentionalist hypotheses.[27] The assumption that writing is produced by another person and that the person was attempting to write or say something intelligible establishes reading as a type of communication, no matter how complex or potentially indeterminate. Dasenbrock is urging a type of faith within the framework of skepticism, similar to what Kenneth Dauber calls "ordinary language criticism":

> One is always someplace, thinking something, or, at least, since the second part of that statement might seem to suggest a naive epistemology based on a shamelessly untheorized ontology in the first part, we might say, instead, that one always speaks *as if* one were somewhere and *as if* what one was doing were thinking. Taking "as if" for "is" is ordinary language criticism's faith. It is faith in one's empirical condition, faith that what one speaks *is* one's empirical condition. And, since it is faith, precisely — that is, since such an empiricism arises in the wake of the collapse of theory, in the failure of epistemology or ontology to ground one's speaking — it is a faith, in every way but the practical, as skeptical as the post-modern assumption that one is always someplace else thinking what can never be thought.[28]

The faith Dauber elaborates is in the situation of speaking or writing, of being "in the middle of things," without a particular grounding other than the writer's own choices, a sort of skeptical self-determination or self-creation afloat on the perpetual uncertainty of language. The consequence of such a skepticism, paradoxically, is a faith that the choices a writer makes are, willy-nilly, his or her own:

> To meet the challenge of skepticism head on, we might say that it is the making good of one's faith, so that it is quite patronizing to say, as most contemporary criticism does, that in writing one falls victim to some hegemonic construction of place and thought, that one subjects oneself to some imperial ordering of extremes. Rather, since extremes do not exist prior to one's possession of them, to write is to construct an imperium whose order, whoever else's it might also be, is inescapably one's own. Here we would happily agree with the new historical criticism that to write is to limit — is to enter, in fact, into the rule of a limitation. But because the rule is one's own, it is a rule difficult to distinguish from liberation, and which is, therefore, not the refusal of limit-making but its greater mastery. (ibid., 134)

The freedom reached here is not idealistic but skeptical: it is the conviction that "one exists only as one gives an account of oneself" (137), which in Dauber's terms is preferable to the anti-idealistic idealism of poststructuralism: "It is better to come to terms with one's writing *in* its limitation than to suppose a 'one' that, free of limitation, must finally prove, with limitation's return, both itself and its writing forever illusory. In this way one may avoid a certain sentimental longing — the pathos of dialectical writing, but a sentimentality, nevertheless — and learn a chastened contentment" (135).

The full acceptance of skepticism posits a speaking agent aware of limits but speaking nonetheless and making choices that really do constitute choices and not merely repetitions of a given scene. With this ability to make choices comes a responsibility for the choices a writer makes. For Dauber, the American exemplar of this position is Benjamin Franklin: "But the real scandal is not [Franklin's] reliance on some ulteriority he is eager to hide, but in his disavowal of the relevance of the ulterior, in his frankness which owns the self's implication in everything it says even where what it says might rather seem to rest on a self already, in some ulterior sense, assumed. For Franklin's selfhood does not disappear in a speech finally not his. Rather, it is present everywhere in the responsibility it takes precisely for whatever it says whenever it says it, and even where what it says is just what others have said first—an audience, say, or a hegemonic discourse, or even, to adapt a remark of Emerson's in 'Self-Reliance,' itself in a previous statement" (ibid., 131–32). In this respect, and most important for this discussion, the writer does not, cannot, escape responsibility for his or her chosen words, even when those words seem to be the product of a cultural construction. Culture cannot consume the self, or fully produce it, because the self exists only insofar as it chooses, through its skepticism, to present itself to the world. Thus, "intentions," whether they appear to escape context or not, are still intentions, are still the writer's own. Context, in this sense, remains of vital importance, but it ceases to be an all-consuming force that overwhelms even the stated choices of the individual. And while it is certainly possible that a particular writer can unconsciously enact a pervasive political or cultural idea, this approach begins with the assumption that an author's conscious choices demand the respect typically accorded our conversational equals.

Granting this acknowledgment of the writer as "other mind," Dauber argues powerfully for a new sort of critical attention: "This would be its question: not whether the self exists, a question no skeptic from Descartes to Hume ever seriously considered, except as a theoretical exercise clearly marked as theoretical, but how far into society it is willing to carry itself, into how many different languages, situations, audiences; not how it always means something other than what it says, but how far it might plausibly mean its meanings to go. . . . Thus [this criticism] might disapprove or be partisan as much as it chose. It might be conservative or revolutionary. But its partisanship and its disapproval would be based not on what a writer failed to say, but on what he did say" (ibid., 133). To accord this respect is essentially to argue for the status of the writer as an ethical subject. It is likewise to foresee a criticism that imagines the engagement between reader and writer, reader and text, as one of mutual responsibility, of a meeting, upon the uncertain ground of language, of equals.[29] For Dauber, who is influenced by Stanley Cavell, the appropriate term might be "acknowledgement," though we could just as easily add "neighboring" or "marriage."[30] Cavell offers several overlapping conceptualizations of the relationship between the self and the world or the self and others, each a subtle combination of closeness and separation. As Russell Goodman explicates, Cavell's metaphor of "remarriage" offers a relation to the world that makes separation the basis for closeness:

> Cavell makes explicit this blend of connection and alterity when he understands Dunne saying to Grant near the end of *The Awful Truth:* "What is necessary now is not to estrange ourselves but to recognize, without denying our natural intimacy, that we are also strangers, separate, different." Indeed, Cavell maintains that the separation of divorce (necessary for remarriage) is an emblem of the freedom that marriage requires. A narcissistic or incestuous intimacy must first be ruptured, he argues, "in order that an intimacy of difference or reciprocity supervene. Marriage is always divorce, always entails rupture from something." Marriages in these comedies, like the Romantic marriages of self and world, are unions that preserve otherness. As Cavell sees it, a marriage is a "scene in which the chance for happiness is shown as the mutual acknowledgement of separateness."[31]

If we imagine this relationship extending to reader and writer (or reader and text), we can see that the awareness of cognitive limit, the intentional limitation of the self in deference to the other, structures all reading. Interpretation becomes "acknowledgement" rather than knowledge, "neighboring" rather than consumption. Rather than opposing knowledge to the unknowable, such an arrangement sees the consciousness of knowledge's limit as the very foundation of what can, or cannot, be said about others.

Interpretation and Respect: Levinas

Cavell's intermingling of nearness and distance establishes an ethical relationship between subject and object that both draws upon and helps illuminate American romantic writers. It is also shares significant interest, though from a somewhat different background, with the ethical philosophy of Emmanuel Levinas.[32] Best known as a philosopher and theologian who blended poststructuralism and rabbinical Judaism, Levinas offers a unique, and sometimes idiosyncratic, revision of Western philosophy's concern with Being. As both student and critic of

Martin Heidegger, Levinas attempted to reformulate the Western understanding of self-knowledge by arguing for the prior and fundamental experience of others (or otherness) as a basis for all philosophy: "One has to respond to one's right to be, not by referring to some abstract and anonymous law, or judicial entity, but because of one's fear for the Other. My being-in-the-world or my 'place in the sun,' my being at home, have these not also been the usurpation of spaces belonging to the other man whom I have already oppressed or starved, or driven out into a third world; are they not acts of repulsing, excluding, exiling, stripping, killing?"[33] To ground consciousness and philosophy in the "Other" is, in part at least, to suggest that Western conceptions of knowledge (as "grasping" or appropriation) are inherently violent, an unethical extension of the self at the expense of "other minds": "Knowledge is re-presentation, a return to presence, and nothing may remain *other* to it" (ibid., 77). The other thus becomes the unthinkable, that which exceeds its own idea, what Levinas in *Totality and Infinity* famously calls the "face": "The way in which the other presents himself, exceeding *the idea of the other in me*, we here name face. This *mode* does not consist in figuring as a theme under my gaze, in spreading itself forth as a set of qualities forming an image. The face of the Other at each moment destroys and overflows the plastic image it leaves me, the idea existing to my own measure and to the measure of its *ideatum* — the adequate idea. It does not manifest itself by these qualities, but καθ' αὐτό. It *expresses itself.*"[34]

Levinas derives this paradoxical face-that-is-more-than-face by aligning it with the idea of infinity. As Krzysztof Ziarek explains, "according to Descartes, the idea of infinity is characterized by two singular features: it cannot be possibly comprehended by the mind hampered by its finite nature, and its *ideatum* cannot be contained by the idea itself. In other words, the idea of infinity, despite its tracing presence in the mind, does not belong to the order of thought, and, unlike other ideas, there can be no adequation between the idea and its *ideatum.*"[35] We can conceive of infinity only as a sort of container the contents of which overflow containment. The other is in this sense infinite, strange, and irreducible to the I, or what Levinas calls "the same." Indeed, the confrontation of the I and the other, the "face to face," "calls into question" the foundation of individual freedom conceived, out of the Cartesian tradition, as Being: "A calling into question of the same — which cannot occur within the egoist spontaneity of the same — is brought about by the other. We name this calling into question of my spontaneity by the presence of the Other ethics. This strangeness of the Other, his irreducibility to the I, to my thoughts and my possessions, is precisely accomplished as a calling into question of my spontaneity, as ethics."[36] This calling into question prompts or arises with a condition of the self that Levinas labels "metaphysical desire," the "desire for the absolutely other": "The metaphysical desire has another intention; it desires beyond everything that can simply complete it. It is like goodness — the Desired does not fulfill it, but deepens it. . . . A desire without satisfaction which, precisely, *understands* [*entends*] the remoteness, the alterity, and the exteriority of the other" (ibid., 34). This metaphysical desire is not to be confused with need; for Levinas, need implies fulfillment of the self, the I, and therefore a reduction of the other to the ego. "Desire implies an entirely different movement, a different direction, as it does not need to return [to the I] and cannot ever be satisfied since it feeds on its own hunger. Moreover, desire conceived in this way is neither a lack nor a failure of thought. In fact, there is no thinking that could recompense desire, because desire does not belong to the order of thinking."[37]

Because this relation to otherness depends upon a "metaphysical desire" that refuses thought or "thinks otherwise," truth too must be refashioned in light of the "face to face," or ethics. Countering the image of truth as a "union of the knower and the known," Levinas insists that the search for truth is guided by the idea of infinity: "Infinity is not the 'object' of a cognition (which would be to reduce it to the measure of the gaze that contemplates), but is the desirable, that which arouses Desire, that is, that which is approachable by a thought that at each instant *thinks more than it thinks*."[38] Desire, rather than fulfilling a need, "measures the infinity of the infinite"; truth is thus not the object of a lack but an event that "arises" in the confrontation of others: "Truth is sought in the other, but by him who lacks nothing. The distance is untraversable, and at the same time traversed. The separated being is satisfied, autonomous, and nonetheless searches after the other with a search that is not incited by the lack proper to need or by the memory of a lost good. Such a situation is language. Truth arises where a being separated from the other is not engulfed in him, but speaks to him" (ibid., 62). The situation of language, of speaking, becomes the primary relationship out of which truth arises, not as a concept or object but as an event, an experience that exceeds its own form: "*The absolute experience is not disclosure but revelation:* a coinciding of the expressed with him who expresses, which is the privileged manifestation of the Other, the manifestation of a face over and beyond form. . . . The face is a living presence; it is expression" (66).

Levinasian ethics, in other words, not only offers a radical shift of perspective in terms of the self's relation to the world; it also highlights a fundamental paradox of interpretive respect. By insisting on the absolute alterity of the world outside the self, Levinas maintains distance (or disengagement) as fundamental to ethics. Engagement, if it is to be ethical, can come only through a prior acknowledgment of separation, through a kind of cognitive withdrawal or refusal. Indeed, it is the very separateness of the other that gives rise to its demand, its "mastery" as the "face" that "calls into question my freedom" (ibid., 84): "The Other, whose exceptional presence is inspired in the ethical impossibility of killing him in which I stand, marks the end of powers. If I can no longer have power over him it is because he overflows so absolutely every *idea* I can have of him" (87). The awareness of the other-*as-other* is the check to the murderousness inherent in freedom; without separation or the acknowledgment of otherness, there can be no shame: "Discourse and Desire, where the Other presents himself as interlocutor, as him over whom I *can*not have power [*je ne peux pas pouvoir*], whom I cannot kill, condition this shame, where, qua I, I am not innocent spontaneity but usurper and murderer" (84).

Despite Levinas's considerable complications, his descriptions of the ethical relation share the general concerns of readers like Cavell, Dauber, and Dasenbrock. Each of these commentators expresses a basic interest in the ways traditional Western conceptions of knowledge work to limit and restrict the object of interpretation. For Dauber and Dasenbrock such an ethical scrutiny, with its fundamental emphasis on self-limitation, founds an approach to interpretation that repeats the basic structure, if not the subtle complexities, of the Levinasian "face to face." For Cavell, "re-marriage" or "acknowledgement" helps us imagine a connection between self and other (or the self and the world) that arises out of, rather than in opposition to, epistemological distance. In other words, all these thinkers posit an approach to "other minds" that preserves ethical separation while demanding, through that separation, an intensified form of obligation or engagement. As Dasenbrock most plainly states it, "We can therefore insist on good faith having priority over bad faith, good will over a will to power, only if we insist on an ethics of interpretation in which because authors are persons, they must be respected in the way persons in general must be respected."[39] This "respect" does not equate text and author, but it does suggest that interpretive situations involving language necessarily presuppose an encounter between a speaker and a listener, a reader and a writer. It also sets at its base the primary experience of estrangement, the unpredictable and in some sense irreducible encounter with otherness.

But can this sort of ethical philosophy be applied to a relationship between a reader and a text or a work of art? For Cavell, Dasenbrock, and Dauber it seems fair to say that it can, that the interpretive relationship they posit applies to the self's encounter with the world outside the self, human or otherwise. For Levinas the situation is less clear. As Jill Robbins explains, Levinas tended to distrust aesthetic figuration, seeing it as a type of egoistic totalization: "Suffice is to say that if the work, in Levinas's view, *cannot* present or signify the other that is precisely *because* it signifies; it signifies with the referrals inherent in sign systems and the constitutive absence that implies. The necessary indirection of a work's mode of signification falls short of the directness of the discourse of the face."[40] Artistic language is fundamentally deceptive, particularly when opposed to ethical language, which is characterized by "straightforwardness and an original sincerity, a sincerity that precedes the opposition between veracity and deceit" (ibid., 78–79).

But as Robbins points out, Levinas's opposition to art fluctuated throughout his career; for while he rejected figuration as either deceitful or ethically destructive, he also argued for the ethical value of various works of fiction and poetry. The art or commentary for which Levinas made this exception is characterized, according to Robbins, by "self-interruption": "Interruption signals the putting into question of the totality. . . . Self-interruption is the trope for a form of ethical discourse in which the interruption is not reabsorbed into thematization and totality, namely, an ethical discourse that *performs* its own putting into question" (ibid., 144–45). This disruption of totality can apparently be found in Paul Celan's poetry or in the multivocal interruptions of midrash: "Levinas's descriptions of rabbinic interpretation emphasize its perpetual, self-renewing mode of questioning that never comes to rest in a single interpretive answer" (138). Furthermore, this stylistic exception is apparently seconded by an occasional thematic preference for works of fiction that seem to illustrate Levinas's conception of the ethical. Thus *The Brothers Karamazov* (and particularly the phrase, "I am the most responsible") can become a touchstone for Levinas's own descriptions of the burden placed by otherness. This reliance on representative textual examples raises the specter of an ethical violation of sorts used in the service of "reading" textual otherness: "This is, then, another instance of Levinas's using a text to illustrate a philosophical argument, thereby reducing it to its denotative terms, eliding its literary specificity. Would this not be a betrayal of Dostoevsky's text, an ingratitude of a kind that similarly was operative in Levinas's readings of the texts of Blanchot and Rimbaud, even when he would mark a debt to them? Yet within the double bind of the hermeneutics of respect . . . — in order to 'do justice' to a text that asserts an asymmetrical ethical imperative, one must be unjust to it—such a betrayal, even when it is neither intentional nor explicit, may be constitutive" (148–49). As Robbins here suggests, not only is it possible to see the text as an object of interpretive "respect," but it is also necessary to understand that an ethics that transcends thematicization must at times be reduced in order to be described as ethics. Self-interrupting art thus becomes a source of example and also a manifestation of otherness, not a Levinasian "face," perhaps, but a manifestation that recalls a face-to-face relation.

The difficulties of applying Levinas's philosophy to art are thus considerable but not insurmountable.[41] And since I consider myself to be offering less a Levinasian than an ethical reading, I am more concerned with the resonances between Levinas and Heidegger, Heidegger and Cavell, Cavell and Dauber or Dasenbrock, than I am with the strict application of Levinas's philosophy. My opposition of a "hermeneutics of respect," to use Robbins's phrase, to the reductive readings of ideological criticism simply proposes a change in the relationship between subject and object, a movement toward the uncertainty of the "face to face" and away from the historical or political "mastery" of ideological readings. This critical humility, with its sense of obligation on the interpreter's part, not only establishes an ethical space by means of which withdrawal comes to demand reengagement but also simultaneously recovers a relation to otherness that resonates strongly with recent descriptions of aesthetic experience.

In Elaine Scary's *On Beauty and Being Just*, we can detect a similar concern about the limitations of political criticism coupled with an attempt to relocate the positive *social* impact of aesthetic attention. Like the Levinasian "face," Scary's "beauty" prompts a response through a "radical decentering" of the self: "At the moment we see something beautiful, we undergo a radical decentering. Beauty, according to Weil, requires us 'to give up our imaginary position as the center. . . . A transformation then takes place at the very roots of our sensibility, in our immediate reception of sense impressions and psychological impressions.' . . . It is not that we cease to stand at the center of the world, for we never stood there. It is that we cease to stand even at the center of our own world. We willingly cede our ground to the thing that stands before us."[42] This diminution of the self echoes the other's challenge to the "same," in Levinasian terms, while setting beauty in the place of astonishment. Both are, figuratively, "disarming," shifting the burden, the sense of obligation or subordination, from the object to the subject, from beauty/other to the self. For Scary this shift signals a movement toward equality or fairness that echoes Dasenbrock's call for a criticism of respect and Cavell's for reengagement after "divorce."[43]

It may be difficult to see Scary's sense of equality in a Levinasian context, given the overwhelming sense of obligation or shame in Levinas's model. But the sort of dialogue initiated in this aesthetic confrontation requires independent agents, each unable to contain or control the other, each surprised by what the other says, by the distance between speakers in a conversation without advantage. The decentering of the self of which Scary speaks is thus a dissolution of the self's dream of oneness, its totalization of the world into its own private thought. Beauty breaks into the self's isolation and, according to Alexander Nehamas, begins an unending conversation: "The conversation is never-ending partly because beauty, as I said, is a promise, an anticipation, a hope as yet unfulfilled. To find something beautiful is, precisely, not to have yet finished with it, to think it has something further to offer. But also because the more we come to know the beautiful thing itself, the more we come to know other things as well."[44]

This compulsion to act in response to an encounter that defies easy analysis returns us to the young Alfred Kazin, feverish in his bed, reading *Oliver Twist* and dreaming. The primacy of that experience, its uncertainty, delight, and danger, suggests not only the foundation of a life's work, a passion to be pursued, but also a structure through which reading can recover its human source. "Why was Dickens compelled to write like that, and why did it work on me like a drug?" What is the strength of this "strange if awful happiness"? And beginning there, how do we pursue this other voice, this strangeness, in a way that refuses to destroy it, that keeps us always within its "effect"? The family of thought I have attempted to outline above offers a way to preserve this experience and to recover reading as an act of ethical approach, a way of reengaging the world through an intimate separation. That it cannot be engaged at all without this awareness, that ethical commitment cannot exist without distinction are its paradoxes. Indeed, it is the separation itself, the distance and isolation (Kazin alone in his room) that produces the demand for reengagement and generates an endless search, a constant conversation between reader and writer or between the observer and the object of beauty.

Hawthorne's Shyness

My own conversation with the major writings of Nathaniel Hawthorne is the main subject of this book. It is, as I believe criticism should be, a personal account, even though the author in question is best known for his resistance to interpretive intimacy.

In an attempt to understand him (as naive as that continues to sound and is) I started with what I knew. The biographies paint a fairly consistent picture: a quiet but ambitious writer, reclusive yes, but active enough in the affairs of his time. I decided that most of us, should we come to deal with him, would simply call him "shy," if not rude or self-concerned. Shy. Without much thought on the matter we would see this as a trait of personality, a weakness for the most part, as is common enough, even a handicap or affliction. In other words, we would presuppose, as we often do, an ideal social self, at ease with others, happy in crowds, whose public and private lives meld seamlessly, without anxiety. And because Nathaniel Hawthorne seems incapable of such fluidity, we would see his evasiveness as a defense, a shielding of what in ideal circumstances would be allowed to move freely, happily.

But is this what it means to be shy, at least in Hawthorne's terms? Is shyness merely a flaw or can it be more? — a philosophy, for instance, a way of seeing the self and its approach to the world? Any survey of Hawthorne criticism can tell us that this writer is known for his veils, but is it possible that these strategies arose not out of defensiveness toward the world but from a higher sensitivity to the interactions of individuals and "others"? I have come to believe that it is, not that Hawthorne disregards his anxious personality but that he transforms nervousness into thoughtful art, a series of questions fundamental to the interpretive placement of the romantic individual.

In this interest he is not alone, though the family of thought in which I hope to place him is not typical. As much as I recognize Hawthorne's indebtedness to certain well-known influences (Scottish Common Sense philosophy, Thomas Reid in particular; eighteenth-century writers, certainly Dr. Johnson), this study places him in the company of romantic skeptics (Emerson and Thoreau) and postromantic philosophers, both continental and pragmatist. This latter lineage marks the threshold of contact between an American line of thought that begins with Benjamin Franklin (and includes the later Emerson, Thoreau, William James, Thomas Dewey, and Stanley Cavell) and the speculative continental tradition that gathers in Nietzsche, Heidegger, Wittgenstein, and Levinas. One of the shared concerns between these philosophical "families" is a fundamental skepticism with respect to large, controlling ideas. These thinkers are particularly concerned with the various ways Western conceptualization, in one form or another, can become destructive or abusive. In this respect they develop a strain of later romantic thought common in British and European writing, but they do so in a way that lifts it beyond the bounds of historical romanticism.

Part One of this study thus attempts to outline Hawthorne's position vis-à-vis both English romanticism and postromantic continental philosophy. It argues that Hawthorne's style of shyness takes in Keatsian negativity while approaching Heidegger's broader and more complex notion of the "poetic." Such an approach depends upon a conception of truth considerably more complex and skeptical than that of his American neighbor Melville — a romantic truth of movement and life, ungraspable, an "event of estrangement."[45] The otherness of truth thus initiates an ethical examination of the individual acting within a world already marked by its fundamental distance. Specific human relationships become touchstones for ethical behavior; ideas, no matter how attractive, yield to the overwhelming demand of the other. Both "The Minister's Black Veil" and *The Scarlet Letter* highlight these tensions between personal and idealistic commitments, arguing for the fundamental role of "facing" the other as the nonfoundational ground for social involvement.

Part Two considers the political complications of this "philosophy of shyness" by examining recent critiques of Hawthorne and by looking closely at the texts most often associated with his political career (the Pierce biography, "Chiefly About War-Matters," *The Blithedale Romance*). It is here that I attempt to take seriously Hawthorne's own desire to separate his ethical and political voices while I also explore the significant hiatus between the ethical content of his fiction and the moral failings of his pro-Unionist, Democratic politics. This is clearly the most contentious ground for the present-day reader of Hawthorne, and I am making an explicit attempt to recomplicate the relationship between Hawthorne's art and his politics — so often taken by current criticism to be unified and inseparable.

Part Three follows the development of Hawthorne's conception of history via Cavell's notion of the symbolic "re-marriage" of the self and the world. This essay looks at Hawthorne's consideration of teleological history and the pattern of escape and reengagement he posits as necessary for an ethical vision. It similarly reconsiders the argument against exile, through which Hawthorne contends for a renewed commitment not merely to the self's community but to America as the site of a democratic future.

What binds these sections together, aside from Hawthorne himself, is a general concern with ethics. In its most basic sense this implies a philosophical interest in relationships and particularly in the effects of interpretation on the treatment of others. As an epistemological skeptic, Hawthorne continually posed fundamental questions of ethics and engagement: how do ideas affect others? How do interpretive decisions determine actions? How does inaction or withdrawal relate to ethical behavior? How does politics express or contradict basic ethical imperatives? and so on. More than anything else, he seems concerned with how the local at its most basic — the self confronting the other — comments upon more familiar questions of social and political engagement. His solution, if we can call it that, is both radical and paradoxical: to argue that social engagement must be predicated on a fundamental sense of self-limitation, on a radical humility that puts the self in deference to the other and thereby both enables and *demands* reengagement through, rather than despite, an awareness of separation.

What makes this approach particularly challenging is that Hawthorne's politics are clearly unacceptable to contemporary audiences. His stubborn antebellum Unionism and its attendant resistance to radical abolition mark him as a peculiar choice for a study of ethics. How can we argue for the ethical content of a writer who failed to oppose slavery more vigorously? How can a writer be concerned with fundamental interpretive abuse and fail to recognize its general function in his own society? But what might seem a contradiction is actually a paradox at the heart of ethical thinking. It is the tension between abstract commitment to a revolutionary idea and the unthinkable demand of the specific stranger, between politics conceived as "reasonable" action through ideological power and an ethics of the single self confronting the infinite "face." Hawthorne's life and work express this tension, highlighting the human complexities of engagement while challenging our own assumptions about the moral sufficiency of political idealism. Reading him, we must recognize not merely his unacceptable nineteenth-century politics but the potential hiatus between ethical theory and its distortion by partisanship and the rhetoric of idealism.

Hawthorne's Shyness is therefore both a book about ethics and an example, to the extent possible, of ethical criticism, of an approach to an author through an awareness of limitation. I present it in part as an example of personal engagement, of an individual struggle with the awareness of the distances between us. To read Hawthorne is to come face to face with the space that separates one from another and to fight the tendency, even the desire, to fill that space illegitimately, through self-extension. But I also offer it as an alternative to critical approaches that work to control the object of attention by partially or entirely dehumanizing the author, by treating writers primarily as symptoms of social and political scenes rather than as difficult, resistant others. This is an attempt, in other words, not to remove culture or politics from consideration in literary criticism but to reassert a realm of personal responsibility that gives meaning to all choices, whether personal or political.

Part I / The Philosophy of Shyness

Moreover I have felt sure of him in his neighborhood, & in his necessities of sympathy & intelligence, that I could well wait his time — his unwillingness & caprice — and might one day conquer a friendship. It would have been a happiness, doubtless to both of us, to have come into habits of unreserved intercourse. It was easy to talk with him — there were no barriers — only, he said so little, that I talked too much, & stopped only because — as he gave no indications — I feared to exceed. He showed no egotism or self-assertion, rather a humility, &, at one time, a fear that he had written himself out. One day, when I found him on the top of his hill, in the woods, he paced back the path to his house, & said, "*this path is the only re-membrance of me that will remain.*" Now it appears that I waited too long.

— EMERSON, *Journals*

A more intrepid talker than myself would have shouted his ideas across the gulf; but, for me, there must first be a close and unembarrassed contiguity with my companion, or I cannot say one real word. I doubt whether I have ever really talked with half a dozen persons in my life, either men or women.

— HAWTHORNE, *The French and Italian Notebooks*

CHAPTER TWO

Romantic Truth

In September 1850, a month or so after their first meeting, Herman Melville spent five days with Nathaniel Hawthorne and Hawthorne's wife and children in the "little old red farm-house" at Lenox, Massachusetts. When not staying out of Hawthorne's way, "Mr. Typee," as Sophia Hawthorne sometimes called him, accompanied his older colleague around the Berkshire countryside: "In the afternoon he walked with Mr Hawthorne. He told me he [Melville] was naturally so silent a man that he was complained of a great deal on this account; but that he found himself talking to Mr Hawthorne to a great extent. He said Mr Hawthorne's great but hospitable silence drew him out — that it was astonishing how *sociable* his silence was. (This Mr Emerson used to feel) He said sometimes they would walk along without talking on either side, but that even then they seemed to be very social"[1] In a curious way, Mrs. Hawthorne's account of the week mirrors what we find in Melville's letters: an exuberant voice, unstoppable really, responding to a friend's encouraging silence. This is partially a trick of history, of course; Hawthorne's letters to Melville have not survived. And yet their absence seems strangely appropriate or at least partially reflective of this famous relationship. Even at this point the roles seem set: one to talk, the other to be "hospitable" — "sociable" but silent.

These opposing personalities suggest, at least metaphorically, distinct attitudes toward language and relationships. It is not that Hawthorne refused to speak to others or that Melville was never silent but that between the two they represent significantly different ways of approaching the world outside the self. Melville's, if I can overgeneralize for a moment, is aggressive and inquisitive, a probing intelligence that tends to imagine knowledge as hidden and volatile. Hawthorne's is passive, receptive, able to be both sympathetic and distant. Melville talks, in other words, and Hawthorne *listens*. And it is this "listening" — as a style of thought, as an approach to the world — that characterizes his epistemological stance. It is "sociable," which is to say that it allows for a certain closeness, Emerson's "proximity," but it is also silent, reserved, separate.[2] And rather than picture knowledge of the world or of others as concealed or secretive, he prefers to step back from mystery, to be attuned to surfaces. He is interested, that is, but skeptical, aware of the secret but suspicious of his own desire and ability to know.

The difference between the two men appears even more forcefully in their writing, particularly the major theoretical works of the early 1850s. Melville's "Hawthorne and His Mosses," for instance, may have begun as a tribute from the young writer to his older model, but it ended up as a platform for Melville's own theories of knowledge. As though in response, Hawthorne's preface to *The House of the Seven Gables* registers the sort of quiet skepticism and stylistic withdrawal that its author's "hospitable" silence only suggests.

A Dark Little Black-Letter Volume

"Hawthorne and His Mosses" (1850) is one of the most famous book reviews in literary history.[3] Ostensibly an anonymous account of Hawthorne's latest short story collection, the essay actually crystallizes the rapidly developing aesthetic and philosophical theories of the explosive author of *Redburn* and *White-Jacket*. As a consequence, it has been repeatedly mined for information on Melville's literary and political goals, his sexuality, and his conception of Hawthorne as both a potential soul mate and an "American Shakespeare."[4] More basically, it can also tell us a great deal about how the young Melville of 1850–51 understood relationships, particularly the degree of knowledge and understanding that may pass between two potential friends. Indeed, one of the essay's most remarkable features is the presumptive intimacy between the narrator, the self-styled "Virginian," and the subject of his analysis, for though the Southerner's comments may suggest little more than youthful enthusiasm, they also depend upon an invasive epistemology that Hawthorne's fiction consistently condemns.

In the essay's initial section its highly strung voice admits to a kind of dizziness, to being "spun . . . round about in a web of dreams"; he succumbs to the "soft ravishments of the man" but then is dismissed "with but misty reminiscences, as if I had been dreaming of him" (ibid., 241). This withdrawal is presumably Hawthorne's familiar exit from "The Old Manse," the introductory sketch in which he denies claims of intimacy and reveals his perpetual distance: "Has the reader gone wandering, hand in hand with me, through the inner passages of my being, and have we groped together into all its chambers, and examined their treasures or their rubbish? Not so" (*CE*, 10:32). For Hawthorne, the reader's assumption of communion functions as a tool, a device by which to gain authorial control: the reader believes himself privy to the author's inner life, but in fact he knows only what the writer wishes him to know. Or does he? The narrator of "Hawthorne and His Mosses" simply pushes past this delicacy; he refuses to let the ravishing figure slip away. Indeed, he moves closer and closer as the essay progresses, becoming as he nears more and more certain of the "truth" about Nathaniel Hawthorne.[5]

But how is one to know another person? The essay's initial description suggests an Emersonian method, by which "greatness" is found through "intuition." And yet the Virginian has trouble resting in so elusive a construction, adding that to "touch" such knowledge is to "find it is gold." It is the same "Truth" found in Shakespeare, he tells us, the "vital truth" of Lear when he "tears off the mask": "For in this world of lies, Truth is forced to fly like a scared white doe in the woodlands; and only by cunning glimpses will she reveal herself, as in Shakespeare and other masters of the great Art of Telling the Truth, — even though it be covertly, and by snatches."[6] This frightened truth, elusive though it may be, is nevertheless depicted as an object, a thing to be hunted, caught, or missed in the woods, but a definable substance just the same. In other words, Melville is relying upon objective metaphors and a quasi-Platonic division of worlds to describe the kind of truth he finds in Shakespeare and Hawthorne. He thereby implies that the skilled reader can, if only for a moment, reach the "place" of truth or, by extension, the deep "inside" of the usually hidden author. Not many months later, while writing *Moby-Dick*, he would call this movement "diving," reading as a metaphysical quest.[7] Hawthorne and Shakespeare become targets, white whales (or "does") that contain the truth.

It is a self-fulfilling form of inquiry: by imagining a truth in others, the individual is creating his own dream of union, an erasure of difference. This is clearest in the essay's most famous passage, the much-discussed erotic recompense of penetration: "But already I feel that this Hawthorne has dropped germinous seeds into my soul. He expands and deepens down, the more I contemplate him; and further, and further, shoots his strong New-England roots into the hot soil of my Southern soul."[8] The shift from aggressive to passive on the part of the reader implies a process: the quester seeks truth only to find himself overtaken, possessed by that which he had hoped to possess. And yet the reader himself is responsible for the structure of this encounter, from the imagined site of truth to the vision of the author as seedsman. The result is a self-invasion in which Melville's conception of himself finds his image of the author, a solipsism that simply confirms a preexisting unity.

This figuration continues in Melville's letters from the period, particularly that of April 16, 1851, in which he "reviews" *The House of the Seven Gables* for Hawthorne and indulges in what he will later call "ontological heroics." Melville begins his discussion of the recently published romance by imagining it as the titular house itself: "There is old china with rare devices, set out on the carved buffet; there are long and indolent lounges to throw yourself upon; there is an admirable sideboard, plentifully stored with good viands; there is a smell as of old wine in the pantry; and finally, in one corner, there is a dark little black-letter volume in golden clasps, entitled 'Hawthorne: A Problem'" (*C*, 185). A comfortable conventionality (book as house, author as book) animates these figures. It suggests a similar degree of readability, though of course houses can be dark and books closed. But whether or not reading in either case is easy or difficult, the images offered depend for their coherence on the implied reality of substance or depth, a valued interiority. The house is full and so too the man, though the nature of that fullness remains uncertain. More simply, if "Hawthorne" is a problem, he can be solved or at least submitted to a process of solution. Thus he comes to embody, through his characters, "a certain tragic phase of humanity." He has the "intense feeling of the visable truth . . . the absolute condition of present things as they strike the eye of the man who fears them not, though they do their worst to him" (*C*, 186). And there is a "grand truth" about him: "He says NO! in thunder. . . . For all men who say *yes*, lie" (*C*, 186).

Echoing his own language in "Mosses," Melville again divides the cognitive field into surface and depth, false and true. He offers a solution to the Hawthorne problem by setting up a framework that will allow truth to emerge and Hawthorne to be read. Admittedly, this truth is dark and destructive, a great and thunderous NO!, but it is graspable; it is an answer, which is more perhaps than is available from that other "book," the Universe: "We incline to think that the Problem of the Universe is like the Freemason's mighty secret, so terrible to all children. It turns out, at last, to consist in a triangle, a mallet, and an apron, — nothing more! We incline to think that God cannot explain His own secrets, and that He would like a little information upon certain points Himself. We mortals astonish Him as much as He us. But it is this *Being* of the matter; there lies the knot with which we choke ourselves. As soon as you say *Me*, a *God*, a *Nature*, so soon you jump off from your stool and hang from the beam. Yes, that word is the hangman. Take God out of the dictionary, and you would have Him in the street" (*C*, 186). This passage, full of romantic bravado, provides a sense of just how complicated Melville's idealism could be. After designating his friend as a "problem" text and before giving us the paradoxical answer to that problem, he shifts into another mode, upsetting his own reasoning. The universe appears to be a "problem" with a secret center, and yet perhaps this secret is but the shape of our thinking, of language itself. By "naming" God and thereby possessing him, we lose him. Our very grasp is our undoing. Despite this sophisticated glimpse of his own philosophical limitations, however, he continues to grasp at everything — God, nature, *and* Hawthorne. The problem without an answer is answered just the same with a "NO!," a darkness, without substance yet substantive, a negation but still a "truth."

Of course, Melville does doubt the availability of truth, but its cryptic nature is more the result of the world's blindness than its inherent slipperiness. Even the dark "NO!" is present and available if we can adjust our sight correctly, if we can see and receive it: "But Truth is the silliest thing under the sun. Try to get a living by the Truth — and go to the Soup Societies. Heavens! Let any clergyman try to preach the Truth from its very stronghold, the pulpit, and they would ride him out of his church on his own pulpit banister. It can hardly be doubted that all Reformers are bottomed upon the truth, more or less; and to the world at large are not reformers almost universally laughing-stocks?" (*C*, 191). There is sufficient evidence to argue, as many readers have, that Melville saw himself as a prophetic reformer, the truth-teller *contra mundum*.[9] It is not the existence or availability of truth that is here questioned but its reception, the failure of his audience to accept the unpleasant negation he offers. "Truth is ridiculous to men" not because it cannot be grasped but because the "world of lies" prefers a pleasing illusion. Even Solomon, "the truest man who ever spoke," had to "manage" his message "with a view to popular conservatism" (*C*, 193). Only in rare moments of "atmospheric skepticism" is there a sense that Melville's truth is anything less than certain, stable, or at least conceivable for the author who imagines himself writing "the Gospels" in his century (*C*, 191, 193, 213, 192). Even the relationship between author and reader, fraught as it is with threats of failure, offers no fundamental barrier to its transmission, for if truth can be known and "preached," so can a fellow author or human being. It is in this way that the "Hawthorne" of the letters becomes a present, finite conception, eventually a part of Melville himself: "Whence come you, Hawthorne? By what right do you drink from my flagon of life? And when I put it to my lips — lo, they are yours and not mine. I feel that the Godhead is broken up like the bread at the Supper, and that we are the pieces" (*C*, 212). Though admittedly the result of his "pantheistic" euphoria at his friend's response to *Moby-Dick*, this description simply extends previous conceptions of the reader-writer relationship. The optimism is temporary, of course, as *Pierre* and *The Confidence-Man* dramatically demonstrate. But at what must have been the high point of Melville's writing life, such intimacy, gained through reading, seemed both desirable and possible.

A Pin through a Butterfly

We may never know Hawthorne's specific reaction to Melville's declarations, but his tendency to avoid and distrust such unities, whether real or imagined, is abundantly clear. The evidence of his personal reticence is plentiful. He resisted touch, according to his wife, avoided meetings, slipped away whenever possible from strangers and even friends.[10] The thought of unnecessary social intimacy appears to have disturbed him; he describes the Shakers of the Hancock settlement as "a filthy set," "and their utter and systematic lack of privacy" as "hateful and disgusting to think of" (*CE*, 8:465). His reserve, even in "sociable" silences, defines him, especially when compared to the notably demonstrative Melville. More important, his fiction and the philosophical ground on which it rests share this "shyness," a commitment to keeping a distance between reader and author, subject and object. The complete collapse of one self into another is seldom if ever permitted in Hawthorne's writing, and when it does occur it is an unmistakable evil, an invasion and violation of selfhood.[11]

The closest thing from Hawthorne to a statement similar to "Mosses" is the preface to *The House of the Seven Gables* (1851). Long considered a key to Hawthorne's literary theory, the *Gables* preface can be read as a reply of sorts to

Melville's letters and review, for whether intended as such or not, it gives the clearest available picture of his thinking during this period. It also addresses the same issues Melville raises: the nature of the reader-writer relationship and the potential shape and availability of romantic truth. Like most of Hawthorne's prefaces, the introduction to his third novel is a masterpiece of ironic self-stylization; designed both to invite and frustrate, it functions in part as an elaborate mask that often hides as much as it tells. Even so, it seems serious enough in its desire to claim for the romance "a certain latitude," a freedom from the "very minute fidelity" to the "ordinary course of man's experience" (*CE*, 2:1). This familiar plea for the imaginative space of the *kunstmärchen* carries with it a larger agenda both political and philosophical. The "novel," through its close observance of the everyday, is restrictive, controlling; the romance offers freedom. Faithful to the "ordinary," the novel must swear to the validity of "probable" experience and to an epistemology that constructs such a category. It must believe, in other words, that experience *is* ordinary. The romance resists such constraints; it has the latitude not merely to imagine improbable experience but to propose alternate ways of seeing that deny or transcend the ordinary.

Still, the romance has its limits: it "has fairly a right to present . . . truth under circumstances, to a great extent, of the writer's own choosing or creation," but "as a work of art, it must rigidly subject itself to laws," and it is capable of "sin[ning] unpardonably, so far as it may swerve aside from the truth of the human heart" (*CE*, 2:1). This qualification seems straightforward enough, but what sort of truth can be ascribed to "the human heart"? The figure, though apparently conventional, is somewhat hard to handle. It suggests the wedding of concept (truth) and feeling (heart), for though it may be tempting to alter the phrase to read "the truth about the human heart [emotions]," the connecting "of" remains faintly ambiguous. Heard this way, the phrase implies both a conceptual truth concerning emotional states and a nonconceptual truth figured by the heart—a formulation that puts pressure on both possibilities. The question it poses might be put this way: How do we locate the truth of the human heart? through thought or feeling? Can it be expressed in a statement, a moral? Or can it only be shown indirectly, through metaphor? In other words, is this a truth susceptible to the language of philosophy or is it a "poetic" truth and as such both presentable and inexpressible at the same time?[12] And what does it mean to "swerve aside" from it? Is it a beacon, a guide, something distant but not necessarily attainable in itself? Or is it the path itself, suggesting a way but not limited to a specific place or moment?

Whichever the case, it is clearly not Melville's "black-letter volume." There is a sense of distance, a stable but unreachable end — and no sense at all that what we are after is an object, a definable thing that can be handled, possessed, read. This may be the reason Hawthorne quickly shifts figures, describing the romance first as a "picture" with "lights" and "shadows" and then as a meal delicately flavored with hints of the "Marvellous." In other words, the truth he imagines is not an object that can be seized but an elusive effect of individual experience. Because the romance does not restrict itself to the collective vision of society, it is associated with the freedom to reconceive the world, to see it as something other than what society has agreed to call ordinary or probable. The "truth of the human heart" in this sense is the truth of desire: the reimagination of the world as a changing and changeable reality, part of the life in a democratic society. Admittedly, the "actual" — what society calls normal — cannot be ignored; the artist must realize that an audience requires the stability of a generally agreed upon interpretation of reality. To alter that view is, as the Scottish Common Sense philosophy warned, dangerous and disruptive, in the same sense that democracy in its purer forms courts interpretive anarchy. The romancer must suggest, hint at (through "flavoring" and "shadow") other ways of seeing (the marvelous) and offer freedom within order.

The subsequent paragraphs of the preface serve to clarify this new understanding of truth by elaborating its paradoxical doubleness and contrasting it with the limited statement of a "moral." Hawthorne was certainly fond of thinking about his fiction in such terms. His journals are full of ideas that cluster around brief thematic statements, and *The House of the Seven Gables* is no exception. What is interesting here, however, is how he chooses to qualify the moral he offers. After telling us that he "has provided himself with a moral" — "the truth, namely, that the wrong-doing of one generation lives into the successive ones, and, divesting itself of every temporary advantage, becomes a pure and uncontrollable mischief" — he quickly backtracks, noting that romances rarely "teach anything" except "through a far more subtle process than the ostensible one": "The Author has considered it hardly worth his while, therefore, relentlessly to impale the story with its moral, as with an iron rod — or, rather, as by sticking a pin through a butterfly, — thus at once depriving it of life, and causing it to stiffen in an ungainly and unnatural attitude. A high truth, indeed, fairly, finely, and skilfully wrought out, brightening at every step, and crowning the final developement of a work of fiction, may add an artistic glory, but is never any truer, and seldom any more evident, at the last page than at the first" (*CE*, 2:2–3). The imagery here is remarkably different from that of the opening paragraph. The truth captured by the moral is now "an iron rod," or "a pin," that impales the butterfly of romance, "causing it to stiffen" unnaturally. The "high truth" that is "seldom any more evident at the last page than at the first" is both expressed and not expressed, apprehended in movement and life, like the butterfly, and thus never quite captured at all. To catch it, as Wordsworth might have said, is to kill it; to define it is to "pin" it down, losing it through appropriation.[13]

The distance to Melville's "black-letter volume" now seems striking. Whatever their other similarities, Hawthorne's attitude toward truth-seeking is fundamentally passive, including the need for ethical distance. Even Melville's "white doe" in a "world of lies" relies upon the stark contrast between true and false that Melville found so compelling. It may be as elusive as Hawthorne's butterfly, but Melville's seeker seems more than able to catch and express it, if only he could find an audience brave enough to listen. This is not to suggest that Melville's fiction is reducible to simplistic "morals," but it is to notice his habit of thinking in terms of definite answers to indefinite questions.[14] Hawthorne, it seems fair to say, approaches truth with greater delicacy, with conceptions that seem designed to keep him away from all reductive tendencies, from thinking of himself as a truth-teller or even a truth-seeker in the Melvilleian mold.[15] As late as 1856, on the beach near Liverpool, he found the contrast just as pronounced: "Melville, as he always does, began to reason of Providence and futurity, and of everything that lies beyond human ken, and informed me that he had 'pretty much made up his mind to be annihilated'; but still he does not seem to rest in that anticipation; and, I think, will never rest until he gets hold of a definite belief. It is strange how he persists — and has persisted ever since I knew him, and probably long before — in wandering to-and fro over these deserts, as dismal and monotonous as the sand hills amid which we were sitting" (*CE*, 22:163).

Readers have long recognized that this famous passage says as much about Hawthorne as it does about his turbulent guest. The traditional interpretation casts the younger man as the despairing idealist (either heroic or foolish, depending upon the reader's temperament) and the consul to Liverpool as a fatalist — different goals, different epistemologies. One struggles with impossible questions; the other accepts the limitations of human understanding. After all, to seek a "definite belief" presupposes knowledge that can be defined — limited, capable of possession. To see that such a search is futile implies that Hawthorne, whatever his other limitations, at least understood Melville's trap: the idealist is caught not only because he seeks "what lies beyond human ken" but also because he believes such knowledge exists in a form he can seize and control. He sees it as finite when it is, if it exists at all, infinite and therefore other than thought.

Negation and Veiling

This, then, might be called Hawthorne's philosophy: a passive but ethical skepticism, wary of ideas, attuned to the local. His suspicion of the ordinary includes the concern that custom tends to reduce life's strangeness, particularly the resistant individuality of other minds. In this respect, at least, Hawthorne is a thoroughgoing romantic, in tune with the major interests of Wordsworth, Coleridge, and especially Keats. "The Custom-House" section of *The Scarlet Letter* makes this clear in its famous "moonlight" passage, where the romance is described as a "neutral territory" somewhere between dream and reality. Here the "Actual and the Imaginary may meet, and each imbue itself with the nature of the other," and the solitary watcher, in the shadows of moon and firelight, can "dream strange things and make them look like truth" (*CE*, 1:35, 36). The passage, in both image and theory, bears a strong resemblance to the plan for *Lyrical Ballads:*

> It was agreed, that my endeavours should be directed to persons and characters supernatural, or at least romantic; yet so as to transfer from our inward nature a human interest and a semblance of truth sufficient to procure for these shadows of imagination that willing suspension of disbelief for the moment, which constitutes poetic faith. Mr. Wordsworth, on the other hand, was to propose to himself as his object, to give the charm of novelty to things of every day, and to excite a feeling analogous to the supernatural, by awakening the mind's attention from the lethargy of custom, and directing it to the loveliness and the wonders of the world before us; an inexhaustible treasure, but for which in consequence of the film of familiarity and selfish solicitude we have eyes, yet see not, ears that hear not, and hearts that neither feel nor understand.[16]

The emphasis on perception dominates both statements: actual and imaginary, everyday and supernatural reflect binary modes of seeing that romantic poetics hopes to collapse. The goal is to make "strange things . . . look like truth," exposing the limits of custom or, more accurately, overcoming the oppositional dialectic between "familiar" and "strange." According to Wordsworth and Coleridge, the division can be attacked from either direction; strangeness can be made familiar or familiarity strange. And Hawthorne agrees, claiming that "a different order of composition" might have allowed him to "spiritualize . . . the opaque substance of to-day" by focusing on the daily life of the customhouse. His failure to do so, to write what he calls the "better book," is a failure of attention: "The fault was mine. The page of life that was spread out before me seemed dull and commonplace, only because I had not fathomed its deeper import" (*CE*, 1:37).

This failure suggests interference, the self in its own way. And if "moonlight" is an insufficient remedy at times, Hawthorne can point to a second method for displacing the customary limitations of the observer — self-veiling. Here the approach seems to owe more to Keats than to Coleridge, though its basic goals can still be described as romantic and, at least poetically, revolutionary. For Keats, the overwhelming concern is attitude, self-conception; like Hawthorne, he objects to the rough groping of intellect in the service of conceptualization. The poetic mind is passive, refusing both limitation and certainty. It must be "capable of being in uncertainties, mysteries, doubts, without any irritable reaching after fact and reason."[17] For Walter Jackson Bate "the significant word . . . is 'irritable.' We should also stress 'capable' — 'capable of being in uncertainties, Mysteries, doubts' without the 'irritable' need to extend our identities and rationalize our 'half knowledge.' "[18] As with Hawthorne's "high truth," the poet must resist the impulse to "extend" his identity and move instead toward self-negation as a way of acknowledging others. As Paul De Man says of *Endymion*, "it is a dream about poetry as a redeeming force, oriented toward others in a concern that is moral but altogether spontaneous, rooted in the fresh sensibility of love and sympathy and not in abstract imperatives."[19]

In this respect Hawthorne's "shyness" functions in much the same way as Keats's "negative capability," as a desire to receive the world through an intentional self-negation.[20] In Keats's language the "poetical Character . . . does no harm from its relish of the dark side of things any more than from its taste for the bright one; because they both end in speculation. A Poet is the most unpoetical thing in existence; because he has no Identity — he is continually in for — and filling some other Body."[21] To surrender to the other is thus to lose one's identity, making the poet a momentary receptacle for strangeness. By apparent contrast, Hawthorne, whose interest in sympathy is equally crucial, seems to offer a "poetical Character" not so much empty as set aside:

> Thou wilt not think that it is caprice or stubbornness that has made me hitherto resist thy wishes. Neither, I think, is it a love of secrecy and darkness. I am glad to think that God sees through my heart; and if any angel has power to penetrate into

> it, he is welcome to know everything that is there. Yes; and so may any mortal, who
> is capable of full sympathy, and therefore worthy to come into my depths. But he
> must find his own way there. I can neither guide him nor enlighten him. It is this
> involuntary reserve, I suppose, that has given the objectivity to my writings. And
> when people think that I am pouring myself out in a tale or essay, I am merely telling
> what is common to human nature, not what is peculiar to myself. I sympathize with
> them — not they with me. (*CE*, 15:612–13)

There are differences here, primarily between Keats's cultivation of vacancy and
Hawthorne's flirtation with "secrecy" and "darkness." Since Hawthorne's terms
imply hidden depths of potentially "truer" content, we are forced to imagine
some sort of identity behind or beneath the surface. It is his peculiar gift, however, to permit such thinking while distancing himself from its implications. By
sympathizing with his readers, Hawthorne is opening himself to otherness and
expressing "what is common to human nature." Consequently, his own hidden,
or veiled, self is displaced, removed from consideration through the process of
imaginative sympathy. Only another such discerning "mortal" "capable of full
sympathy" can "come into [his] depths."

Even so, to announce a hidden self is to highlight its hiddenness, to make of
the structure of hiding an irritation and an anxiety that seems mostly absent from
Keats's formulation. A purely negative space lacks the dramatic hold the veil
creates, even if the veil is nothing more than the enactment of its own structure.
Apparently incapable of the total passivity Keats desires ("but let us open our
leaves like a flower and be passive and receptive"), Hawthorne retains not so
much a self as the conceptual arrangement through which privacy becomes possible.[22] He maintains a structure of secrets even while placing that structure in
ironic lights that reveal it as a product of thought and a creative positioning vis-
à-vis the world. Such ironies inform a style designed both to receive and to step
away from the otherness it engages. That is, Hawthorne's style uniquely combines Keatsian negativity with a conscious hiddenness to produce a doubled
stance through which the self can both open and close without compromising
either sympathy or privacy.

The well-known passage from the preface to *The Snow-Image* (1852) describes
its own seductive combination of invitation and withdrawal:

> There is no harm, but, on the contrary, good, in arraying some of the ordinary facts
> of life in a slightly idealized and artistic guise. I have taken facts which relate to
> myself, because they chance to be nearest at hand, and likewise are my own prop-

erty. And, as for egotism, a person, who has been burrowing, to his utmost ability, into the depths of our common nature, for the purposes of psychological romance, — and who pursues his researches in that dusky region, as he needs must, as well by the tact of sympathy as by the light of observation, — will smile at incurring such an imputation in virtue of a little preliminary talk about his external habits, his abode, his casual associates, and other matters entirely upon the surface. These things hide the man, instead of displaying him. You must make quite another kind of inquest, and look through the whole range of his fictitious characters, good and evil, in order to detect any of his essential traits. (*CE*, 11:4)

This passage is as complicated as it is nonchalant. Its movement depends upon the simultaneous offering and denial of access to Hawthorne "himself." Yet, depending as it does upon the ironies of surface and depth, such a double move-ment cannot yield substantial truth without questioning its existence; it cannot give us "Hawthorne" except as an enactment of its own, substantially empty structure. In this respect, the style of the passage is the equivalent of the smile it describes: a sign that both connects and separates, a sign of outwardness as well as inwardness.[23] The passage's final allurement, too often taken at face value, ap-pears to provide a way into the "essential" Hawthorne through the truth-telling powers of fiction. But by enticing readers to "detect" hidden essences, Haw-thorne is merely resetting the trap he has just described. According to the pre-vious sentences, "matters entirely upon the surface . . . hide the man, instead of displaying him," a statement that knowingly implies the impossibility of detec-tion itself. In other words, "essential traits" can never be known as "surface matters" because in order to become a part of definite knowledge they must cease to be "essential"; they must rise to the surface and become a part of the veil. In this sense the structure upon which detection depends never changes; essence, though present as a goal, is always out of reach.

This is the point at which philosophy and style meet. Hawthorne's conception of truth, like Keats's, demands an artistic strategy that is, at the very least, sus-picious of the reductions carried out by one mind upon another. While not entirely negative, his self-veiling nevertheless finds expression in a style aware of its own seductive engagement with surface and depth. To seek transparency from such a language is therefore to misunderstand the philosophical ground on which it is built. For when style is constructed as a form of veiling, as a part of the author's withdrawal from the scene of his writing, it establishes its own parame-ters of response. It tells us how to read by forcing us to give up preconceptions about the deeper place of truth. It is meant, in other words, to frustrate, as well as instruct, by refusing anything more than its chosen mask.

This is also the point at which Hawthorne meets the romantic and post-romantic tradition that moves from Emerson and Thoreau through Nietzsche, Heidegger, Levinas, and Cavell. The list may surprise, given the history of Hawthorne criticism. It should not. Despite his resistance to Emerson and transcendentalism, it is clear that Hawthorne shared more than the streets of Concord with these American inheritors of German idealism. And the steps from Emerson to Nietzsche, Nietzsche to Heidegger, Heidegger to Levinas and Cavell are well established in the commentary on each of these figures. It is a line of thought concerned with the effects of ideas, with the shape and construction of thought, its limitations and its potential liberation from both Platonic and Cartesian suppositions. Traditionalist though Hawthorne was in many respects, his work, particularly his theorizing of the romance and its approach to representation, places him squarely in this skeptical, philosophically radical company.

The Poetics of Shyness

According to Gerald Bruns, for the later Heidegger "poetry has now to be understood as the way of entering into the mode of being of *Gelassenheit*, the letting-go of things." "Poetry," he continues, "now has to be understood in terms of the renunciation (*Verzichten*) of linguistic mastery. This means understanding poetry as the *Sichversagen* of the poet, where poetry opens itself—enters into, listens or belongs to—the mystery of language, its otherness, its nonhumanness, its density, its 'danger.' "[24] Like its romantic predecessors, this is a negative position, a withdrawal: the observer who foregoes the desire to master (know) the world must also forego language as the tool of mastery. Language (as poetry) is no longer a speaker or speech but a listener, a listening. In the place of transparency, it offers its own thickness, a resistant strangeness.

Famous for its "indeterminacy," Hawthorne's writing may well participate in a similar resistance, if at times it struggles against it. By undermining the exchange between dream and everyday reality, his sentences pull away from interpretive categories toward themselves. They force us to accept language as surface rather than medium, as a series of interruptions of a presumed transparency.[25] In this sense Hawthorne's language can, at important moments, be remarkably "silent," refusing clarity. It works seductively, relying on the desire for light to demonstrate vulnerability. After all, flaunting an impenetrable thickness would simply free us from responsibility. And Hawthorne is interested in choices, even — or especially — when they are unclear.

His style might, then, best be described as *darkness in the desire for light*, his authorial positioning, his attitude, as *withdrawal in the desire for connection*, what I have previously called "shyness." As Emily Miller Budick has shown, such paradoxes bring to mind Cavell's meditations on the philosophical orientations of Thoreau and Emerson.[26] Thoreau first — his withdrawal, neighboring, and "nextness":

> The writer keeps my choices in front of me, the ones I am not making and the ones I am. This makes me wretched and nervous. My choices appear as curiosities, and to be getting the better of me. Curiosity grows with every new conjecture we find confirmed in the words. It seems all but an accident that we should discover what they mean. This becomes a mood of our acts of reading altogether: it is an accident, utterly contingent, that we should be present at these words at all. We feel this as the writer's withdrawal from the words on which he had staked his presence; and we feel this as the words' indifference to us, their disinterest in whether we choose to stay with them or not. . . .
>
> What is next to us is what we neighbor. The writer has spoken of finding himself suddenly neighbor to the birds; and he speaks of the pond in neighborly terms. . . . Our relation to nature, at its best, would be that of neighboring it — knowing the grandest laws it is executing, while nevertheless "not wholly involved" in them.[27]

The problem of Thoreau's words, the problem of reading "Thoreau," rests upon his simultaneous presence and absence in those words, and the "mood" Cavell invokes is certainly not unfamiliar to the reader of Hawthorne. The complex interplay of distance and nearness, whether in relation to nature or society, suggests both separation and connection and, in terms of language, both resistance and yielding. Though Hawthorne does not position himself "one mile from any neighbor," he does in terms of his language "neighbor" the world, his readers, us. Like Emerson in "Self-Reliance," he "will have no covenants but proximities."[28] *Veil* is Hawthorne's word for the separation from and connection to "what is next to us." It shrouds, brings darkness but initiates desire, and in this respect is a means of negative seduction, a drawing in, a "sociable silence."

It seems remarkably significant in this context that Sophia Hawthorne should invoke the opinion of Emerson to speak of her husband's conversational reticence. That the "sage of Concord" should understand what it means to be "sociably" silent, to think of silence, that is, as a kind of speech, is certainly no surprise. According to Cavell, seduction is also a property of Emerson's "aversion" to conformity, a "double" turning: "Since his aversion is a *continual turning away* from society, it is thereby a continual turning *toward* it. Toward and away; it is a motion of seduction—such as philosophy will contain. It is in response to this seduction from our seductions (conformities, heteronomies) that the friend (discovered or constructed) represents the standpoint of perfection."[29] Taking the Hawthorne-Melville relationship as a model for this sort of friendship, we can see that silence, or "darkness," negativity, is precisely and paradoxically this turning away and toward. Or, as Bruns explicates Heidegger's similar interests: "There is, for example, keeping silent (*das Schweigen*). '*Keeping silent,*' Heidegger says, 'is another possibility of discourse, and it has the same existential foundation,' namely talk. Moreover, there is more to keeping silent than to speaking. Understanding, taken in Heidegger's sense of understanding as an *existentiale* or mode of being of *Dasein*, follows from listening rather than from speaking."[30] "Silence," both in and out of language, even if understood as a type of resistance, can also be taken as a requirement for understanding through "listening," or openness. The turning away that is silence thus becomes the negativity of listening, the "sociable silence" of Hawthorne in his walks with Emerson and Melville, the "darkness" of his language, which invites readers but refuses at times to speak to them. Again, to repeat, Melville talks and Hawthorne *listens;* to say so is to describe their attitudes toward language and thought, toward knowledge and the availability of others through that knowledge.

For Hawthorne it is style that enacts this sort of "listening." It invites and, in certain respects, teaches listening through its own stubborn combination of invitation and refusal. Through this doubleness it approximates Emerson's "aversion" or Thoreau's "neighboring" and approaches what, according to Bruns, Heidegger calls "poetry": "Rather, poetry is closer to listening than to speaking, that is, it is less a form of linguistic competence or a *poiesis* than a hermeneutical condition of openness to what is said, or more accurately to what is unsaid: openness, perhaps, to the unsayable, or to what cannot be put into words—as language, for example, cannot be put into words. Rather we will need to think of poetry as openness to the *otherness* of language" (ibid., 24). Poetry understood in these terms expresses or simply is an attitude toward language and toward the world. More particularly, for the later Heidegger, it describes an approach to thinking and to that "truth," which, through the activity of poetry or "poetic thinking," becomes entangled with darkness or otherness. Thinking here is the negative approach to the world that Hawthorne offers. What it is not is "grasping," Emerson's "clutching," Hawthorne's "impaling": "Emerson's image of clutching and Heidegger's of grasping, emblematize their interpretation of Western conceptualizing as a kind of sublimized violence. (Heidegger's word is *greifen*; it is readily translatable as 'clutching.') Heidegger is famous here for his thematization of this violence as expressed in the world dominion of technology, but Emerson is no less explicit about it as a mode of thinking. The overcoming of this conceptualizing will require the achievement of a form of knowledge both Emerson and Heidegger call reception, alluding to the Kantian idea that knowledge is active, and sensuous intuition alone passive or receptive."[31]

This conjunction of violence with understanding gathered in the notion of "mastery" may very well be the overriding (negative) theme of the American romance. Its presence in Hawthorne's work, especially the short stories, has been noted for some time, and its important role in such a later piece of self-conscious "romancing" as Henry James's *The Turn of the Screw* has been explored at length by Shoshona Felman in her essay "Turning the Screw of Interpretation." Explaining the paradoxical connection between the governess's repression of information and the "mastery" of her situation, Felman points to the ironic loss associated with such control: "The principle of totality being the very principle of a *boundary* and of the repression inherent in it, the text's irony here lies in the suggestion that the illusion of total *mastery*, of 'seeing *all*,' is in reality a counterpart to the act of '*shutting one's eyes* as tight as possible to the truth.' . . . To 'master,' therefore, to understand and '*see it all*,' as the governess complacently puts it to herself, is in this text, ironically enough, to occupy the very place of *blindness*: of the blindness to which the Master voluntarily commits himself at the outset of the story, by ordering the suppression of all information."[32] In this sense, "blindness," or the repression of what falls outside the limits of conceptual truth (the repression of otherness), results inevitably from the move to master, to totalize. Totality cannot allow for the existence of otherness; conceived as knowledge or "light," it cannot allow the presence of the unknowable, of "darkness."[33]

But while the critique of mastery may be the negative theme of the romance, the form promotes the positive value of "aversion" to modes of philosophical "conformity." The focus for this shift in understanding is "truth," conceived either as a limited, formal statement or as a phenomenon, an event. We have already seen the extent to which Hawthorne's description of "the truth of the human heart" resists or reformulates the notion of truth as graspable or otherwise strictly defined. His evasive description implies motion and elusiveness. His suggested attitude, as implied through metaphor, is a *letting be* as opposed to the obvious violence of "sticking a pin through a butterfly." If we accept the connection between this attitude and Heidegger's notion of "poetry" or "poetic thinking," then we can also see that the *Gables* preface depends upon a similar understanding of the otherness of truth itself. Such a notion appears in Heidegger's "The Origin of the Work of Art" in rather more startling form: "Truth is un-truth, insofar as there belongs to it the reservoir of the not-yet-uncovered, the un-uncovered, in the sense of concealment."[34] Of course, "un-truth" here equates to otherness, not falsehood, what is other than rather than the opposite of truth, or, what is beyond the boundaries of the concept "truth." Again, I rely upon Bruns for gloss: "The otherness of truth is not merely an accidental divergence from essence, an error or mistake or falsehood. It is rather that truth itself is inscribed by a rift that splits it, so to say, lengthwise, joining the familiar and the strange, openness and refusal, clearing and dissembling, darkness and light. Clearly, truth here is no longer that which takes up its residence in knowledge and the discourse of propositions. . . . Truth is always historical; it is always an event." Here is truth, in Bruns's phrase, as "an event of estrangement."[35] For Hawthorne it is the "high truth" that is "never any truer, and seldom any more evident, at the last page than at the first." We experience such "knowledge" as a confrontation with a resistant other, as an overflowing of limits. What we so confront can be neither placed nor located; nor can it be grasped or pinned down without violence. In other words, to conceive of truth as other is not merely to register an epistemological problem; it is to describe a relationship with the world, an ethics.

CHAPTER THREE

Ethics and the Face

Hawthorne and Levinas

To speak of Hawthorne and ethics has probably never been easy. Any author who so clearly declares his own disengagement, his "childish" retreat into moonlit fantasies, is either genuinely uninterested in worldly behavior or is so completely interested that he insists on highlighting the problematics of engagement. In recent years, this subdivision of the so-called Hawthorne problem has grown in complexity owing in large part to the dominance of revisionist political criticism. In a theoretical period deeply concerned with worldly engagement, as ours is, authorial strategies that rely on withdrawal or "veiling" (for which Hawthorne is famous) can seem irresponsible, otherworldly, and potentially evasive of ethical concern. Accordingly, some readers have chided Hawthorne for failures to commit himself linguistically, personally, or politically to direct or "correct" action in the material world. Jonathan Arac, for example, argues that Hawthorne established "indeterminacy" as an excuse or as protection from direct action: "Hawthorne's derealizing style represents objects so that we doubt their reality, yet while thus questioning what offers itself as our world, he refuses to commit himself to the authenticity of any other world or way of seeing."[1] Criticizing at once Hawthorne's aesthetic strategy, the "hermeneutics of indeterminacy" in "current criticism," and the "politics of Freudian compromise-formation," Arac suggests that Hawthorne's failure to advocate active opposition to slavery undermines the ethical content of his work by exposing a connection between aesthetic withdrawal and inaction.[2]

This line of argument is opposed by critics such as Emily Miller Budick, who, like Kenneth Dauber in *The Idea of Authorship in America*, argues that separation, the freedom to turn away, is a necessary condition for commitment. Citing Cavell's description of Emerson's "aversive thinking," Budick underscores the necessary relationship between skepticism and responsibility: "Aversive thinking, by preserving the force of both metaphysical and linguistic skepticism, compels readers and writers, listeners and speakers, to take responsibility for their words."[3] A similar notion, without direct reference to Cavell, is put forth by Dauber: "And yet the hard truth which Hawthorne is asking his readers to face is that, despite any longings to the contrary, they must take the passage at 'face' value precisely. It is *in* the difficulties the passage raises, not in resolving them, that Hawthorne exists. Or better, if he appears to conceal himself in the face he puts on, then as one declaring his concealment exactly, he takes responsibility for himself all the more."[4] In this sense, the ethical basis of Hawthorne's work, as these readers describe it, rests upon an acknowledgment of otherness, an insistence upon separation as a precondition for any sort of meaningful connection. To conceive the relationship in different terms, as simple "commitment," for instance, raises the possibility of compromising the autonomy of that to which one commits. The appropriative grasp of thinking, even if understood as a provisional agreement on an "authentic" reality, reduces otherness to an idea; it transforms the other by replacing it within a totality. That Hawthorne at times resisted such "custom house" reductions and cherished the resistance of experience to systematic thought is clearly evident; that this resistance is the basis for the ethical function of his work may be more difficult for current readers to accept.

The introductory sketch that Hawthorne called "The Old Manse" offers a clear starting point. How are we to take so blatant a refusal of the intimacy readers commonly seek?

> Has the reader gone wandering, hand in hand with me, through the inner passages of my being, and have we groped together into all its chambers, and examined their treasures or their rubbish? Not so. We have been standing on the green sward, but just within the cavern's mouth, where the common sunshine is free to penetrate, and where every footstep is therefore free to come. I have appealed to no sentiment or sensibilities, save such as are diffused among us all. So far as I am a man of really

individual attributes, I veil my face; nor am I, nor have ever been, one of those supremely hospitable people, who serve up their own hearts delicately fried, with brain-sauce, as a tidbit for their beloved public. (*CE*, 10: 32–33)

This famous step back echoes the similarly defensive letter to Sophia Peabody in which Hawthorne tells his fiancée that only God, an angel, or "any mortal . . . capable of full sympathy" can "come into [his] depths" (*CE*, 15: 612). There he calls his attitude an "involuntary reserve" and insists upon his distance from all readers, both of his "heart" and of his fiction. He "veils his face" to his individual peculiarities, discussing only general characteristics shared by all. In other words, he insists upon his own ability to withdraw from the presence of the reader/other at the same time that he remains in that presence as "objective" author. He seeks both connection and separation and uses his fiction at least in part as a means to realize this double desire.

In *Totality and Infinity* Levinas describes the "face" as "the way in which the other presents himself, exceeding *the idea of the other in me*" (50, original emphasis). The face is a "mode" that, like the idea of infinity, overflows its own limits, becoming "expression" (51). What he designates the "face to face" is thus a confrontation between self and other that exceeds thought and yet initiates "discourse," "the relationship of language": "The relationship of language implies transcendence, radical separation, the strangeness of the interlocutors, the revelation of the other to me. In other words, language is spoken where community between the terms of the relationship is wanting, where the common plane is wanting or is yet to be constituted. It takes place in this transcendence. Discourse is thus the experience of something absolutely foreign, a *pure* 'knowledge' or 'experience,' a *traumatism of astonishment*" (73, original emphases). This astonishment might be thought of simply as unpredictability, the freedom of others to speak beyond the thematic limits imposed upon them. Such a situation requires a recognition of the self's vulnerability, its inability to extend through the exterior world. The ego is "put into question" under a prohibition that is fundamentally ethical: "The reason for this is relatively simple: the Other makes me realize that I share the world, that it is not my unique possession. . . . The Other puts me into question by revealing to me that my powers and freedom are limited. But the face does not annihilate the self; on the contrary, it is the condition of its separateness. It instigates dialogue, teaching, and hence reason, society and ethics. It also gives a proper foundation to freedom. The transcendental Ego would like to be the sole source of its own knowledge, actions and meanings; the encounter with the Other shows such freedom to be egotistical, arbitrary and unjustified."[5] This relationship suggests a choice between an illegitimate self-extension and an intentional withdrawal that recognizes the demand of otherness — the choice between "knowledge" and "respect," between "grasping" and "welcoming."[6]

What then does Hawthorne mean when he tells readers of "The Old Manse" that he veils his face? Clearly, he is not, like Mr. Hooper of "The Minister's Black Veil," walking around Concord with a "piece of crape" over his eyes. Perhaps he is simply withholding personal information, private details. In this reading, "face" would refer to a set of facts or feelings associated with the private self. And yet, the face itself is the site of public identity, the set of features that determines the public self, what one shows to the world. So Hawthorne chooses an image of public or external identity to figure the private or internal self. He then offers to "veil" that public/private self by presumably withholding one set of information and simultaneously offering another. In this way "veiling" is not so much hiding one's "face" with a blank mask as it is refusing to show one face by showing another in its place. And what is this other "face" but the "veil" itself, the "sentiment or sensibilities . . . diffused among us all." Thus, when Hawthorne "veils his face" he is assuming the general characteristics of human personality; he is displacing his private self in order to receive and perceive the thoughts and feelings of others.

This ability to take on common attributes, to be "objective," does not imply special knowledge of the private selves of others. Hawthorne's "involuntary reserve" is an epistemological position that contains an awareness of both the limits of knowledge and the limitations on the aggressive understanding of the artist. "Veiling" then can be seen as a way of expressing an understanding of such limits, of the distance between author and audience. To "veil the face" is to acknowledge the otherness of the world, to see one's separation from it and one's connection to it as a product not of knowledge but of the sympathy made possible through withdrawal. In this respect, Hawthorne's artistic choice to "veil his face" stands on the same ground, oddly enough, as Levinas's philosophical injunction to come "face to face" with otherness. Face to face implies a revelation based upon withdrawal, an approach to otherness made possible only by the surrender of attempts at knowledge.

"Face to Face" with Hooper: "The Minister's Black Veil"

In addition to Hawthorne's representations of his own "self-veiling," there are well-known and much-discussed instances of veils and veiling in his fiction, the most famous of which is clearly "The Minister's Black Veil." The story has attracted an astonishing number and variety of readings, including unusually lengthy accounts from Michael Colacurcio and J. Hillis Miller.[7] Despite this abundant response, those wishing to understand how Hawthorne's "self-veiling" relates to Mr. Hooper's donning of a "piece of black crape" may find that significant questions remain — not so much unanswered as answered in ways that deserve further consideration.

Colacurcio's historicist reading attempts to cover every angle, including both general context (the Great Awakening) and specific reference (Hooper gathers John Hooper, Thomas Hooker, and William Cooper). Colacurcio examines the romantic interest in "sorrow" and weighs it in the story's scales against the Puritan "true sight of sin," concluding at the end of some seventy pages that the story's author is probably not a Puritan sympathizer but something like a pragmatist:

> Surely Hawthorne knew — as sorrowfully as any seventeenth-century Puritan — that the "self" was "the very figure or type of Hell." He might even accept, more tentatively, a whole class of Puritan propositions about Sin and the Self. But in his view the last thing anybody should have to endure was a whole life looking at (or for) that self. The thing might not, in itself, even exist; and even if it did, it never *could* be adequately expressed. No one can show forth his inmost heart. But cannot one show his face? The literal face will be, of course, partially deceptive: a parson will smile and smile and be a sinner still. . . . But the alternative turns out to be worse: the symbolic veil will always be destructive of available community; it will continuously heighten and feature what cannot be overcome. Better not wear it. Better do what one can.[8]

Colacurcio describes a Hawthorne potentially sympathetic to the pragmatic turn of William James: "Our account of truth is an account of truths in the plural, of processes of leading, realized *in rebus*, and having only this quality in common, that they *pay*."[9] The tone in James's *Pragmatism* may be a good deal less anguished, but the surrender of ultimate knowledge (whether of truth or self) that Colacurcio depicts rests upon the same basic contention: Knowledge should be restricted to what is knowable; the search for ultimate truths is futile and self-destructive.

For Miller, on the other hand, Hawthorne is less the pragmatist than the deconstructor, a connoisseur of conceptual vertigo. "The Minister's Black Veil," Miller argues, is a story designed at least in part to "unveil" the "ideology of unveiling."[10] This ideology is precisely the trap of seeing everything on the surface as a deception, a mask, so that truth is hidden forever or at least until the apocalypse. Referring to the story's final scene, Miller explains that "the most disquieting effect of Hooper's veil, as the story makes clear in Hooper's last speech, is to show the face itself as already an impenetrable veil. A veiled face is a veil over a veil, a veiling of what is already veiled" (ibid., 100). Rather than pragmatically refusing such conceptual hazards, Miller's Hawthorne, like Miller himself, both criticizes and participates in such thinking. As the deconstructive position would have it, the ideology of the veil can be exposed only from within that ideology: "Have I not . . . through an ineluctable compulsion, unavoidably used as the 'tool' of reading the very thing I have most wanted to put into question, just that ideology of apocalypse with its associated figure of the veil and prosopopoiea?" (123).

Despite their exhaustive attentions, these two readings continuously beg a central question: How close is Hawthorne to Hooper? For Colacurcio the distance appears to be substantial; in order to demonstrate the practical failure of Hooper's ideology, Hawthorne cannot afford to disappear into Hooper. From a pragmatic perspective, Hooper is mistaken or mad, and even if we sense some sympathy in the presentation, Hawthorne ultimately turns away from Hooper's self-imposed "death" toward the uncertainties of preapocalyptic existence. Miller's reading suggests a much closer relationship, not full identity but a likeness so near that what he calls the "story's" horror and Hooper's darkened vision become very nearly the same. Hooper's point, that faces are veils and "unveiling" an earthly impossibility, feeds the story's argument that the "ideology of unveiling" must be "unveiled." Hawthorne may be aware of the problems of his minister's position, but as a self-conscious critic of such thinking, he is also aware that he shares those problems.[11]

Given these possible relationships, where does the "self-veiling" Hawthorne of "The Old Manse" stand? If, as I have argued, the "self-veiling" he describes is an expression of epistemological and ethical distance, how does this stance relate to Hooper's self-veiling and its possible purposes? For Hooper the veil has both positive and negative results. It makes him a more effective minister, gives him greater sympathy with sinners and "all dark affections," and makes him a well-known if somewhat suspect religious leader. On the other hand, it divides him from the community, ruins his engagement and potential family life, and leaves him gloomy and possibly deranged. This double effect suggests that Hooper may be Hawthorne's stand-in, the isolated artist who participates in communal life but only from behind a protective mask. And yet Hooper's veil is also the veil of a

Calvinist and as such implies an attitude toward knowledge and otherness difficult if not impossible to ascribe to Hawthorne. Hooper's veil and its attendant theology depend upon the Calvinist understanding of history as it is reflected in predestination and apocalypse. In this sense Hooper's history is already written, already complete. There can be no actual mystery in his world because all answers exist; even his own uncertain fate (salvation or damnation) has already been decided and, in this sense, is already certain. Answers exist for Hooper in a system "solved" to its last degree; the veil, while it divides in life, implies a unification in death and apocalypse, where all deception vanishes in the face of a single, knowable truth — a single history.

While Hawthorne's "self-veiling" produces some of the same effects that Hooper's veil creates, the difference in philosophical context undermines any easy similarities. In terms of sympathy, for instance, both appear to rely upon separation to enable a sympathetic response to others. However, Hooper's sympathy is not an "involuntary reserve" that allows him to see "what is common to human nature." Instead, the veil creates an "awful power, over souls that were in agony for sin. . . . Its gloom, indeed, enabled him to sympathize with all dark affections" (*CE*, 10:104). Hooper's sympathy is for sin or darkness, for the hidden truth beneath the veil of secular history. In this sense it is less the sort of sympathy Hawthorne describes than it is an effect of what Hooper treats as absolute knowledge. The truth of Calvinist history is the sinfulness of humankind and its eventual redemption or damnation. As Hooper says at the end of the story, everyone sins and everyone hides it; therefore, the truth of every individual is hidden behind a false front, and every individual can and will be reduced to that hidden truth at the apocalypse. Hooper's smile reinforces this perception. Described as "sad" and "faint," it not only suggests an ironic perception of his isolation but also reflects the voyeur's privileged position. It is a knowing smile, and while the knowledge may be painful to Hooper, it is also satisfying. Like that of his counterpart, Wakefield, his smile suggests "craftiness," not so much a tendency to play tricks as a desire to adopt the privilege of secret knowledge.

In contrast, Hawthorne tells Sophia Peabody that his resistance to self-exposure is not due to "caprice or stubbornness" or to "a love of secrecy and darkness" (*CE*, 15:612) but follows instead from an understanding of how knowledge, especially knowledge of others, is limited. Only "full sympathy" enables another to "come into [his] depths," and even this fullness is not necessarily the same as the complete knowledge ascribed to God or angels. As a Calvinist with a special insight into sin, Hooper believes that he does or will have complete knowledge of others; as a romantic influenced by the "noble doubt" of skepticism, Hawthorne suggests that "full sympathy," not knowledge, is the best that any "mortal" can do.[12] The self and other are mysteries that resist definition and limitation. They will not and should not be "pinned down."

The story's most important scene in terms of this contrast is the encounter between Hooper and his fiancée, Elizabeth. It is important first because Elizabeth presents an alternative to Hooper's apocalyptic thinking:

> "Have patience with me, Elizabeth!" cried he passionately. "Do not desert me, though this veil must be between us here on earth. Be mine, and hereafter there shall be no veil over my face, no darkness between our souls! It is but a mortal veil — it is not for eternity! Oh! you know not how lonely I am, and how frightened to be alone behind my black veil. Do not leave me in this miserable obscurity for ever!"
>
> "Lift the veil but once, and look me in the face," said she.
>
> "Never! It cannot be!" replied Mr. Hooper.
>
> "Then, farewell!" said Elizabeth. (*CE*, 9:47)

Hooper bases his plea on Elizabeth's "patience" for the apocalypse. The present, he implies, is false; therefore, she should be able to devalue the physical world in favor of the spiritual truth to come. But Elizabeth insists upon Hooper's physical presence in or through his face. She does not ask for truth or certainty, only presence and language with all the uncertainty that accompanies them. "First lay aside your black veil: then tell me why you put it on" (*CE*, 10:46). First join me on an equal footing where we both realize how difficult it is to know ourselves and others; then talk to me. Her position may not be fully expressed, but it is fully implied by contrast to Hooper's. "'No,' she said aloud, and smiling, 'there is nothing terrible in this piece of crape, except that it hides a face which I am always glad to look upon'" (*CE*, 10:46). A face that she is "always glad to look upon" is not a mask that hides spiritual truth through potential hypocrisy. It is the experience itself, without pretensions to the secret knowledge or penetration that Hooper's conception demands.[13] In this sense Elizabeth comes closer to Hawthorne's sense of "self-veiling" than does Hooper. Her request to see the face is, ironically, more accepting of mystery than is Hooper's insistence that she wait until the apocalypse to see his "true face."

It is also useful in this regard to contrast Elizabeth's attitude toward what Miller identifies as the story's central horror — the perception that the face is already a veil. For Hooper such an insight prompts the assumption of the "two folds of crape"; that is, it pushes him to "reveal" the horror of the face as veil in order to restate his faith in apocalyptic truth. For Elizabeth such a perception is not necessarily horrific as long as she can "face" Hooper on equal terms. " 'Lift the veil but once, and look me in the face,' said she" (*CE*, 9:47). Hooper's veil terrifies her only when she surrenders to his ultimate refusal to enter into the uncertainty of earthly knowledge, his refusal of the skeptical acceptance of otherness.

But while Elizabeth may be the romantic alternative to Hooper's Calvinism, that alternative does not succeed within the story. In what can be read as a tragic loss, Hooper's apocalyptic thinking overcomes Elizabeth's desire for equality and acknowledgment, even to the point that she is forced to cover her eyes as she leaves the room. She succumbs to Hooper's conception of the world and, at the same time, to the Calvinist vision of history. As we will see in Part Three of this study, the moment is similar to the encounter between Holgrave and Phoebe in *The House of the Seven Gables*. There Holgrave refuses to take his revenge and so reduce Phoebe to playing a part in the history of guilt. His "withdrawal" from the moment suggests a momentary transcendence of (Calvinist) history similar to what Elizabeth offers to Hooper. Unlike Phoebe, however, Elizabeth assumes her own mask because she is "mesmerized" by Hooper and so reduced to his "totalized" vision of history.

The failure of acknowledgment in this case suggests that Hawthorne placed himself somewhere between Hooper and Elizabeth, aware of the need for a "veil" but suspicious of the assumption of masks: "An essay on the misery of being always under a mask. A veil may be needful, but never a mask. Instances of people who wear masks in all classes of society, and never take them off even in the most familiar moments, though sometimes they may chance to slip aside" (*CE*, 8:23). This notation in Hawthorne's journal not only records the germ of "The Minister's Black Veil" but it also establishes a crucial distinction between a veil and a mask. In this case Hawthorne appears to use both terms as figures for different attitudes toward the exterior world. To wear a mask is to hide, to be cut off from the world and therefore miserable. The veil, on the other hand, here implies some limitation within the relationship with otherness, a permeable barrier that represents a heightened awareness of distance. Hawthorne himself may have found this type of veil "needful" and so rejected Elizabeth's (or Sophia's) appeal for simple revelation. But he also considered this sort of mask a terrifying possibility, one that the philosophically veiled individual should avoid. Despite the shift in terms, Hooper's *veil* is or becomes a *mask*; it is not a permeable barrier that regulates the relationship with otherness. It destroys otherness by reducing it to the terms of Hooper's apocalyptic thinking.

Hawthorne's middle ground, between masking and revelation, returns us to the Levinasian "face." The "veiled" self that Hawthorne describes does indeed reflect the "metaphysical desire . . . without satisfaction which, precisely, understands [*entend*] the remoteness, the alterity, and the exteriority of the other."[14] "Veiling" includes such an understanding as part of its complex representation of encountering other people. Clearly, for Hawthorne, anyone can "wear" a "veil" or "mask" without wearing a piece of crape; to come "face to face" then, as Levinas describes it, is closely related to coming before the world "veiled" — with an understanding of the limitations that the other (as "face") imposes upon the self. As Colin Davis explains, "The face may be a real part of the human body available to be encountered, seen and experienced; but for Levinas it is before all else a channel through which alterity presents itself to me, and as such it lies outside and beyond what can be seen or experienced."[15] The face overflows all ideas that might be used to reduce or control it. Its main effect is to initiate the "idea of infinity," the idea that "overflows itself." For Hawthorne, this might be modified to say that the "veiled" face is a "mode" that recognizes the limitations of the self with respect to the other. In this sense the other does indeed "overflow itself"; it can be understood only through sympathy — that is, through a relinquishment of the narrow confinements of conceptual knowledge.

The Scarlet Letter: Ethics as First Philosophy

The ethical implications of Hooper's failure to face the world receive extended attention in *The Scarlet Letter.* Just as Dimmesdale is often seen as a development of Hooper, so can Hester Prynne be considered a more complicated Elizabeth, a working out of the earlier figure's implied positions. As is true of all Hawthorne's veil-centered fictions, the relationship between truth and ethics, between knowledge and behavior, remains central. As a result, Hester's relationships become the focal point for Hawthorne's increasingly powerful assertion that personal, one-to-one encounters precede and provide a basis for the individual's orientation toward society.[16] Just as Hooper's failed engagement to Elizabeth figures his larger failure to engage his community, so do Hester's face-to-face encounters with Pearl, Dimmesdale, and Chillingworth allow her to see the primacy of responsibility over abstraction. The approach to the other, the primary ethical relation, founds (and confounds) Hester's attempts to idealize her struggle. At the same time, such a relation establishes, through the course of her experience, a vision of truth that insists upon its own limitations, one that, in other words, acknowledges its own partiality and thereby its secondary status to the unpredictable "astonishment" of the other.[17] The most obvious starting place for such a discussion is Hester's relationship to Pearl. If any character in *The Scarlet Letter* can claim to exceed understanding, it is Pearl, the uncontrollable, "bewildering," and "baffling" "outcast of the infantile world" (*CE*, 1:92, 93). Critics have described her as representing, among other things, "the intuitive, lawless poetic view of the world," the "volatile forces at the center of the self," the Wordsworthian "child of nature," and, more recently, the political power of communal conformity.[18] She is, in general terms then, beyond limits ("The child could not be made amenable to rules" [*CE*, 1:91]), though it is her very externality, her existence beyond understanding, that gives her the power to disrupt Hester's thoughts. Most significantly, through this disruption, she paradoxically keeps Hester in the world, forcing her to deal with individuals rather than abstractions, to face others, to speak to them rather than reducing them to a part in a systematic vision of society.[19]

Pearl's function arises clearly enough in Hester's famous defense of her right to keep and raise her child: " 'God gave me the child!' cried she. 'He gave her, in requital of all things else, which ye had taken from me. She is my happiness! — she is my torture, none the less! Pearl keeps me here in life! Pearl punishes me too! See ye not, she is the scarlet letter, only capable of being loved, and so endowed with a million-fold the power of retribution for my sin? Ye shall not take her! I will die first!' " (*CE* 1:113). Hester's language recalls Mary Rowlandson's: "Yet the Lord still showed mercy to me and upheld me, and as He wounded me with one hand, so He healed me with the other."[20] The paradox of the blessing-blow, the wounding as healing, operates here but less to demonstrate the unfathomable grace of God than to recover, through its very paradox, Hester's humanity (or alterity), her existence as something more than an icon or a figure for punishment. "Pearl keeps me here in life!" This is not merely a threat of suicide, which surfaces elsewhere in the text, but a significant declaration that to be "here in life" is to be involved with others as individuals, in agreement or disagreement, to speak and be spoken to, to look someone else in the face.

In terms of Levinas's project, the appropriate term here is *shame*, and though this special definition no doubt differs from nineteenth-century uses of the word, it can serve to highlight the ethical implications of Hester's defense. In a section of *Totality and Infinity* titled "C. Truth and Justice: 1. Freedom Called Into Question," Levinas first connects "knowing" to a theoretical stance that "puts itself into question, goes back beyond its origin" (82): "This self-criticism can be understood as a discovery of one's weakness or a discovery of one's unworthiness —either as a consciousness of failure or as a consciousness of guilt" (83). This "guilt" and its manifestation as "shame" are not the result of specific violations; instead, they form the very ground of the relationship with others, the basis from which truth can be said to arise: "The freedom that can be ashamed of itself founds truth (and thus truth is not deduced from truth.) The Other is not initially a *fact*, is not an *obstacle*, does not threaten me with death; he is desired in my shame" (83–84, original emphasis). Hester's passionate declaration acknowledges these limitations even as it suggests a basic understanding that the limits she faces are integral to her condition—are, in fact, her very condition. Hester acknowledges Pearl as in some sense unfathomable while seeing herself as bound to the fundamental demand Pearl makes upon her. In this sense her insistence that Pearl "is the scarlet letter, only capable of being loved" transforms the Puritan punishment for adultery into a figure for human relationships; the punishment Hester feels is not for her violation of Puritan law but for her tendency to withdraw from the world, to harden herself against it and so transform both herself and the world into petrified figures.[21] Pearl, who exceeds any attempt at figural control, provides moments of rupture and astonishment that allow Hester to avoid the sort of premature death already experienced by Dimmesdale.

Understood in this way, Hester's famous "freedom of speculation" passage, in which she theorizes social revolution, directly opposes, and is opposed by, Pearl's insistent, painful questioning about the letter and her own origins. There is no need to summarize the well-known section of "Another View of Hester," except to say that the passage has a definite trajectory that moves from a consideration of revolution to the thought of suicide. Political critics, particularly Sacvan Bercovitch, have argued that this is part of Hawthorne's attempt to contain dissent by eventually rechanneling it into process and consent.[22] But if we follow the passage through to the chapter's end we can see how the "office" of the scarlet letter, in this particular context, is not to bring Hester to the limits of Puritan law but to bring her back into the world, to enable her to acknowledge that the immediate demands of others precede and supersede idealized conceptions of social reformation.

The primary distinction that governs the speculation passage appears in its first sentence: "Much of the marble coldness of Hester's impression was to be attributed to the circumstance that her life had turned, in a great measure, from passion and feeling, to thought" (*CE*, 1:164). There follows a description that not only connects Hester to other revolutionary figures but also establishes her theoretical tendency to abstraction: "Indeed, the same dark question often rose into her mind, with reference to the whole race of womanhood. Was existence worth accepting, even to the happiest among them? As concerned her own individual existence, she had long ago decided in the negative, and dismissed the point as settled" (*CE*, 1:165). The emphasis here falls on "the whole race of womanhood" rather than on the particular condition of individuals. Hester uses her own experience as a figure for all women and thereby reduces their condition to the operations of her own ideas. The danger of such a reduction Hawthorne makes plain by referencing Poe's favorite subject: the self caught within the maze of its own mind: "Thus, Hester Prynne, whose heart had lost its regular and healthy throb, wandered without a clew in the dark labyrinth of mind; now turned aside by an insurmountable precipice; now starting back from a deep chasm" (*CE*, 1:166). Such an excess of interiority leads to suicide unless the individual can find a way to break out into the world of others. That is, it is precisely the ethical failure of Hester's abstract speculations that Hawthorne seems intent on highlighting—her inability to see and acknowledge other individuals outside the limits of her own thinking.

In this particular context, then, the office of the letter is very much the office of Hawthorne's authorial veil: to indicate the space between individuals, to highlight the limitations of thought that are already in force for Hester. Thus, again in this specific context, the letter is less an agency of Puritan law than it is a force for romantic self-limitation; after all, what follows the notation of its failed office is nothing less than Hester's return to others, in this case Dimmesdale: "Now, however, her interview with the Reverend Mr. Dimmesdale, on the night of his vigil, had given her a new theme of reflection, and held up to her an object that appeared worthy of any exertion and sacrifice for its attainment. She had witnessed the intense misery beneath which the minister struggled, or, to speak more accurately, had ceased to struggle. She saw that he stood on the verge of lunacy, if he had not already stepped across it" (*CE*, 1:166). The shift to the present should not be underestimated here. "Now" Hester has returned to the present because of her "interview" with the minister. It is through speaking to another person, through the unpredictability of that interview, that coming face to face, that Hester is brought out of the abstract and into the uncertainty of human relationships. Now she "witnessed," now she "saw" what was before her: another person in trouble, facing madness at the hand of an enemy in whose crimes Hester is implicated. It is almost as if Hawthorne is suggesting that the failed office of the letter is being accomplished after all. "Now, however . . ." (as opposed to her earlier speculativeness), Hester is leaving the trap of abstraction and reentering the unpredictable, human world.[23]

That such a reentry is difficult and therefore momentary is evident from Pearl's persistent attempts to goad her mother into just this sort of "interview." However, Hester's resistance converts the potential conversation into an interrogation:

> "What does the letter mean, mother? — and why dost thou wear it? — and why does the minister keep his hand over his heart?"
>
> "What shall I say?" thought Hester to herself. — "No! If this be the price of the child's sympathy, I cannot pay it!" (*CE*, 1:180–81)

This seemingly innocent maternal evasion fails to satisfy Pearl, who pushes Hester to a threat: "Do not tease me; else I shall shut thee into the dark closet!" (*CE*, 1:181). The choice that here faces Hester — between speech and silence, opening and closing — is the same choice she faces in her interactions with other characters and with the community. It is Hooper's choice between veiling and masking or, in Levinasian terms, between "facing" and the frozen figuration of the face. As Jill Robbins explicates it, Levinas's distrust of figuration shares significant ground with Hawthorne's warnings about self-allegory: "To speak, then, of the petrification of the face is to announce an event which, within the terms of Levinas's ethical thought, is one of the worst things that could happen. . . . This 'image' of the petrified face, the frozen face, denotes at once the violence directed at the face of the other — the loss of the other's face — and also the loss of face on the part of the figural interpreter. . . . To take on a character (*une figure*) is to risk *becoming* a figure, and thereby to lose what is human, to be turned into a statue, to be turned into stone."[24] We have only to recall Richard Digby, the "man of adamant," to realize the threat to Hester and to recover for Hawthorne the powerful opposition between unpredictable human interaction and the "certainty" and finality of the hardened face: "He had discovered the entrance of a cave, closely resembling the mouth of a sepulchre, within which sat the figure of a man, whose gesture and attitude warned the father and children to stand back, while his visage wore a most forbidding frown" (*CE*, 11:168). This is the end Hester risks, from which Pearl, by demanding speech, by being aggressively "in her face," saves her.

Hawthorne presents a similar situation, though with a different outcome, in his earlier story, "The Gentle Boy." In a communal and dramatic situation notably like those of *The Scarlet Letter*, a persecuted Quaker (Catherine) follows her religious "enthusiasm" — the religious and political fight to end the persecution of her sect — at the expense of her relationship with her son, Ilbrahim, the gentle boy of the title. Her intense devotion to spiritual idealism contrasts with the simpler actions of Tobias Pearson, a Puritan of "military rank" (*CE*, 9:86), who repeats the samaritan's act of taking in his enemy. Throughout the tale Hawthorne's emphasis falls on the destructive effects of zealotry, of placing the idea over the individual, or worse, of converting individuals into ideas. At its most basic level, his critique aims not at any particular doctrine or historical set of beliefs but at a systematic, totalizing thought that translates all personal relationships into preestablished intellectual categories. In this sense Catherine, who, like Hester, has "raven hair" and "dark," "wild" features, comes off no better than the Puritans who persecute her (*CE*, 9:81). She reluctantly chooses her wilderness quest over the needs of Ilbrahim and so is faced at the tale's end with her son's death, a sacrifice of sorts to her absence and a rupture within her idealism. Ilbrahim's death teaches her "a true religion" (*CE*, 9:104) that has less to do with domestic ties than with the disruption of thought by the demands of responsibility.

The tendency in recent criticism has been to read this opposition between ideal and personal commitments as Hawthorne's way of celebrating middle-class domesticity and motherhood. And while it is certainly true that the cult of domesticity plays a role in Hawthorne's works, it is more often than not a symbolic language used to suggest a larger, and more complex, ethical vision. Thus, T. Walter Herbert's assertion that Hester is "preserved from the wilder excesses of rebellion by the devotion she pours into the rearing of Pearl" is accurate to an extent, but only if we understand "rebellion" to denote a particular type of idealistic thinking and "devotion" to encompass genuine engagement with Pearl as an individual.[25] The tendency of Herbert's reading is to flatten Hester into "mother" and Pearl into "child" without considering the larger implications of their relationship as a model for *all* human interaction. Hester's resurgent "feminine nature" — as opposed to Chillingworth and Dimmesdale's intellectual "masculinity" — is more than a model for nineteenth-century mothers; it is just as clearly an ethical force capable of structuring relationships of all sorts, regardless of gender. "The Gentle Boy" points the way: Catherine's failure as mother encapsulates the inability of the community to transcend ideology and recognize Ilbrahim as a fellow human. Her abandonment of responsibility *as a mother* becomes a powerful symbol of all abandonments in which individuals are sacrificed to idealistic orders.

A similar symbolic dynamic operates in *The Scarlet Letter*, in which Hester's relationship with Pearl sets the terms for her interactions with Dimmesdale, Chillingworth, and the Puritan community. In the case of Dimmesdale, for instance, their "interview" on the scaffold leads to her decision to reveal Chillingworth's secret as a way of restructuring the one-sided, parasitic bond between the two men. The process follows this pattern: from the face-to-face meeting on the scaffold to Hester's understanding of "the intense misery beneath which the minister struggled" (*CE*, 1:166) to her new resolution to "reveal the secret" (*CE*, 1:173) — to speak, that is, where speech has been hostage. This shift of concern appears most forcefully at the beginning of chapter twelve, "Another View of Hester":

> In her late singular interview with Mr. Dimmesdale, Hester Prynne was shocked at the condition to which she found the clergyman reduced. . . . Knowing what this poor, fallen man had once been, her whole soul was moved by the shuddering terror with which he had appealed to her, — the outcast woman, — for support against his instinctively discovered enemy. She decided, moreover, that he had a right to her utmost aid. Little accustomed, in her long seclusion from society, to measure her ideas of right and wrong by any standard external to herself, Hester saw — or seemed to see — that there lay a responsibility upon her, in reference to the clergyman, which she owed to no other, not to the whole world besides. The links that united her to the rest of human kind — links of flowers, or silk, or gold, or whatever the material — had all been broken. Here was the iron link of mutual crime, which neither he nor she could break. Like all other ties, it brought along with it its obligations. (*CE*, 1:59–60)

The emphasis here is on the movement from personal encounter to the recognition of responsibility. Admittedly, this is the responsibility of "mutual crime," but it is precisely this understanding of her guilt toward him and his toward her that initiates a new sense of ethical obligation for Hester. Her recognition that she has a "responsibility" to Dimmesdale, whose presence asserts a "standard external to herself," underscores her turn away from the general and toward the specific, from the idea to the other being whose suffering she cannot ignore. Put another way, we might say that she here moves from monologue to dialogue, from dangerous isolation to the uncertainty and risk of facing others.

What partially enables this step is Hester's pragmatic conception of truth. Unlike Dimmesdale, who finds himself trapped in the Platonic-Calvinist division of worlds, Hester seems capable of a sophisticated withdrawal from the opposition of surface and depth. She is far less concerned than the minister that the truth about the self or the soul be absolutely known and far more aware of the limitations of self-knowledge and the knowledge of others. The contrast repeats the similar split between the Reverend Mr. Hooper and Elizabeth, between Calvinism and skeptical romanticism. First Dimmesdale: "As concerns the good which I may appear to do, I have no faith in it. It must needs be a delusion. What can a ruined soul, like mine, effect towards the redemption of other souls? — or a polluted soul, towards their purification? . . . Canst thou deem it, Hester, a consolation, that I must stand up in my pulpit, and meet so many eyes turned upward to my face, as if the light of heaven were beaming from it! — must see my flock hungry for the truth, and listening to my words as if a tongue of Pentecost were speaking! — and then look inward, and discern the black reality of what they idolize? I have laughed, in bitterness and agony of heart, at the contrast between what I seem and what I am!" (*CE*, 1:191). Like Hooper, Dimmesdale is caught in a conception of Being stringently isolated from action. The "true" Dimmesdale is the hidden, inner self, whose falseness deprives his work of all meaning. Thus, to his thinking, the truth and value of all action depend upon the inner condition of the actor. The outer self can be valid only when it expresses the inner; any disjunction between the two renders the world false.

For Hester, such a strict distinction between the material and spiritual or actual and ideal no longer holds this sort of power. She replies to Dimmesdale's self-pity with the worldliness of a late romantic pragmatist: " 'You wrong yourself in this,' " said Hester, gently. 'You have deeply and sorely repented. Your sin is left behind you, in the days long past. Your present life is not less holy, in very truth, than it seems in people's eyes' " (*CE*, 1:191). Hester's ability to see the value of action regardless of intent, to place the practical over the essential, drives her attack on Dimmesdale's Calvinism. Her radicalism is thus primarily philosophical rather than political; that is, she begins by advocating a pragmatic conception of truth that approximates, though with a tragic tone, the thought of William James: "Pragmatism, on the other hand, asks its usual question. 'Grant an idea or belief to be true,' it says, 'what concrete difference will its being truth make in anyone's actual life? How will the truth be realized?' "[26] "Your present life is not less holy, in very truth, than it seems," to repeat Hester's assertion. The "very truth" of seeming, because of its attentions to the world of others, fractures the binary dilemmas of hypocrisy; in a Jamesian sense, it matters not and so has no claim to recognizable truth.

She makes the point again, more dramatically, in the forest scene: "Begin all anew! Hast thou exhausted possibility in the failure of this one trial? Not so! The future is yet full of trial and success. There is happiness to be enjoyed! There is good to be done! Exchange this false life of thine for a true one. Be, if thy spirit summon thee to such a mission, the teacher and apostle of the red men. . . . Preach! Write! Act! Do any thing, save lie down and die!" (*CE*, 1:198). The primary note of Hester's plea is for action, work in the world. The impulse to escape the strictures of Puritan punishment arises only as a means toward making action real again. It is, in another sense, a metaphor for what Dimmesdale must accomplish mentally, philosophically; he must "leave this wreck and ruin here," abandon the pattern of thinking that has convinced him of the falseness of appearance and reenter the world. The plea echoes Elizabeth's simple request in "The Minister's Black Veil": "First lay aside your black veil: then tell me why you put it on," with its faith that speech, conversation, can bring the self back to the world.

Hester's approach to Chillingworth is made on much the same basis, though the "leech" represents an even harsher version of the idealism that makes Dimmesdale his victim. What she objects to most is Chillingworth's privileged position; like Mr. Hooper, the physician wears a mask that enables special sight into sin and creates a voyeuristic advantage. "You burrow and rankle in his heart! Your clutch is on his life, and you cause him to die daily a living death; and still he knows you not" (*CE*, 1:170–71). Hester determines to expose Chillingworth and thus bring the two onto a potentially equal basis; she wishes to bring about a "face to face" of sorts and so disrupt the monologic power of Chillingworth with the uncertainty of dialogue. Or, brought closer to Levinasian terms, she wishes to disable Chillingworth's idealistic objectification of truth (as totality) and create an ethical space in which Dimmesdale can emerge as a human being rather than an idea.

It is abundantly clear, both in the text and its critical responses, that Chillingworth is the "man of knowledge," an intellectual, in other words, who has certainly placed "head" over "heart." But what sort of knowledge does Chillingworth represent? How does he conceive of truth and how does that conception structure his responses to others, his actions? In some respects, his approach recalls the Melville of "Hawthorne and His Mosses": "Never know him! Believe me, Hester, there are few things, — whether in the outward world, or, to a certain depth, in the invisible sphere of thought, — few things hidden from the man, who devotes himself earnestly and unreservedly to the solution of a mystery. . . . I shall seek this man, as I have sought truth in books; as I have sought gold in alchemy. There is a sympathy that will make me conscious of him. I shall see him tremble. I shall feel myself shudder, suddenly and unawares. Sooner or later, he must needs be mine!" (*CE*, 1:75). It is not difficult to hear an uncanny anticipation of Melville's language in the "Mosses" essay or, more important still, his attitude toward reading and the search for "truth in books." This is not to suggest that Melville equates to Chillingworth but that the intimacy Melville proposes curiously echoes the parasitic bond of the doctor and the minister. Chillingworth clearly objectifies his search for truth and envisions total possession, a union not without its sexual tinge. He sees the minister as entirely knowable, the "mystery" of his very self not really a "mystery" at all, but a puzzle the solution to which has already been posited and imaginatively seized.

Hester's response suggests that she understands precisely the ethical dangers of "burrowing," "rankling," and "clutching" at another self. "You cause him to die daily a living death," she argues, noting not only the physical threat to Dimmesdale's life but the ethical threat to his existence as a separate being. Her language recalls the dynamic of the *Gables* preface: the pinning down of a moral onto the elusive substance of life destroys the life through appropriation. If we add to the literary moral the notion of a "moralistic" truth, the fixation of Calvinist guilt, we can begin to see Chillingworth as a somewhat secularized version of the reductive tendencies of Puritan history, though, in this case, the Calvinist vision of hidden sin leads not to redemption but to revenge: "He had begun an investigation, as he imagined, with the severe and equal integrity of a judge, desirous only of truth, even as if the question involved no more than the air-drawn lines and figure of a geometrical problem, instead of human passions, and wrongs inflicted on himself. . . . He now dug into the poor clergyman's heart, like a miner searching for gold; or, rather, like a sexton delving into a grave, possibly in quest of a jewel that had been buried on the dead man's bosom, but likely to find nothing save mortality and corruption. Alas for his own soul, if these were what he sought!" (*CE*, 1:129). The connection here between Chillingworth's self-delusion that he is an objective judge and the "miner's" quest for "gold" or "jewel" is the basis of Hawthorne's conception of ethical violation. Digging into another's "heart" is likened to a sexton robbing a grave; it leads the investigator to find "nothing save mortality and corruption," in other words, not merely death and decay but the "corruption" of his own soul. The shortcoming that makes such an attitude possible is Chillingworth's failure to recognize his own implication in the search for truth. He cannot see his own necessary blindness, and without a consciousness of his limitations, he fails to recognize the strangeness of others, risking trespass onto the sacred.[27]

As in "The Minister's Black Veil," Hawthorne chooses a woman to speak for his skeptical pragmatism, though Hester, like Elizabeth, is successful only to the extent that she suggests a possible, rather than a probable, revision of human relationships. In this sense Hawthorne might best be thought of as a tragic pragmatist, one who lacks confidence in society's ability to allow for the sort of ethical distance necessary to protect the "sanctity of the human heart." In Hester, however, he creates his most resilient and powerful representative of the struggle to maintain both distance and connection, to enact his own artistic "shyness." Marginalized by her punishment and the limitations of the letter, Hester "stood apart from mortal interests, yet close beside them, like a ghost that revisits the familiar fireside, and can no longer make itself seen or felt" (*CE*, 1:84). This banishment, painful though it is, gives her a unique perspective on both herself and her relation to the Puritan community. At the same time, the letter, like Hooper's mask, seems to give her special insight, the dark vision of secret sin: "She felt or fancied, then, that the scarlet letter had endowed her with a new sense. She shuddered to believe, yet could not help believing, that it gave her a knowledge of the hidden sin in other hearts" (*CE*, 1:86).

Unlike many of Hawthorne's male protagonists, however — Young Goodman Brown, Hooper, Aylmer, Richard Digby — Hester uniquely rejects this temptation. She struggles against the letter's insinuations, no matter how satisfying they may be: "She was terror-stricken by the revelations that were thus made. What were they? Could they be other than the insidious whispers of the bad angel, who would fain have persuaded the struggling woman, as yet only half his victim, that the outward guise of purity was but a lie, and that, if truth were everywhere to be shown, a scarlet letter would blaze forth on many a bosom besides Hester Prynne's? Or, must she receive those intimations — so obscure, yet so distinct — as truth?" (*CE*, 1:86). This temptation, the same yielded to by Hooper and Young Goodman Brown, is the desire to see the surface of the world as false and thereby grant the self an exclusive vision of its own goodness. Hester rejects the thought, offering instead her own limitations, her own vision of knowledge such as Levinas presents it — as that which founds knowing on its own self-critique, that which "puts itself into question": "Such loss of faith is ever one of the saddest results of sin. Be it accepted as a proof that all was not corrupt in this poor victim of her own frailty, and man's hard law, that Hester Prynne yet struggled to believe that no fellow-mortal was guilty like herself" (*CE*, 1:87).

What separates Hester from Hawthorne's destructive male protagonists is her attempt to structure her relationships to others on the basis of her own limitations. Rejecting the logic of hypocrisy, she works, often against her own desires, to avoid reductive thinking and the fantasy of control it brings. The result of these efforts is a position of distance and sympathy that reproduces Hawthorne's authorial stance. Hester can help others both practically and emotionally because she recognizes the limits of her own knowledge and places herself in the position of the artistically veiled listener. The displacement of the self in deference to the other thus grounds her experience and sets the terms for her much-discussed return. By displacing abstract notions of political revolution with individual interactions, Hester realizes Hawthorne's startling revision of the relationship between ethics and politics: the ethical demand of the specific other, the sufferer, both founds and upsets all attempts at idealistic political revolution.

Part II / The Politics of Shyness

No doubt it seems the truest of truth to you; but I do assure you that, like every other Abolitionist, you look at matters with an awful squint, which distorts everything within your line of vision; and it is queer, though natural, that you think everybody squints except yourselves. Perhaps they do; but certainly *you* do.

— HAWTHORNE TO ELIZABETH PEABODY, 1857

You can no more keep out of politics than you can keep out of the frost.

— EMERSON, *Journals*

CHAPTER FOUR

Ethics and Politics

The Question of Engagement

If the ethical basis of Hawthorne's fiction has received less attention than it deserves of late, the same cannot be said for its politics. The last twenty years have seen an increased tendency to question Hawthorne's fictional techniques by reference to the author's political statements or activities. In some instances the lesser known nonfiction texts — particularly the campaign biography of Franklin Pierce, the children's stories, and the essay "Chiefly About War-Matters" — have been used to give context to the novels and short stories, functioning as interpretive templates for the more familiar fiction. In others, the emphasis has fallen directly on *The Scarlet Letter* as both the key to Hawthorne's oeuvre and the dominant expression of American middle-class culture circa 1850.[1]

The best known and most widely discussed of these readings is Sacvan Bercovitch's *Office of "The Scarlet Letter."* Building on the related work of Larry Reynolds and Jonathan Arac, Bercovitch contrasts American and European attitudes toward revolution as part of an attempt to link Hawthorne's evasive literary techniques with conservative or "compromise" politics. The result is less a reading of *The Scarlet Letter* than an extension of Bercovitch's often-repeated theory of the consensual power of American pluralism.[2] What is lost in the reading, according to Richard Millington for one, is the novel's resistant complexity, particularly as it concerns questions of personal and political commitments: "Bercovitch's *Scarlet Letter* is a text without relationships, except for the paramount relation between the individual and her sense of the possibilities for her autonomy — or, to put this more precisely — relationships, Bercovitch argues, are construed by character, author, and reader alike as allegories of one's own path down the road marked 'freedom' on one side of the street and 'consensus' on the other. But think of what this leaves out."[3] "What this leaves out," according to Millington, is the complexity of Hester's interactions with others, particularly the important opposition in the text between the local demands of interpersonal responsibility and the broader goals of liberal self-realization: "Perhaps Hester's most *radical* move, both in the context of Puritan Boston and in relation to the freedom-obsessed consensus ideology Bercovitch describes, is to propose that the pursuit of happiness might be as authentic a goal as liberty."[4]

Among other things, Millington's response reestablishes the ethical question. It makes an important claim for a realm of personal responsibility disallowed by Bercovitch's political determinism. As Millington points out, Bercovitch's reading is based on a stark division between individual autonomy and communal consensus. Even more, it poses the starkest of choices: either the individual reforms society or society reforms the individual. There is no middle ground; or rather, what middle ground there is falls within the borders of acquiescence, since all but total opposition equates to inaction. Compromise no longer exists except as an elaborately disguised social control.

This is how Hester Prynne, despite her rebelliousness, fails to escape "process," that is to say, consensus disguised as conflict: "Conflict is also a form of process, of course, but one that assumes inherent antagonism; it derives from a partiality that inspires partisanship. Conflict forces us to take positions and thus issues in active oppositions: one certainty against another, one generation against the next, one class or gender against another. Process (for Hawthorne) is a form of partiality that accepts limitation, acknowledges its own incompleteness, and so tends toward tolerance, accommodation, pluralism, acquiescence, inaction."[5] It is difficult to see what Bercovitch is getting at here. He seems to be offering a more robust form of pluralist politics to counter what he sees as Hawthorne's insufficiently oppositional "process." And yet what he actually proposes is a form of individual idealism ("one certainty against another") *in place of* his own parody of democratic philosophy.[6] It makes little sense to suggest that pluralist debate can function as a complete conflict of absolute positions without acknowledging the necessity, at some point, for the sort of "tolerance, accommodation, plural-ism" and "acquiescence" he attributes to Hawthorne's political philosophy. It is worth asking, in other words, where such conflict is meant to stop, given the mechanisms of a pluralist government. Bercovitch seems to imagine the proper conclusion as a revolutionary reversal, but instead of an argument for revolution we get an insinuating blur of distinctions — from tolerance to accommodation, from pluralism to acquiescence and inaction. The sentence might win an award for begging questions: Does pluralism, Hawthorne's or anyone else's, necessarily lead to acquiescence? Does political "action" emerge only in "conflict," while everything else not sufficiently oppositional equates to "inaction"?[7] And is it clear, finally, that attempting to describe the self in society is actually a covert or unconscious mechanism for keeping dissenters in their places?

In his 1993 article "Emerson, Individualism, and the Ambiguities of Dissent," Bercovitch offers a similar, if somewhat more subtle, argument. Here he at-tributes the opposition between self and society to the myth of America, which produces a "constant conflict between . . . the self in itself, a separate, single, resistant individuality, and society en masse, individualism systematized."[8] He then finds in Emerson a complex approach to such division, an attempt to re-imagine the opposition as a unique combination of individuality and participa-tion, what Cavell might call a "marriage" of self and world. But such a position, inventive though it may be, cannot help but erase its own activity: "Translated in the terms of Emersonian dissent, these dynamics issue in a vision of autonomy preserved, precariously but decisively, and all the more decisively for its pre-cariousness, within the bounds of community; a form of protest that is bound to challenge (subvert, deny, resist) the consensus its represents — *bound* to challenge and by that act authorized to sustain the polarity of self and society upon which consensus depends" (ibid., 124–25). We might call this a sort of structural soph-istry: the self that opposes the group unwittingly reinforces the group through its opposition. Meaningful opposition — individuality that would escape this con-sensual trap — is impossible short of a total attack on the structure itself. True "conflict" then, as Bercovitch defines it in *The Office of "The Scarlet Letter,"* must be action against the structure of pluralistic society; "process," because it fails to attack that structure, must be "inaction."

For Bercovitch, therefore, Hester can do little more than reinforce the com-munal will — *no matter how resistant her actions.* If she opposes the community, as readers have long suggested, through limited acts of self-assertion (embroidering the letter, dressing Pearl, even helping the sick), she reinforces her position as the (internal) outcast and thereby reaffirms the oppositional structure. If she acquiesces to the letter, she likewise confirms the consensus. In this sense her return and resumption of the letter can only be proof of her consensual patience brought about by a faith in process: "Once, long before, she transformed the A into a symbol for able, admirable. Now she transforms herself, able and admirable as she is, into an agent of socialization," in part at least, by prophesying "an age of love to come."9

But does Hester offer such a prophecy, and is her return best thought of within the stark opposition between "conflict" and "process" that Bercovitch establishes? Hawthorne begins his explanation of Hester's return by contrasting a potential life abroad with Pearl (as the "sad and lonely mother at her fireside") with the resumption of "her long-forsaken shame" (*CE*, 1:262, 263): "But there was a more real life for Hester Prynne, here, in New England, than in that unknown region where Pearl had found a home. Here had been her sin; here, her sorrow; and here was yet to be her penitence" (*CE*, 1:263). The key phrase is "a more real life." What is "more real" about the life in New England than in "that unknown region" with Pearl? The third sentence appears to answer the question by noting that Hester's personal history (sin, sorrow, penitence to come) is inseparable from its scene. In this respect Hester chooses a type of Emersonian "proximity" as the key to her new understanding of individuality. Such "nextness" or "neighboring" opposes the escapist vision of individuality Hester herself proposes in the woodland scene with Dimmesdale: "Deeper it goes, and deeper, into the wilderness, less plainly to be seen at every step; until, some few miles hence, the yellow leaves will show no vestige of the white man's tread. There thou art free!" (*CE*, 1:197). The emphasis on the location of her history reflects a more complex understanding of what it means to be an individual engaged in a community. It suggests that escapism does little more than allow the community to define not only who you are but also where you may and may not go; the freedom of the wilderness offers no freedom at all, proscribed as it already is by communal definition and de facto banishment. What must be fashioned instead is an individuality within/against community, precisely the sort of "both/and" thinking that for Bercovitch equates to compromise and inaction.10 And yet, Hester does act, comforting and counseling "as best she might" as one "who had herself gone through a mighty trouble" (*CE*, 1:263).

Such counseling includes, as Bercovitch emphasizes, a sort of visionary statement concerning the future, an assurance and a "belief":

She assured them, too, of her firm belief, that, at some brighter period, when the world should have grown ripe for it, in Heaven's own time, a new truth would be revealed, in order to establish the whole relation between man and woman on a surer ground of mutual happiness. Earlier in life, Hester had vainly imagined that she herself might be the destined prophetess, but had long since recognized the impossibility that any mission of divine and mysterious truth should be confided to a woman stained with sin, bowed down with shame, or even burdened with a life-long sorrow. The angel and apostle of the coming revelation must be a woman, indeed, but lofty, pure, and beautiful; and wise, moreover, not through dusky grief, but the ethereal medium of joy; and showing how sacred love should make us happy, by the truest test of a life successful to such an end! (*CE*, 1:263)

In Bercovitch's view such a prophecy transforms Hester into an "agent of the law, the sainted guide" who is reconstituted "*as a marginal dissenter*, into an exemplum of historical continuity": "Hester neither reaffirms her adulterous affair nor dis-avows it; her actions neither undermine the social order nor celebrate it; and at the end she neither reinstates the old norms nor breaks with them. Instead, she projects her dream of love onto some 'surer ground' in the future. . . . In other words, her return deliberately breaks with tradition by its emphasis on the politi-cal implications of process as closure."[11]

So, as marginal rebel Hester (unwittingly?) preaches conformity. More accu-rately, we might say instead that she preaches patience or that she offers a vision of human progress that is less idealistic than it is tragic. For what is the alternative at this point? Escape only reinforces the existing communal pattern, and com-plete acquiescence opposes the spirited nature of Hester's personality. For Ber-covitch, then, the final choice is revolution, the course pursued by the mother in "The Gentle Boy." But Hawthorne has already suggested the very real ethical toll such revolutionary zeal can take on those nearest to the idealist. If Hester's life with Pearl has taught her anything, it is that the unqualified demand of the individual other cannot be displaced onto an idealism that transforms that de-mand into simple thought. In this sense, Bercovitch's critique of Hawthorne amounts to little more than a difference of opinion about the potential dangers of idealism. For Hawthorne there is no easy choice between conformity and re-bellion; there is instead a set of choices with political effects that are limited by ethical concerns. Unfettered idealism and self-reliance may be just as dangerous as absolute conformity; revolution leads to violence and often unchecked abuse through idealism.

Seen in this light, Hester's prophetic comfort can just as easily be understood as a description of the tragic limitations of human reformers, "the impossibility that any mission of divine and mysterious truth should be confided to a woman stained with sin" (*CE*, 1:263). Her imagined "angel" seems to be just that, an otherworldly figure unlikely to appear in human form given the corruptions of power.[12] In this respect Bercovitch's underlying argument—that conflict in America must be revolutionary to escape conformity—reduces Hawthorne's critique of idealism to nothing more than a politically expedient conservatism. In doing so it ignores what Charles Swann has called "Hawthorne's sheer tough-mindedness, his willingness to accept that the past (to say nothing of the present) is rarely pure, that historical change is not only inevitable but also bound to be marked by moral complexities and ambiguities, yet to take the position that this does not mean that the artist should retreat from history and politics, and indifferent, sit there paring his fingernails *à la* Stephen Daedulus."[13]

For Swann, such a story as "My Kinsman, Major Molineux" undermines Bercovitch's criticism by pointing to "Hawthorne's tragic (not negative) view of Revolution," particularly the ways in which public politics can create private suffering: "But what happens in the story is that justifiable revolutionary activity against the representative of the British imperialist state tragically involves the humiliating suffering of a private man. The consequence is a *private* agony" (ibid., 13, 14). Hawthorne's insistence on the specific, individual consequences of revolutionary politics argues that the ethics of encountering the singular other cannot be easily absorbed by the mechanisms of idealistic struggle. As Pearl is to Hester so is the Major to his "kinsman" Robin: as "kin" Robin is inevitably linked to and therefore responsible for the Major. The moment their eyes meet produces "pity and terror" in Robin because he recognizes his connection to Molineux and is therefore faced with the tragic reality of human suffering. The mob, their own faces masked, have reduced the Major to an inhuman target; tarred and feathered, he is similarly "masked" by the politics of revolution and therefore susceptible to idealistic violence.[14] In this context Robin's laughter seems less an endorsement of revolution than a recognition of his own untenable position. He can neither avoid his connection to his kinsman nor ignore his own implication in the violence of the mob. Thus "weary of a town life," he tries to return to the country, presumably to escape this "tough-minded" question. But as the story's ending suggests, Robin, like Hester, will need to remain *within* the community if he is to become an individual and "rise in the world" on his own.

The Ethical Nonposition

Whatever its limitations, Bercovitch's analysis does point toward a serious, and somewhat neglected, question about the author of *The Scarlet Letter:* What is the relationship in Hawthorne's life and work between ethics and politics? Modern criticism has for many years offered essentially consistent depictions of Hawthorne's political allegiances. F. O. Matthiessen, for instance, provides a summary in *American Renaissance* that anticipates the more recent criticisms of revisionists while it highlights the paradoxes of Hawthorne's self-critical stance:

> To holders of the opposite position, Hawthorne's distrust of purposive action presents a wide-open target. It might be necessary even for believers in dialectical process to grant some truth in his statement that "there is no instance, in all history, of the human will and intellect having perfected any great moral reform by methods which it adapted to that end," since every step of progress seems to call into being some new, not wholly foreseen evil, which has to be wrestled with in turn. But when he took the line to which Coverdale tended, on being struck, in the picnic spirit of Blithedale, by "the folly of attempting to benefit the world," Hawthorne could lay himself open to the full charge of obscurantism.

> A peculiar kind of social understanding made Hawthorne hold to both the contrasting terms of this paradox of being at once a democrat and a conservative. It enabled him to give a clear impression of human dignity in his character sketches of common men like those in "The Toll-Gatherer's Day" or of "The Old Apple Dealer," and caused him also to praise Pierce for daring "to love that great and sacred reality — his whole, united, native country — better than the mistiness of a philanthropic theory." As a result Hawthorne's views outraged everyone on the left, and their depth of spiritual integrity was doubtless lost on most of Pierce's conservative supporters among the Southern planters and the Northern proponents of the cotton interest.[15]

What newer historicists would change in this analysis is not the way Matthiessen understood Hawthorne's political positions but the way he interpreted the relationship between Hawthorne's artistic and political voices.[16] Unwilling to allow any separation between artistic and political discourse (even, or especially, when the author asserts such a distance), more recent readers have often flattened art into politics or, in Matthiessen's terms, turned the "contradictory aspects" of "human situations" into the "simple contrasts of black and white" associated with the pamphleteer.[17] Relying on various constructions of "ideology" to undo this division, such criticism has produced both useful expositions of context and an abusive erasure of authorial intention, stylistic registers, and rhetorical situations. As Myra Jehlen worried in her 1986 introduction to *Ideology and Classic American Literature*, "it now seems rather that critics are in danger of ignoring the more explicit content of a work as superficial or even as misleading. . . . The work that presents its conception of the world as natural through the apparent spontaneity of character and story conceals that way 'its real ideological determinants,' which it is the critic's task to reveal."[18]

It is clear, then, that ideological criticism — despite its purported poststructuralist sophistication — too often works from within the very idealism of unveiling that Hawthorne investigates and criticizes. What Hawthorne is *really* doing, such readings argue, is supporting the politics of compromise, arguing against abolition, or replicating the American ideology of dissensus. His fiction, as art, is a veil over these more tangible concerns, and it is the job of current criticism to remove that veil, to tell the truth, even if the critical methods at work have little room for truth-telling as such. And if Hawthorne himself claims that revelation is not so simple a matter — that it always involves concealment, that truth is fluid rather than fixed — such claims will simply become part of the veil that hides his true, political purpose. Every aesthetic or stylistic device will be read quite simply as a ploy (conscious or not) whose value can be measured only by a retrospective analysis of political effect.

Again we can turn to *The Office of "The Scarlet Letter"* for an example. A key element of Bercovitch's argument is his reconsideration of Hawthorne's famous ambiguity, specifically Hawthorne's technique of offering multiple interpretations of given situations or events. For Bercovitch, such stylistic "multiple choice" undoes choice itself:

> I have been using the term "option" in connection with Hester's return in order to stress the overriding distinction in Hawthorne's "device of multiple-choice" between making choices and having choice. His point is not that Hester finally makes a choice against adultery. It is that she has no choice but to resume the A. To make choices involves alternatives; it requires us to reject or exclude on the ground that certain meanings are wrong or incompatible or mutually contradictory. To have choice (in Hawthorne's fiction) is to keep open the prospects for interpretation on

the grounds that reality never means either one thing or another but, rather, is Meaning fragmented by plural points of view, for, although the fragmentation is a source of many a "tale of frailty and sorrow," such as *The Scarlet Letter*, it is also, as *The Scarlet Letter* demonstrates, the source of an enriched sense of unity, provided we attend to the principles of liberal exegesis. And by these principles, to opt for meaning in all its multifariousness — to have your adulterous love and do the work of society too — is to obviate not only the conflicts embodied in opposing views but also the contradictions implicit in the very act of personal interpretation between the fact of multiple meaning and the imperative of self-assertion.

In other words, to interpret is willfully, in the interests of some larger truth, *not to choose*. (21–22)

Hawthorne's ambiguity, then, far from offering many choices, according to Bercovitch, offers only one choice between two alternatives: to support pluralism or to reject it. If Hawthorne's characters agree that meaning is "fragmented by plural points of view," they cannot make choices but must refuse in light of larger truths. The only true choice, then, would necessarily involve a complete rejection of pluralism, essentially an absolutism of "self-assertion" that believed its point of view to be total, unlimited. Bercovitch's argument thus accuses Hawthorne of promoting liberal pluralism at the expense of revolutionary action, but he does so by offering a vision of choice that is itself antidemocratic, authoritarian, and potentially dangerous. As Peter J. Bellis argues, Bercovitch is doing little more than replacing one ideology with another: "But just what are the political or revolutionary alternatives excluded or foreclosed by nineteenth-century American ideology? For Bercovitch, these are embodied in the 'European Forty-eight,' by which he primarily means the Paris uprising of June 1848. These are the events that loom over Bercovitch's American Renaissance as the political road not taken."[19] This idealistic preference for modes of political violence over compromise may be little more than twentieth-century academic nostalgia, but for Hawthorne the choice between violent self-assertion and pluralistic dialogue has serious ethical implications.

Indeed, it is precisely the danger of such idealistic choices to those nearest to the individual that Hawthorne is most interested in revealing. In fact, it would appear that the sort of idealism underlying Bercovitch's analysis is Hawthorne's greatest concern, for if idealistic choices can harm those nearest to us, how do we justify that harm through our claims to a greater good? What level of sacrifice is acceptable? To what extent will violence solve problems without destroying others in the process or begetting further violence in the name of idealism? These are serious questions that cannot be ignored or simply absorbed by ideological analysis. They are, fundamentally, ethical rather than political questions. That is, they involve the basic question of the relationship between self and other and place that relationship at the basis of all further thought or action. Accordingly, the self—and the idealism it promotes as self-extension—finds its fundamental existence through the limitations established by the other. An idealism that, directly or indirectly, claims dominion over the other can only be a violation of those fundamental limits. Politics, at least as Bercovitch defines it, will necessarily require such violations and will, therefore, always fail to live up to the demands of the other. Conflict, as Bercovitch demonstrates, will be allegorized into simplified terms; the transcendent demand will be reduced to an objectified idea.

Against this idealistic vision of conflict Hawthorne proposes an ethic based in part on what critics have called "historical consciousness." In her discussion of "Young Goodman Brown," Emily Miller Budick argues that historical consciousness undermines individual point of view while demanding, nevertheless, an engagement with the world beyond the self: "History, for Hawthorne, records the world from a point of view that is not the self. It demands that the self acknowledge a world it did not create, cannot transform, and cannot finally even verify."[20] In this respect the individual must make specific decisions within the context of the self's own limits and must measure the value of those decisions by reference to specific, local concerns—the real effects of choices on the lives of others. Such decisions will be made not on the basis of abstract principles; for Goodman Brown there are no principles available in the woods, only specters, each as dubious as the next. Decisions will be made as though from no rational or otherwise systematic foundation but out of the knowledge of the self's own limits and with an eye to the probable effects on the people most likely to be helped or harmed by the decision.

Again, we can draw on Emmanuel Levinas to help characterize such a paradoxical position, for according to Thomas Carl Wall, Levinas describes a similar dilemma:

> This strange ethics . . . can only be included in any morality, politics, or community whatever *as excluded* (or, as Levinas puts it, as "betrayed"). . . . Giorgio Agamben puts it this way: "The fact that must constitute the point of departure for any discourse on ethics is that there is no essence, no historical or spiritual vocation, no biological destiny that humans must enact or realize. That is the only reason why something

like ethics can exist, because it is clear that if humans were to be this or that substance, this or that destiny, no ethical experience would be possible — there would only be tasks to be done."

The "point of departure" here is in fact the absence of anything that would constitute a point of departure, which is why ethics will always have been, as Agamben puts it, "something like ethics." There will be something *like* ethics because there will be no ethics *proper*. . . . That is to say, the "ethical experience," outside essence, will be an experience of an improper, incoherent, indeterminate obligation.[21]

In this sense, ethics becomes not a system of behavior based on concepts but "a responsibility propriety cannot satisfy" (ibid., 52). The demand of the other is "incoherent" and therefore incapable of being institutionalized, rationalized, or, most important for Hawthorne, allegorized. Such a disjunction between the conceptual and the ethical does not lead to paralysis but to an improvisation of action through an awareness of interpretive limits. Simon Critchley has described a similar sort of "hiatus" between ethics and politics in his reading of Jacques Derrida's encounter with Levinas: "Derrida emphasizes how the very indeterminacy of the passage from ethics to politics entails that the taking of a political decision must be a response to the utter singularity of a particular and inexhaustible context. The infinite ethical demand of deconstruction arises as a response to a singular context and calls forth the invention of a political decision. Politics itself can here be thought of as *as the art of response to the singular demand of the other*; a demand that arises in a particular context — although the infinite demand cannot simply be reduced to its context — and calls for political invention, creation."[22]

It is precisely ethics' resistance to the allegorical tendencies of idealism — the way the face of the other demands more than I can think or contain — that drives Hawthorne's critique of the limitations of "political" thinking.[23] For if politics, as Matthiessen suggests, is inevitably allegorical — inevitably reductive in its figuration of ideas and points of view — ethical experience will indeed be an experience of "impossibility." And it is precisely this impossibility that structures Young Goodman Brown's decision. In the absence of idealistic certainty, he must choose whether to read the world as an extension of himself or as otherness itself. By choosing the first alternative, he transforms the world and others in it into his own idealistic drama, sacrificing the world to the self. The result of this choice, while it may indirectly assert the values of pluralism, most clearly emphasizes the harm done to Brown's family and to himself through his basic ethical violation.

The great challenge that "Young Goodman Brown" poses to current criticism thus arises from its insistence on the groundlessness of decision-making, on the often terrifying space between systematic principles and ethical choices.[24] Hawthorne refuses to allow the easy passage from epistemological uncertainty to determined action without at least acknowledging the necessary damage done in the translation from ethics to politics. As Critchley further argues, this troubled relationship is both a potential weakness of Levinasian ethical philosophy and its essential insight:

> In Pascalian terms, when I say, "this is my country, my child, my place in the sun," the usurpation of the whole world begins. When the infinitude of ethics contracts into the finite space of an *ethos* — a site, a plot, a space for the sacred . . . — then the very worst becomes possible. I admit that ethics without *ethos* or, better, without a relation to a plurality of *ethoi*, is empty, and this is a weakness of Levinas's work, a weakness that runs like an open wound through his exaggerated polemics against Heidegger and his inability to criticize Israel as a nation-state.
>
> Rather, what is required is that democracy be driven by a concern for justice, an infinite responsibility, a formal universality, that arises in a singular experience or in the experience of indebtedness towards a specific singularity, and which is the condition (but not a recipe) for politicization. In my view, political decisions have to be invented in relation to a conception of justice that is never integrable or presentable within the institutions and practices of a given society. There is no just society, no just decision and justice can never be done; which does not mean that the demand for justice should be given up, but precisely the reverse.[25]

Here we have the horns of Hawthorne's own ethical/political dilemma. For to insist on this separation of ethics and *ethos* is to risk either quietist failure (as in the Pierce biography) or the sacrifice of the ethical to political expediency and partisan power. His most infamous political statements — particularly his often-repeated claim that attempts at reform rarely or never accomplish their goals — can be seen as efforts to base choices upon a fundamental skepticism similar to Critchley's comments on justice.[26] Such a position is particularly vulnerable to the rhetorical reductions of specific political moments or decisions that, by their very nature, work to ignore or elide the infinite demand as impractical. In such a story as "Young Goodman Brown" the title character is not relieved of the obligation of ethics simply because there is no interpretive certainty from which to proceed. If anything, the demand to acknowledge others is intensified by its groundlessness, and it is Brown's greatest failure that he grasps at the certainty of an available politics (witchcraft paranoia) rather than the uncertain ethicality of skepticism.

The "sort of politician I am"

In many respects, Young Goodman Brown might be seen as a thinker similar to the young Melville in his letters to Hawthorne: both are idealistic seekers, both make quick, presumptive interpretations of others. And thinking this way, we might again take Hawthorne's reaction to and friendship with Melville as a guide to his other, more controversial political involvements. That is, if Hawthorne resists the sort of allegorical appetite shown by Melville (the younger man's troping of his friend as a "black-lettered volume"), how will Hawthorne translate that resistance into the allegorical world of politics? What will his political voice look like, how will it act, and, most significant, will it function at all in this context? And if it fails to function, in one way or another, what is the meaning of that failure?

We can begin to address these questions by returning briefly to Matthiessen's comments about the essay "Chiefly About War-Matters." Matthiessen uses as an example what he calls a "typical reflection" of Hawthorne's that "no human effort, on a grand scale, has ever yet resulted according to the purpose of its projectors." He then plays this comment against its accompanying note (also by Hawthorne): "The author seems to imagine that he has compressed a great deal of meaning into these little, hard, dry pellets of aphoristic wisdom. We disagree with him. The counsels of wise and good men are often coincident with the purpose of Providence; and the present war promises to illustrate our remark." The conjunction of the two voices — one presumably autobiographical, though parodic at times, the other "fictional" in its way — creates a remarkably complex sensibility or voice that inherently resists reduction.[27] It is a style of self-resistance, brought about by intentionally limiting point of view and thereby creating a historical vision that works against political allegory. Along the same lines, the opposition pits the historical vision against the local consideration; it divides "the truth of the human heart" from its specific application by suggesting that local concerns often exist in their own economy of choice, regardless of long-term implications.

That such a position is likely to fail in a way — to be unable, that is, to engage the political debate by insisting on taking a broader view of the historical moment — seems quite clear and was no doubt just as clear to Hawthorne. In fact, the great majority of his statements regarding his political voice are similarly self-critical and, if taken seriously, point toward an important distinction often overlooked by readers hoping to categorize all of Hawthorne's writings as equally politicized.[28] In one of the letters defending his term in the Salem Custom House, for instance, Hawthorne insists on maintaining the distinction between his own writing and that of "politicians":

> I am accused, you tell me, of writing political articles for a democratic paper here — the Salem Advertiser. My contributions to that paper have been two theatrical criticisms, a notice of a ball at Ballard Vale, a notice of Longfellow's Evangeline, and perhaps half a dozen other books. Never one word of politics. Any one of the articles would have been perfectly proper for a Whig paper; and, indeed, most of them were copied into Whig papers elsewhere. You know, and the public know, what my contributions to the Democratic Review have been. They are all published in one or another of my volumes — all, with a single exception. That is a brief sketch of the life of my early and very dear friend, Cilley, written shortly after his death, at the request of the Editor. I have not read it for years; but I am willing to refer to it, as a proof of what sort of a politician I am. Written in the very midst of my grief, and when every other man in the nation, on both sides, was at fever-heat, it is, though very sad, as calm as if it had been written a hundred years after the event; and, so far as I recollect it, it might as well have been written by a Whig as by a Democrat. (*CE*, 16:277)

As the editors of the *Centenary Edition* tell us, despite these claims, the Cilley article does contain "the typical rhetoric of Jacksonian primitivism," and it clearly played a part in securing for Hawthorne his position at Salem. (Hawthorne himself obviously knew this and deliberately excluded it from his reprinted collections.) What sort of voice is this, then, that tries to separate itself from politics while participating to a degree in political activity? Is it merely a deception, an argument for political immunity that is itself a political argument designed to allow him to retain his position? Or did Hawthorne seriously believe that his writing had avoided political partisanship (even when it was in some sense political), and, if so, why would he have made such a claim?

If we take these statements as they present themselves, we might do well to remember Hawthorne's explanation to Sophia about the "involuntary reserve" that gives his writings "objectivity." For if Hawthorne's fictional voice strives for "historical consciousness" or ethical vision, then his principal problem when entering the world of politics would be to preserve that "involuntary reserve," to create a voice that engages political issues without itself becoming "political" in a reductive or allegorical fashion. The description of the Cilley article, for example, stresses the author's "calm" or detachment, "as if it had been written a hundred years after the event." This historical perspective sets up a type of engagement that is based upon disengagement. That is, only through the adopted vision of a hundred years hence can Hawthorne attempt to enter the political debate without sacrificing a voice insistent upon its ethical rather than political interests.

The results of this attempt are mixed, however. On the one hand, it creates a political language that often mocks itself, both stating and undercutting positions as part of an apparent strategy to preserve artistic or historical perspective. Such a voice works against the rigidity of political idealism to make room for an ethical vision that refuses the limitations of political debate. It is at once an entrance into and an escape from the political, an aversion that works toward ethics through self-limitation.[29] In many respects it might be thought of as the continued sacrifice of Hawthorne "the politician" in order to secure the authority of Hawthorne the artist. This strategy is most evident in the "Custom House" section of *The Scarlet Letter* and in "Chiefly About War-Matters," where the complex language of Hawthorne's prefaces creates a "self-veiling" that enables a unique sort of artistic and political gesture. However, in situations where a "veiled" language would be insufficiently allegorical for the rhetorical purposes of the writing, Hawthorne's ability to maintain his artistic voice collapses under the weight of a purely political vision. This failure is most evident in the Pierce biography, in which the requirements of political rhetoric clearly overwhelmed whatever attempts Hawthorne occasionally made toward preserving his position as artist rather than "politician."

Rereading *The Life of Franklin Pierce*

As Hawthorne's most controversial piece of political writing, the Pierce biography has become the key text for critics interested in reading the fiction in light of Hawthorne's politics. The charge of "obscurantism" made in 1941 by Matthiessen has essentially remained, renewed by a more flexible concept of ideology into an overall examination of the "cultural work" of his writing. By placing the relatively fixed political position of the campaign biography against the seemingly open politics of *The Scarlet Letter*, Jonathan Arac attempts to recover a political context for the novel and connect its aesthetic strategies to the compromise politics of the biography. After offering such a reading, his essay concludes with an attempt to qualify, or more accurately identify, his critical methodology. Attempting to revise Frederic Jameson's "notion of a 'political unconscious,'" Arac argues that we should understand the relationship between literature and politics in the nineteenth century as "*juxtaposed* to one another" rather than "superimposed one upon the other": "In juxtaposing the *Life of Pierce* and *The Scarlet Letter* I have operated by adjacency, rather than trusting that I could uncover with *The Scarlet Letter* alone all that I needed for its interpretation. Although the two works could be analyzed as narratives together, the Life was 'closed' in its unequivocal endorsement of Pierce as representing the ideal combination of future and stability; *The Scarlet Letter,* by contrast, was 'open' in its refusal to make similarly absolute claims for Hester's transcendence of the contradiction between passion and principle, and also in the overall mobility among the ideological positions that its characters were granted."[30]

This explanation raises two important questions. First, by opposing historical "juxtaposition" to formalism, is Arac simply replacing one set of restrictions with another? In other words, he does not trust that he could "uncover within *The Scarlet Letter* alone all" that he "needed for its interpretation," but he does appear to have found all he needs to read the novel in *The Life of Franklin Pierce.* In place of formalism's willful dissociation of context, he offers a willful dissociation of text, carrying out a similar sort of reduction under the guise of historical reading. Second, does he adequately account for the differences between the "closed" biography and the "open" novel? If they are to be "analyzed as *narratives* together" or by juxtaposition, it would seem that the two texts' fundamentally different attitudes toward language and artistic/political statement should be accounted for by more than just a flimsy dismissal of "art" as mystification.

In light of these questions, I would like to approach the Pierce biography from the following set of assumptions: (1) that this difference between "closed" and "open" texts does matter and should be more thoroughly accounted for; (2) that Hawthorne understood this difference and attempted to negotiate a stance as a (closed) political writer that did not compromise his (open) artistic voice; and (3) that consequently Hawthorne's definitions of his own role as "politician" should be read as a serious attempt, not always successful, to define or maintain the ethical space of his fiction.

The first mention of Hawthorne writing a campaign biography occurs in a letter to Pierce in June of 1852. Anticipating a possible invitation to help his college friend's presidential campaign, Hawthorne ostensibly tries to get out of the job: "Whatever service I can do you, I need not say, would be at your command; but I do not believe that I should succeed in this matter so well as many other men. It needs long thought with me, in order to produce anything good, and, after all, my style and qualities, as a writer, are certainly not those of the broadest popularity, such as are requisite for a task of this kind. I should write a better life of you after your term of office and life itself were over, than on the eve of an election" (*CE*, 16:545). It might be easy enough to dismiss this self-deprecation as conventional modesty designed in part to secure the job it protests against.[31] But Hawthorne's attitude toward political writing is notably consistent here and elsewhere. He takes a practical view of the matter and sees, quite clearly, that his sort of writing ("my style and qualities") are not appropriate to the sort of political writing usually associated with campaigns. He strives, that is, to maintain the position of the romancer, the artist better able to capture the historical perspective of Pierce's life after his "term of office and life itself" are over rather than in the midst of political debate. In this sense, he wishes to remain free of the limitations of narrow perspective in order to see more broadly. He then suggests in his place as biographer a much more "political" substitute in the editor of the *Boston Times*, "a man of excellent ability, and extensive information on political and other subjects" (*CE*, 16:545).

That Hawthorne was eventually persuaded to write the biography may well be a testament to the political capital of his avowedly apolitical, artistic position. As Arac has argued, his use to the Democratic party lay in part in his ability to describe and emphasize character and, presumably, to do so without overtly political motive. But the fact that such a position can have a political use (or that Hawthorne may very well have wanted, at some point, a political appointment) does not alter his basic concern about maintaining an historical/ethical position within his artistic language. Nor does his past participation in Democratic politics elide all anxiety about the potential effects of such overt political writing on his role as romancer. That anxiety remains, though often lost on his audience (both then and now) because of the inevitable reductions of political language.[32] As a result, the biography incongruously combines similar attempts to maintain artistic distance with the inevitably reduced perspective demanded by the genre itself. The campaign biography, as Hawthorne clearly knew, required an inherently simplified language, a consciously limited perspective — the one-sided vision that he consistently criticized in his fiction. Whatever attempts he might make to free himself from that demand were undercut by the rhetorical energy of the form itself, not to mention the interpretive conventions of a "political" audience.[33] The result is a reluctant voice, happiest when quoting others, diligent only in attempts to step away from the demands of the form. And it is important to note that this reluctance occurs *in spite of* his basic agreement with and support of the Democratic platform. That is, his concern is for the integrity of the fictional voice, the ability to speak historically, ironically, to control point of view, to pit voices one against another. Though a Democrat, he still hoped to escape the limitations imposed by Democratic campaign rhetoric.

This problematic position is evident from the first page of the author's preface:

> The author of this Memoir — being so little of a politician that he scarcely feels entitled to call himself a member of any party — would not voluntarily have undertaken the work here offered to the public. Neither can he flatter himself that he has been remarkably successful in the performance of his task, viewing it in the light of a political biography, and as a representation of the principles and acts of a public man, intended to operate upon the minds of multitudes, during a Presidential canvass. This species of writing is too remote from his customary occupations — and, he may add, from his tastes — to be very satisfactorily done, without more time and practice than he would be willing to expend, for such a purpose. If this little biography have any value, it is probably of another kind — as the narrative of one who knew the individual of whom he treats, at a period of life when character could be read with undoubting accuracy, and who, consequently, in judging the motives of his subsequent conduct, has an advantage over much more competent observers, whose knowledge of the man may have commenced at a later date. Nor can it be considered improper, (at least, the Author will never feel it so, although some foolish delicacy be sacrificed in the undertaking,) that when a friend, dear to him almost from boyish days, stands up before his Country, misrepresented by indiscriminate abuse, on the one hand, and by aimless praise on the other, he should be sketched by one who has had opportunities of knowing him well, and who is certainly inclined to tell the truth. (*CE*, 23:273–74)

This opening paragraph can be, and has been, dismissed as a conventional strategy to gain authority through self-deprecation. But if we take Hawthorne as he presents himself to us, the passage clearly demonstrates its author's uneasiness with political language as such, particularly insofar as it conflicts with "his customary occupations," namely, writing fiction. He thus begins with a repetition of his previous claim that he is not a "politician" and, to an extent, not a partisan, claims that can certainly seem deceptive given his previous patronage jobs and his connections to prominent Democrats. But while not disavowing his political ties, Hawthorne is making a serious distinction, one that appears, no matter how insignificant to later readers, to mean a great deal *to him*. He is engaged in political activity; he is writing a biography for a presidential candidate, but he is also writing on behalf of an old friend, from the perspective of friendship rather than partisanship. Again, the distinction is important: first, because he wishes to preserve his role as a romancer, a writer of fictions that take a broader view of history than is possible in overtly political writing; second, because the perspective of friendship makes such a preservation possible, opening up a space where "truth" can be told in opposition to "indiscriminate abuse" and "aimless praise." That such an attempt is problematic, that it may in fact fail or be impossible in the context of a political campaign, seems equally clear to Hawthorne: his paren- thetical notation of his "foolish delicacy" that must be "sacrificed in the under- taking" registers his doubt even as it reinforces his assertion that friendship, to his mind at least, extends beyond reductive political allegiance. That he was willing to write the biography with such concerns in mind complicates recent attempts to portray him as a politically savvy office-seeker willing to do whatever it takes to secure a diplomatic post. Even Scott E. Casper, who distrusts Haw- thorne's qualifications, admits that Hawthorne paid a price for supporting Pierce, gaining the consulship but losing "the esteem of much of his literary commu- nity."[34] But this was hardly an unpredictable result, as Casper would have it.

One way of measuring the importance of the distinctions Hawthorne main- tains in the Pierce preface is to look at his approach to a similar situation some years later. In 1863 he was set to publish *Our Old Home*, the public version of his *English Notebooks*. Because of his friendship with Pierce and his appointment by Pierce to the consulship at Liverpool, Hawthorne decided to dedicate the volume to the now widely reviled ex-president. Hawthorne's publisher, James Fields, warned him against it, even recruiting Ellery Channing — and through Chan- ning, Hawthorne's sister-in-law, Elizabeth Peabody — to persuade him to drop the dedication. As Arlin Turner summarizes the situation, "Hawthorne's decision to dedicate *Our Old Home* to Franklin Pierce was the only one open to him, given his loyalty to friends and his unwillingness to be drawn into the camp of the abolitionists on this occasion, out of what might seem to be deference to his neighbors and relatives and to his own financial interests. The issues were the same he had faced in deciding to write Pierce's campaign biography, but now they were more sharply and more emotionally conceived." To placate Fields,

Hawthorne would "rewrite the last paragraph in such a way that, while doing justice to his friend, it would contain 'not a word that ought to be objectionable to any set of readers.' "[35] This compromise produced the following language:

> And now farewell, my dear friend, and excuse, if you think it needs any excuse, the freedom with which I thus publicly assert a personal friendship between a private individual, and a Statesman, who has filled what was then the most august position in the world. But I dedicate my book to the Friend, and shall defer a colloquy with the Statesman till some calmer and sunnier hour. Only this let me say, that, with the record of your life in my memory, and with a sense of your character in my deeper consciousness as among the few things that time has left as it found them, I need no assurance that you continue faithful forever to the grand idea of an irrevocable Union, which, as you once told me, was the earliest that your brave father taught you. (*CE*, 5:5)

Without a viable political motive other than stubborn consistency, Hawthorne's defense of Pierce at this point can seem either foolish or heroic. More important for this discussion, however, is his desire to preserve the distinction between "friend" and "Statesman" (or candidate) that he relied upon in the preface to the campaign biography. (If, as some might contend, marketing was the major motivation for such language in the biography, Hawthorne here used this distinction with the full knowledge that it would not prevent a marketing disaster.) Hawthorne had known the "friend" for many years, both before and then after the political campaign, and this knowledge over time afforded a perspective that permitted political statement (e.g., the Unionist sentiment of the final sentence) without being limited to the restrictions of political debate. In this same respect, he argued that the dedication should go forward despite Pierce's unpopularity because "if he is so exceedingly unpopular that his name is enough to sink the volume, there is so much more the need that an old friend should stand by him."[36] He also offered Elizabeth Peabody a complicated picture of both his dedication to Pierce and of his friend's strengths and limitations:

> I expressly say that I dedicate the book to the friend, and decline any present colloquy with the statesman, to whom I address merely a few lines expressing my confidence in his loyalty and unalterable devotion to the Union — which I am glad to have the opportunity of saying, at this moment, when all the administration and abolition papers are calling him a traitor. A traitor? Why, he is the only loyal man in the country, North or South! Every body else has outgrown the old faith in the

Union, or got outside of it in one way or another; but Pierce retains it in all the simplicity with which he inherited it from his father. . . . The dedication was written before the New Hampshire Convention, and when I had not seen him for months; but I speak of his faith with the same certainty as if I had just come from a talk with him. Though I differ from him in many respects, I would fain rather that he should die than change. There is a certain steadfastness and integrity with regard to a man's own nature (when it is such a peculiar nature as that of Pierce) which seems to me more sacred and valuable than the faculty of adapting one's self to new ideas, however true they may turn out to be. (*CE,* 18:589–90)

In this context, Hawthorne's loyalty to Pierce extends beyond his own political position, which by then supported the war but envisioned the breakup of the Union as a sort of tragic necessity.[37] What he admired was Pierce's fidelity to his "own nature" and "noble character (though one of limited scope)" (*CE,* 18:589). Again, he tended to emphasize the value of the historical perspective and the limitations of political debate, asking Elizabeth Peabody not to circulate the letter, "for this is the first time that I have written down ideas which exist in a gaseous state of mind, and perhaps they might define themselves differently on another attempt to condense them" (*CE,* 18:591). As she herself later commented in a letter to Horatio Bridge (June 4, 1887), "It was only his mature thoughts, his *final* conclusions after surveying the appearance of the moment in the light of *the great whole* that he meant to print & give to the *human race.* In this particular letter, he himself suggests that his mind is in 'a *gaseous* state,' & that things may seem to him *different,* & it was in fact not a week after that the publication of Frank Pierce's letter to Jefferson Davis . . . *came out in the [New York] Evening Post (Bryant's)* & showed under Pierce's hand that he had encouraged Davis *to secede* & trust that the war would at once be transferred to the streets of the north where the Democrats would fight on the Southern Side" (*CE,* 18:593). For Peabody, this revelation proved Hawthorne's political naivete: "I know that he knew *nothing* about Slavery. He had never been in the South. He never saw a slave or a fugitive slave. He looked at all antislavery literature as beneath the consideration of a reasonable man. It was perfectly true that he often said that he knew nothing about contemporaneous history, that he could not understand history until it was at least *a hundred years old!*" (*CE,* 18:593–94).

It is in this context that we should understand Hawthorne's attempts to distinguish between his limited role as "politician" and his position as a writer who strove to combine distance and engagement as an observer of human activity.

That such an artistic strategy helped create his unique historical/ethical vision is evident, but his struggle to retain that historical position even in midst of political conflict often failed; indeed, it seems both destined and designed to fail given the perspective Hawthorne chose. For the very language of his "hundred years" vision cannot function in the heat of immediate political debate; it introduces a register of distance that neither the form of the biography nor the interpretive conventions in which partisan language functions can allow.

This is notoriously the case for the single most quoted passage of the biography, in which Hawthorne addresses slavery as a national issue. In a chapter titled "The Compromise, and Other Matters," he outlines the political moment by reference to the Compromise of 1850 and Pierce's support for it as "the unshaken advocate of Union" (*CE*, 23:350). He then contrasts Pierce's view of the Compromise with those of abolitionists: "He will stand up, as he has always stood, among the patriots of the whole land. And if the work of anti-slavery agitation — which, it is undeniable, leaves most men, who earnestly engage in it, with only half a country in their affections — if this work must be done, let others do it" (*CE*, 23:352). This opposition between radicals bent on dissolving the Union over slavery and "conservatives" determined to maintain the present Union at all costs then sets up the paragraph on slavery and its likely future:

> Those Northern men, therefore, who deem the great cause of human welfare all represented and involved in this present hostility against Southern institutions — and who conceive that the world stands still, except so far as that goes forward — these, it may be allowed, can scarcely give their sympathy or their confidence to the subject of this memoir. But there is still another view, and probably as wise a one. It looks upon Slavery as one of those evils, which Divine Providence does not leave to be remedied by human contrivances, but which, in its own good time, by some means impossible to be anticipated, but of the simplest and easiest operation, when all its uses shall have been fulfilled, it causes to vanish like a dream. There is no instance, in all history, of the human will and intellect having perfected any great moral reform by methods which it adapted to that end; but the progress of the world, at every step, leaves some evil or wrong on the path behind it, which the wisest of mankind, of their own set purpose, could never have found the way to rectify. Whatever contributes to the great cause of good, contributes to all its subdivisions and varieties; and, on this score, the lover of his race, the enthusiast, the philanthropist of whatever theory, might lend his aid to put a man, like the one before us, into the leadership of the world's affairs. (*CE*, 23:352)

This is, of course, an attempt to move away from a contentious issue, and it is simple enough to register its obvious callousness, lack of imagination, and deplorable quietism. Within the context of mid-century politics, Hawthorne's partisan perspective offers little more than an excuse for doing nothing about anything, a distrust of action so complete that it advocates a sort of paralysis. Likewise, his Democratic allegiances show clearly, and there is little point in questioning his point of view since it, too, is presented clearly, without irony or distance. In other words, this passage contains a manifestly political statement—Hawthorne the "politician" essaying the "species of writing . . . remote from his customary occupations"—that is, expressing the procompromise, Democratic party line. The voice is controlled by its partisan purpose, by the function of the genre, and by the interpretive conventions of those who read campaign biographies. It is, in fact, a narrowly partisan statement, promoting the virtues of a conservative, Unionist stance toward slavery in stark opposition to the idealism of the abolitionists.[38] There is nothing skeptical about such a position, no attempt to qualify its location, to fragment point of view or undercut the speaker's certainty; it is remarkably unlike what we expect from the Hawthorne of *The Scarlet Letter* or "Young Goodman Brown." In this respect, Hawthorne's reluctance to engage in such writing is certainly understandable as a function of his fictional critique of limited point of view. If partisan politics precludes irony, it also precludes the fundamental strategy and critical interest of his art.

If we can agree, then, that writing a campaign biography and writing a romance involve significant differences in the author's attitude toward language, how are we to read the resemblance between the compromise rhetoric of the biography and Hester's counsel to troubled women at the end of *The Scarlet Letter*? For those, like Bercovitch and Arac, who wish to highlight the novel's cultural power, the likeness converts *The Scarlet Letter* into virtual propaganda.[39] In other words, Hawthorne's narrative has been engineered to produce precisely this message as a sort of preview of the campaign rhetoric of the biography. Its pretense to historical truth only masks a preference for inaction over social reform. Thus, though one is "closed" and the other "open," the difference is negligible; the Pierce biography allows us to close both texts into the same political argument and erases any attempt to escape that argument by the sheer force of its materiality.

But for Hawthorne this difference was obviously not negligible, and though the thinking behind each passage may be similar, his attitude toward truth-telling in each is notably distinct. Perhaps no one was as aware as he of the limitations automatically imposed by entering into the volatile rhetoric of a political campaign. To be a *politician*, as he uses the word, indicates a willingness to promote a narrow point of view, to sacrifice irony for enthusiasm, to risk the clearer sight of historical distance for the power of adversarial language. And if we are to understand the relationship in his work between art and politics, it is in this context that we should read Hester's final counsel. For as ill-fitting and inappropriate as it may be for revolutionary action, the novel's concluding vision resonates with Hawthorne's repeated skepticism about the *long-term* efficacy of reform. Viewed from the perspective of "one hundred years" hence, it reflects its author's tragic conservatism, his understanding of the weakness of human beings, and his critique of ameliorative models of human progress.

Far from simply expressing a mid-century Democratic political perspective, such a vision draws from the tradition of Western tragedy, the literature of human weakness and frailty. This is clearly where Hawthorne wished to place himself, within an ongoing critique of absolutism and egocentrism that understands all political arguments, both conservative and liberal, to be inherently limited and therefore prone to abuse. As Arlin Turner explains, "It was Hawthorne's nature to distrust enthusiasm and to ask that advocates of social reform consider the full and ultimate effects of the action they proposed. This he thought the radical abolitionists failed to do. It was in such a context that he wrote Elizabeth Peabody from England, August 13, 1857, in returning an abolitionist essay of hers she had sent him in manuscript: 'No doubt it seems the truest of truth to you; but I do assure you that, like every other Abolitionist, you look at matters with an awful squint, which distorts everything within your line of vision; and it is queer, though natural, that you think everybody squints except yourselves. Perhaps they do; but certainly *you* do.' "[40]

What happens, then, when an author whose work is built upon such basic skepticism attempts to import his vision and style into the limited rhetoric of a political campaign? Hawthorne squints; tragic truth becomes partisan argument, and a voice built upon self-limitation, upon the critical vision of irony, becomes nothing more than a repetition of the party line. To insist on this distinction is not to accept or ignore the general political implications of Hawthorne's art, nor is it to understate the resemblance between Hester's final position and her creator's procompromise rhetoric. Rather, it allows us to see that Hawthorne's attempt to write fiction from an ethical perspective — to critique the limitations and dangers of point of view — is altered by his entrance into the political rhetoric of the campaign biography. His ability to speak of "the great whole" — and to

criticize the narrow vision of Elizabeth Peabody — is lost in the inevitable thin-
ness of adversarial debate.

The Double Voice: "War-Matters"

Just how stubborn could Hawthorne be in his attempt to import a historical
vision into political debate? "Chiefly About War-Matters" offers a remarkable
example and a clear indication of its author's desire to undercut political statement via the style of shyness. Along with "The Custom House," "Chiefly About
War-Matters, By a Peaceable Man" is arguably Hawthorne's most complex piece
of autobiographical "nonfiction." Also like "The Custom House," the essay is in
many respects a study in political language and the limits of artistic freedom
within and against overtly political thought. Unlike the Pierce biography, however, this text reasserts Hawthorne's desire to be both engaged and disengaged
and to pit the simplicity of partisan rhetoric against the natural complexity of
historical truth.

Based upon his visit to Washington, D.C. and environs in 1862, "War-Matters"
begins with one of Hawthorne's typical oppositions, reality versus "Romance."
The authorial voice (fictionalized as "The Peaceable Man") presents itself as
emerging from seclusion, suspending "the contemplation of certain phantasies,"
to go forth and "look a little more closely" at the war. From the opening sentences, however, the tone is remarkably unwarlike. Light, playfully ironic, and
yet at the same time serious in its irony, the voice takes every opportunity to upset
wartime rhetoric by insisting on multiple points of view. Despite the professed
desire to see the conduct of the war at close range, Hawthorne never misses a
chance to pull back from the scene before him and insert his preferred "hundred
years" perspective. Looking at Fort Ellsworth, for instance, he seems less interested in its present than its future, when the overgrown "moat" will become the
stuff of historical legend: "It may seem to be paying dear for what many will
reckon but a worthless weed; but the more historical associations we can link with
our localities, the richer will be the daily life that feeds upon the past, and the
more valuable the things that have been long established; so that our children will
be less prodigal than their fathers, in sacrificing good institutions to passionate
impulses and impracticable theories. This herb of grace, let us hope, may be
found in the old footprints of the war" (*CE*, 23:418–19). The most remarkable
quality of such an observation is its inconsistency with the mood of war. Such
observations may be true, in their way, but to make them during the actual

conflict seems either insensitive or strangely hardheaded. Or is something else at work? Is this, yet again, Hawthorne's compromise rhetoric, advising against ill-considered revolution, employing history as a tool to promote Democratic politics? Certainly, at this point in his career and in the political history of the country, there could be no personal advantage to Hawthorne to write political argument for a defeated party. But as someone never enthusiastic about the war, he could be expected to maintain his opinions and to insert them in a form just qualified enough to avoid direct censure. As he wrote to James T. Fields, "For my own part, I found it quite difficult not to lapse into treason continually; but I made manful resistance to the temptation."[41]

His strategy, then, involved the insertion of political speech but within a form that intentionally makes such speech suspect in itself. For aside from the general irony of the essay, Hawthorne ultimately decided to employ a basic fictional device in the essay's form. Not only did he create the voice of an indignant editor to harass the author from the footnotes, but he likewise dramatized the differences between the bellicose rhetoric of the notes and the sometimes dreamy detachment of the "Peaceable Man." The two fictional figures, each a parody in its own way, have the effect of placing both sides of the rhetorical battle (Hawthorne's "treason," the editor's loyalty) in a critical light.[42] Similarly, in responding to criticism of his depiction of Lincoln, Hawthorne seems to have been keenly aware of the difference between a vision of language that sees all speech as either treasonous or loyal and one that still allows for some notion of complex truth: "What a terrible thing it is to try to let off a little bit of truth into the miserable humbug of a world!"[43] Arguing that his depiction of the president seemed "to have a historical value," he clearly understood not only his own political bias against Lincoln but also the way in which the current climate was affecting the perceptions of those on all sides of the conflict.

A similar complexity emerges in his treatment of John Brown. Visiting Harper's Ferry and the scene of Brown's "deadly mischief" (*CE*, 23:427), the speaker makes no attempt to hide his opinion of the "sturdy old madman": "I shall not pretend to be an admirer of old John Brown, any further than sympathy with Whittier's excellent ballad about him may go; nor did I expect ever to shrink so unutterably from any apophthegm of a Sage, whose happy lips have uttered a hundred golden sentences, as from that saying (perhaps falsely attributed to so honored a source,) that the death of this blood-stained fanatic has 'made the Gallows as venerable as the Cross!' Nobody was ever more justly hanged" (*CE*, 23:427). Whether he would consider this opinion "treasonous" is difficult to tell, but it is clear that the passage fairly sums up Hawthorne's view of Brown. Aside from his general disagreement with radical abolitionists, the creator of Richard Digby could hardly be expected to sympathize with the "fanatic" aspect of Brown's raid. Likewise, Emerson's sanctification of Brown suggests precisely the sort of idealization of violence Hawthorne distrusted. And yet, in the essay's final note (appended to its final sentence), Hawthorne turns the John Brown passage against the "Peaceable Man": "We should be sorry to cast a doubt on the Peaceable Man's loyalty, but he will allow us to say that we consider him premature in his kindly feelings toward traitors, and sympathizers with treason. As the author himself says of John Brown, (and, so applied, we thought it an atrociously cold-blooded dictum,) 'any common-sensible man would feel an intellectual satisfaction in seeing them hanged, were it only for their preposterous mis-calculation of possibilities.' There are some degrees of absurdity that put Reason herself into a rage, and affect us like an intolerable crime—which this Rebellion is, into the bargain" (*CE* 23:442).

As a counterbalance to the essay's final call for reunion ("We woo the South 'as the lion woos his bride'"), the note offers "Northern" war rhetoric as a further demonstration of the two-sided "enthusiasm" of conflict. What is the result, then, of the two voices together? Is Hawthorne arguing at this point for an end to the war, for a compromise position that will reform the union short of Northern domination? Is he attempting to forestall conflict, to expose the limitations of bellicose language as a way of bringing about consensual inaction? More generally, does "Chiefly About War-Matters" even qualify as political speech in the simple sense of the term? Is it of a piece with the rhetoric of the Pierce biography? Or is it something else—an ironic dramatization? a satirical debate? and if so, from what perspective? What is the authorial position that allows for such a presentation? Where, as a "politician," does Hawthorne stand if his political speech is created through fictional device rather than war or campaign rhetoric?

The answers, I think, rest in Hawthorne's continued insistence that he is a romancer rather than a politician—not that he has no political opinions but that he prefers to engage the political from within the framework of his fictional method. The Pierce biography is an exception to this practice; "Chiefly About War-Matters" recovers it. Recall his sense of detachment from his audience, his Keatsian withdrawal in favor of the effect, at least, of artistic "objectivity." Though it may be impossible in the contexts he has sometimes chosen, such a vision of engagement through distance emerges from Hawthorne's attempts to draw character, to see historical truth as something that exists independent of individual visions and that therefore places those visions in the critical light of skepticism.[44] His entrance into overtly political controversy is thus marked by precisely the same set of goals: to offer a position even while showing it to be limited, even while opposing it with similarly compromised language. Does this produce paralysis, does it strip conflict of meaning and value? Not at all. Such a strategy never stopped Hawthorne from being a Democrat. His political opinions remained the same throughout his career, regardless of their usefulness to him. He continued to be a Democrat and to promote the political vision he held. But as a writer who held such positions he also understood their inherent limitations and took pains to demonstrate those limitations whenever the form permitted.

CHAPTER FIVE

Chiefly about Coverdale

The Blithedale Romance

The most brilliant example of Hawthorne's work as a political writer is clearly *The Blithedale Romance.* By "political" I mean of course his sense of himself as a romancer engaging a topic with clear political implications but doing so through the disengaged point of view made possible through fiction. For someone who has expressed anxiety about the effects of partisan politics on his artistic voice, *Blithedale* offers an astonishing recovery of that voice through a reexamination of Hawthorne's own artistic strategies. The result is perhaps the most dramatic example of the extent to which Hawthorne was willing to go to establish an ethical position based upon self-limitation.

He begins in his usual way, with a preface that argues quite seriously for the book's generic identity. Though clearly concerned about realist critiques of his unrealistic stories, Hawthorne chose a remarkably real-world, remarkably political topic for a work published the same year as the Pierce biography. And yet, as though in defiance of the obvious, he continues to argue for the separation between the fictional and the real: "He begs it to be understood, however, that he has considered the Institution itself as not less fairly the subject of fictitious handling, than the imaginary personages whom he has introduced there. His whole treatment of the affair is altogether incidental to the main purpose of the Romance; nor does he put forward the slightest pretensions to illustrate a theory, or elicit a conclusion, favorable or otherwise, in respect to Socialism" (*CE*, 3:1). Again, how are we to read such statements? If it is obvious to us that a writer who sets his story in a socialist community cannot avoid commenting on socialism, there is no reason to believe it was less obvious to Hawthorne. So, if we wish to understand his purpose, we can take this claim as yet another preemptive apology, an artful dodge away from a range of critical comments, or we can take it as an enactment of shyness and another demonstration — bolder, more brazen — of the "sort of politician" Hawthorne hoped to be.

The key appears in the following sentence: "In short, his present concern with the Socialist Community is merely to establish a theatre, a little removed from the highway of ordinary travel, where the creatures of his brain may play their phantasmagorical antics, without exposing them to too close a comparison with the actual events of real lives" (*CE*, 3:1). This "removal," this disengagement from the real, is more than just a defense of the imagination; it establishes an ethical space, a space of self-consciousness and self-limitation that allows Hawthorne precisely the sort of statement he has just offered. In other words, he can offer a position on socialism, but only through his denial of such a purpose. Such a deliberate separation does not imply that he has escaped the broad range of the political, but it does suggest that his goal is to avoid the narrow limitations of overtly political language. For that sort of argument we can turn to "some one of the many cultivated and philosophic minds" Hawthorne lists at the end of his preface, those who can write a "history" of the experiment and adumbrate its "lessons."

Without such an opening maneuver, paradoxical though it is, a writer of political fiction might not escape the set patterns of opinion, the overt politics, that already dominated this type of topic. In the case of the Pierce biography these constraints were clearly in place, and their power to reduce any comment to the simplistic binaries of partisan debate clearly troubled Hawthorne, despite his Democratic sympathies. By announcing his separation from such debates he does not propose a formalist isolation, an artistic immunity from the political; he hopes to combine artistic vision with material reality to produce an involvement with the "real" *by means of* imaginative distance: "The Author has ventured to make free with his old, and affectionately remembered home, at Brook Farm, as being, certainly, the most romantic episode of his own life — essentially a daydream, and yet a fact — and thus offering an available foothold between fiction and reality" (*CE*, 3:2). Hawthorne usually couches such explanations in terms of artistic defensiveness. He needs this "foothold" to avoid exposing the "paint and pasteboard" (*CE*, 3:2) of his characters. But the union of fact and dream also establishes a double critique, a twofold vision that anticipates his deliberate self-limitation in "War-Matters." The realist impulse demands a commitment to the real, an immersion in the moment and in the epistemology of the material. The fantasist impulse demands a similar allegiance to the supernatural, the possibility of strangeness. Hawthorne insists on combining these opposing commitments as a way of demonstrating the limitations of each. It is a strategy of checks and balances meant to isolate the individual as an inherently limited subject.

What separates *Blithedale* from Hawthorne's earlier romances is its dramatic presentation of precisely this double critique in the form of its narrator, Coverdale. Clearly the most controversial of Hawthorne's central characters, Coverdale has provoked a variety of responses both as a narrator (or narrative device) and as a potentially autobiographical figure. He has been described as unreliable, crazy, self-absorbed to the point of blindness, ineffectual, and/or a deluded but cunning murderer. But in terms of Hawthorne's position as an artist within/ against politics, there are really only two significant questions to ask about Coverdale: How close is he to Hawthorne? and What is the purpose of his limitations as a narrator?

The relationship between *Blithedale*'s author and its narrator has been the subject of extensive comment. For those interested in portraying Coverdale as partially or totally unreliable the space tends to be sharply defined. Beverly Hume, for instance, finds "a distance which enables [Hawthorne] not only to manipulate Coverdale's conflicting perceptions but also Coverdale's authorial manipulation of those perceptions."[1] Likewise, Harvey L. Gable Jr. notes that "Hawthorne is able to reveal simultaneously the ideology motivating Coverdale's actions, his feelings as he suffers the consequences, and his later reflections upon the experience."[2] Other critics have been less sure of this divide, preferring a more subtle appreciation of Hawthorne's potential for self-masking. Richard Brodhead, for instance, senses that "Hawthorne's distance from Coverdale is not a consistent one. In his evaluations of Blithedale Coverdale's judgments often have a sane balance, suggesting that they have his author's approval, whereas at other points he exhibits a moral obtuseness that makes him seem to be the object of Hawthorne's scorn."[3] In a similar vein, Irving Howe calls Coverdale a "highly distorted and mocking self-portrait," while Edgar Dryden sees the narrator as a "veil or disguise Hawthorne wears" that is both "manifestation" and "distortion."[4]

Most important for the present discussion, however, is the general agreement among *Blithedale's* readers that Coverdale is a notably self-conscious device. Brodhead, for instance, calls the novel "the most self-conscious of all Hawthorne's fictional exercises," which Charles Swann extends to "the most successful skeptical examination of the authority of the author and his narrative."[5] But what specific form does this self-consciousness take? And what is its purpose? It would be possible to argue, for instance, that Hawthorne's strategy is to give a political critique of utopianism the air of objectivity by intentionally criticizing the book's narrative voice. In this sense his skepticism of reform could be disguised, and rendered more powerful, through self-deference. To make such an argument, however, it is also necessary to believe that Hawthorne's career-long investigation of the self's epistemological limits was a sham, conscious or not, nothing more than a rhetorical strategy. That is, Hawthorne either naively offered self-critique as a form of truth when it was nothing more than a politically interested maneuver, or he knowingly employed self-deference as a form of ingratiation in the service of his political position.

These conclusions seem to me equally off the mark, both arrogant and absurdly cynical. That Hawthorne is a notably crafty author is undeniable, as are his awareness of craft and his ability to integrate rhetorical strategy into his thematic interests. But the question to ask is not what political purpose underlies the disposition of craft but in what ways rhetoric or style embodies the philosophical goals of the work. Take, for instance, this passage from late in *Blithedale*, in which Coverdale offers what sounds very much like a Hawthornian position:

> This is always true of those men who have surrendered themselves to an over-ruling purpose. It does not so much impel them from without, nor even operate as a motive power within, but grows incorporate with all that they think and feel, and finally converts them into little else save that one principle. When such begins to be the predicament, it is not cowardice, but wisdom, to avoid these victims. They have no heart, no sympathy, no reason, no conscience. They will keep no friend, unless he make himself the mirror of their purpose; they will smite and slay you, and trample your dead corpse under foot, all the more readily, if you take the first step with them, and cannot take the second, and the third, and every other step on their terribly straight path. (*CE* 3:70)

As Brodhead points out, one of the difficulties of seeing Coverdale as an entirely unreliable narrator is the presence of just such passages. Here Coverdale sounds very much like Hawthorne, rehearsing the familiar criticism of blind idealism and its ethical toll on friendship. The comment might just as well apply to Melville or Elizabeth Peabody as to Hollingsworth, reenacting the Hawthorneian withdrawal from a well-meaning but aggressive personal invasion. In an otherwise positive portrayal, we might well attribute such a voice to the author himself and designate Coverdale as Hawthorne's genuine alter ego.

But by this point in the book we have already seen several of Coverdale's weaknesses: his narcissism, his passive-aggressive voyeurism, and his tendency to favor fantasy over reality. Though it might be said that the passage above is the reflection of the older and wiser narrator rather than the Coverdale within the narrative, such a separation is highly questionable. We have only to look to his infamous "confession" (itself a product of the retrospective voice) to determine that the lessons Coverdale may have learned exist side by side with those traits present from the novel's beginning. In fact, it is questionable whether Coverdale learns anything in the course of the narrative; he does not noticeably "develop" as a character, nor does he show convincing signs of distance from his former self.[6] In this sense opinions offered late in the book tend to have the same status as those offered near the beginning. Even more important, these opinions exist on the same plane, in the same vocal space, as Coverdale's absurd speculations and fantastic self-indulgences. In other words, this is a character who speaks both sense and folly, who mouths Hawthorne's cherished ideas and, at the same time, shows himself to be ineffectual and foolish.

The challenge posed, then, is to read the passage above not simply as a Hawthorneian "moment" in the narrative but as a Hawthorneian position taken up by a foolish, self-centered character. "I will give you my position on idealism," Hawthorne seems to say, "but I will give it to you from the mouth of a sneaky, self-deluded poet, a silly man who hides in trees, ogles women, and fantasizes about what's under their clothes." For what purpose? If this is a rhetorical strategy meant to strengthen the offered argument, it is not very effective. If anything, Coverdale is a poor spokesman for any position Hawthorne might want to promote. Instead of disarming critics, this maneuver is more likely to arm them with precisely the sort of weapon they require — namely, proof that anti-idealism produces an ineffectual, overly aesthetic self-concern.

Given Hawthorne's skepticism, however, his sense that everyone "squints," it seems much more likely that he is attempting to tell his audience something about the nature of point of view. In other words, he offers a position and exposes its limits simultaneously, neither to strip the statement of meaning nor to disarm opposition but to demonstrate what it means to engage not in spite of but *by means of* disengagement. As he will do in "War-Matters," he emphasizes conversation over monologue, listening over conflict. For if conversation requires both commitment and listening, engagement and distance, then Hawthorne has hit upon a fictional method for demonstrating that necessary combination. He has created in Coverdale a type of narrative voice that makes room for and even solicits response and critique, that intentionally opens itself to his readers' alternative "voices."

This approach is evident in Hawthorne's obvious self-parody in chapter twelve, where Coverdale in his "bower" serves to ridicule not only Hawthorne's earlier work — "Sights from a Steeple," especially — but also his cherished historical perspective, his "hundred years" vision: "It may have been the cause, in part, that I suddenly found myself possessed by a mood of disbelief in moral beauty or heroism, and a conviction of the folly of attempting to benefit the world. Our especial scheme of reform, which, from my observatory, I could take in with the bodily eye, looked so ridiculous that it was impossible not to laugh aloud" (*CE*, 3:101). To take such a passage as purely a product of Hawthorne's position we would have to believe not only that Hawthorne is suspicious of reform (which he is) but that he is similarly suspicious of "moral beauty and heroism" (which he clearly is not). In fact, the entire episode in the bower is so much the product of self-scrutiny that even Coverdale senses its potential absurdity. That his distance above the world makes "the whole matter look ridiculous" says as much about the potential distortions of such a perspective as it does about its access to historical truth.[7] But this self-critique does not imply the complete vacancy of the position; it simply shows that all perspectives, both near and far, are inherently limited by their very status as perspectives. Such positions can be held with conviction but should not be held to the exclusion of response, to the point, that is, of monologue or, in the Melvilleian sense, monomania.

This fundamental position is implied in the principle of "responsibility" cited by Coverdale late in the text in reaction to the "pale man in blue spectacles" (*CE*, 3:198): "He cited instances of the miraculous power of one human being over the will and passions of another; insomuch that settled grief was but a shadow, beneath the influence of a man possessing this potency, and the strong love of years melted away like a vapor" (*CE*, 3:198). The mesmeric hold here duplicates both totalitarian politics and deterministic models of human behavior. The "wizard" is in some respects a tyrant and a "scientist" of the Rappaccini variety, able to deprive the "maiden" of free will and to strip any subject of ethical possibility: "Human character was but soft wax in his hands; and guilt, or virtue, only the forms into which he should see fit to mould it. The religious sentiment was a flame which he could blow up with his breath, or a spark that he could utterly extinguish. It is unutterable, the horror and disgust with which I listened, and saw, that, if these things were to be believed, the individual soul was virtually annihilated, and all that is sweet and pure, in our present life, debased, and that the idea of man's eternal responsibility was made ridiculous, and immortality rendered, at once, impossible, and not worth acceptance" (*CE*, 3:198).

Again, the passage appears to duplicate Hawthorne's typical rhetoric, but it does so from within a demonstration of its own compromised position. Hawthorne has created a flawed, obviously limited character as the spokesman for a philosophy of self-restraint, thereby presenting his argument at the same time that he shows us what it means. No one is immune from the fundamental position of Coverdale's speech; that is, we cannot escape the "eternal responsibility" of the ethical subject, no matter how strongly we may believe in the truth of our position. In this sense the passage offers more than a recovery of sin or guilt from a pseudo-scientific determinism. It registers the fundamental relationship of human beings in terms of "response." Responsibility implies interaction, the formal structure of conversation. In order to respond we must listen; in order to be responsible we must understand our relation to the rest of the world, our responsibility to see our actions within the context of human relationships. The mesmerist thus duplicates the nonethical position of the monomaniacal idealist: He sees the world as an extension of the self and others as creatures of his own mind. There is no response from the world outside the mesmerists's self because he recognizes no limits to his own dominion. He is therefore capable of the greatest atrocities because there is no one to "answer to."

This notion of responsibility can be applied broadly, as an antitotalitarian political model, or narrowly, as a structure for personal relationships. Its fundamental position within friendship or love seems the likely focus of Zenobia's veiled lady story, which itself can serve to scrutinize the book's personal relationships. The story's climactic moment, in fact, replays the similarly significant scene from "The Minister's Black Veil" in which the Reverend Mr. Hooper refuses to lift his veil for his fiancée, Elizabeth. In Zenobia's version, however, there is no promise of an apocalyptic unveiling within the historical structure of Christianity. This Calvinist teleology has been replaced by the promise of an earthly revelation as an immediate reward for a faith that transcends the material. Where the two scenes meet is on the issue of social or human faith. Hooper demands a faith in Christian history; the Veiled Lady demands a faith in human relationships. In both cases, the men involved wish to maintain a type of certainty that will reduce or eliminate risk or surprise. Hooper refuses to place himself in the epistemologically limited position of equality with another human being. Theodore likewise cannot relinquish that "natural tendency toward scepticism" (*CE*, 3:113) that otherwise protects him from the risks associated with belief. In the terms of Coverdale's later defense of responsibility, neither Hooper nor Theodore is able to relinquish a controlling interest in the situation sufficiently to escape comparison to the mesmerist. Each wishes to control the situation, philosophically if not physically. And for Hawthorne it seems but a small step from such egoistic rigidity to the "power of one human being over the will and passions of another" attributed to Westervelt. It is even arguable that the refusal to acknowledge limitation of the self, the refusal of responsibility, necessarily creates a battle of wills that cannot help but produce one-sided control within a relationship. In other words, the model of political conflict, when applied to friendship, can render nothing more than the total victory of one self over another.

Blithedale's other relationships bear out this central notion. Each appears to offer pessimistic comment on the realistic possibility of an ideal friendship. The aggressive demands of Hollingsworth on Coverdale, Zenobia, and Priscilla are so clearly the object of critique that they merit little specific comment. Hollingsworth, like his predecessor Chillingworth, is a relatively flat character used to exemplify the specific, local damage caused by absolutism. But his lack of dimension or depth also functions as a representation of the limits of his vision. In this light we should resist the temptation to identify such characters in Hawthorne's work as little more than the quasi-allegorical tools of rhetoric. They are, in addition to their rhetorical function, expressionist distortions meant to communicate the character's inner limitations. Thus Hollingsworth, when compared with the book's other characters, seems the thinnest because he is the thinnest; each of his relationships to specific others serves to highlight his failure to interact, to engage in the richness of human "response."

Coverdale might be thought to be similarly limited, by his own self-concern if nothing else. What separates him from Hollingsworth, however, is his admittedly occasional critique of absolutism — a self-consciousness within self-absorption. As a result we get a much more complex, shifting character, one who attempts to dominate relationships in certain ways but who also withdraws, who manipulates the distance between himself and others as a partially conscious form of self-restraint. He may value privacy for all the wrong reasons, for the opportunities it offers for voyeurism, escapism, or lack of commitment, but he also reveals how privacy can help obviate Hollingsworth's mistakes. In this sense he is both a spokesman for withdrawal and, remarkably, a walking critique of the self in isolation.

Zenobia, by contrast, seems remarkably engaged, both personally and politically. It is only her ultimate commitment to Hollingsworth, her willingness to sacrifice her independence for love, that places her within the range of the book's interrogation of personal relationships. Generally speaking, it is her elevation of love over political purpose that is thought to drive Hawthorne's critique of utopian reform; as this argument goes, even the strongest woman is not immune from the power of the heart and will sacrifice everything when that power calls. But it seems just as likely that she functions primarily as a warning against self-sacrifice, against losing the self inside someone else — the sacrifice of distance. She is willing to give herself totally to Hollingsworth, and this, more than anything, is the cause of her downfall, not because she surrenders her feminism but because she surrenders her self, like Georgiana in "The Birthmark." Her death can then be seen as a symbolic necessity, a way of representing the death of the self through the sacrifice of distance.

Priscilla, on other hand, seems strangely immune from such losses, despite her long sufferance at the hands of Westervelt. She emerges from the veil into a paradoxical figure of "happiness," the curiously powerful helpmeet of the morally wrecked Hollingsworth: "I did meet them, accordingly. As they approached me, I observed in Hollingsworth's face a depressed and melancholy look, that seemed habitual; the powerfully built man showed a self-distrustful weakness, and a childlike, or childish, tendency to press close, and closer still, to the side of the slender woman whose arm was within his. In Priscilla's manner, there was a protective and watchful quality, as if she felt herself the guardian of her companion, but, likewise, a deep, submissive, unquestioning reverence, and also a veiled happiness in her fair and quiet countenance" (*CE*, 3:242).

It is difficult to tell, at first glance, what such a relationship is meant to suggest. Hollingsworth's failures are easy enough to understand, but Priscilla's "submissive" triumph, her "veiled happiness" mixed with "reverence" seems strangely contradictory. Is this the ethical happiness of self-limitation, the "slender woman" who finds joy in helping others, who has emerged from the veil with a clearer sense of her relationship to the world? Or is there, within her "watchful" protection, an air of victory, of having changed places with the "powerfully built" but now powerless man who once enthralled her? It is difficult to see what sort of happiness she can have in this situation, except a sense of self-worth brought on by a version of maternal power. This is certainly not an ideal relationship in Hawthorne's terms; it is just as one-sided, just as monologic as any controlled by Westervelt or the dreaded mesmerists of Hawthorne's imagination. Hollingsworth's "self-distrust," after all, has little in common with a Hawthornian sense of self-limitation. Hollingsworth has moved from blind egotism to complete loss of self, and the pattern of his fall explains the dangers of his type of monomania. Deprived of his only idea, his single meaning, he is now nothing more than a dependent soul, a "veiled lady" of sorts, who can do little more than lean against his "guardian."

On the whole, then, *The Blithedale Romance* has little to offer in the way of ideal relationships. Its critique of socialism, of any large-scale political reform, rests on the primary contention that the political must begin with the ethical, that personal relationships are the foundation and model for societal action. As we saw in his arguments with Elizabeth Peabody, Hawthorne refused to consider ideas about social change without considering their origin within the context of one-to-one human interaction, and he was skeptical of the tendency of activists to elide the often resistant, perplexing aspects of human individuality in the name of a progress of ideas. Such a position can at times produce the quietism with which Hawthorne has been variously charged. However, it also creates a type of engagement that refuses to see the self as separate from the relationships out of which it was formed, an engagement that insists upon the constant self-scrutiny of ethical distance.

The Child's Mission: *Our Old Home*

Two important examples of just such a self-positioning appear in *Our Old Home*, the public version of Hawthorne's *English Notebooks* and the ostensible record of his term as consul to Liverpool. In the first, Hawthorne offers an account of his relationship with Delia Bacon, the American scholar obsessed with demonstrating that a secret society led by Francis Bacon was responsible for writing the plays of William Shakespeare. This tonally complex retrospective includes descriptions of their initial meeting, Hawthorne's imaginative reconstruction of Bacon's attempt to exhume Shakespeare's gravestone, an account of the critical reception of her book, and a brief mention of their falling out. Throughout, Hawthorne presents the eccentric and self-absorbed Bacon as he would one of his fictional characters. Indeed, it is arguable that she interested him precisely because of her resemblance to those isolated, obsessed figures that populate his fiction. And yet this is more than a simple case of artistic voyeurism. Hawthorne is, in a very real sense, involved in Bacon's life, even if for a short time, and his willingness to become involved, combined with his habit of detached observation, produces an interesting model for the type of engagement he prefers. Specifically, it allows us to see how he understood the limitations that exist between human beings and the ways those limitations, if acknowledged, establish ethical boundaries to thought and action.

During the initial meeting, for instance, Hawthorne quickly decides that Bacon is a "monomaniac," completely dependent for her identity and place in the world upon her all-consuming "theory" (*CE*, 5:106–7). He considers debating the matter with her, offering an "explanation for this theory," but understands that dialogue is impossible: "She had as princely a spirit as Queen Elizabeth herself, and would at once have motioned me from the room" (*CE*, 5:107). Instead he takes up his usual position of observer, curious to see the effects of so dominant an idea, ready to help where possible but conscious of the limits of her attention. What he does not do, somewhat surprisingly, is dismiss her as a crank.[8] Nor does he take offense at her imperious egotism. Even after she dismisses him for some less-than-loyal comment, he maintains a sort of distant fidelity to her uniqueness of character: "In consequence of some advice which I fancied it my duty to tender, as being the only confidant whom she now had in the world, I fell under Miss Bacon's most severe and passionate displeasure, and was cast off by her in the twinkling of an eye. It was a misfortune to which her friends were always particularly liable; but I think that none of them ever loved, or even respected, her most ingenuous and noble, but likewise most sensitive and tumultuous character, the less for it" (*CE*, 5:114).

It is possible, of course, that Hawthorne's sympathy here is merely ironic, revealing Bacon's faults while pretending to overlook them.[9] But such a reading misses a crucial attitude shared by Hawthorne with romanticism in general — the admiration for the self's integrity, the ability to be true to oneself. As Isaiah Berlin explains, "The fact that there is admiration, from the 1820s onwards, for minorities as such, for defiance as such, for failure as being nobler in certain respects than success, for every kind of opposition to reality, for taking up positions on principle where the principle itself may be absurd . . . — this is significant. What romanticism did was to undermine the notion that in matters of values, politics, morals, aesthetics there are such things as objective criteria which operate between human beings, such that anyone who does not use these criteria is simply either a liar or a madman, which is true of mathematics or of physics."[10]

The celebration of the failed but true character similarly informs Hawthorne's

descriptions of Pierce, who likewise inspires his loyalty despite, or perhaps because of, Pierce's political losses. In both cases, the celebration of integrity arises
not from a desire to avoid action; in fact, in Bacon's case it is Hawthorne's
potential overreaching that ends the relationship and effectively precludes any
further assistance he might offer. Instead, the appreciation for the truth of character arises out of a sense of the limits of understanding, out of the pluralist
impulse that is based, certainly for Hawthorne, upon the problematic nature of
truth and epistemology. If indeed there are limits to understanding others, then
there should also be limits to action with respect to others. Such a position does
not produce political paralysis; Hawthorne has been able to help Bacon, for
instance, in certain ways but not beyond the boundaries of her own, perhaps
deluded, self-conception.[11] But what separates Hawthorne's sympathy, in this
sense, from the more robust activism of someone like Melville is his unwillingness to sacrifice the autonomy of an individual like Bacon for social action that,
no matter how productive, would strip her of her self-determination.

We have already seen the difficulties of such an approach within the context of
partisan politics. Its limitations within actual relationships, particularly in light of
Hawthorne's personal reticence, appear most forcefully later in *Our Old Home* in
a passage recounting a visit to the West Derby workhouse: "By-and-by we came
to the ward where the children were kept. . . . And here a singular incommodity
befell one member of our party. Among the children was a wretched, pale, half-
torpid little thing, (about six years old, perhaps, but I know not whether a girl or a
boy), with a humor in its eyes and face, which the governor said was the scurvy,
and which appeared to bedim its powers of vision, so that it toddled about grop-
ingly, as if in quest of it did not precisely know what" (*CE*, 5:300). As we know
from the matching pages in *The English Notebooks*, the "member of our party" is
Hawthorne himself, the shy consul who seems more horrified than amused that
this "sickly, wretched, humor-eaten infant" has taken "an unaccountable fancy"
to him (*CE*, 5:300): "It said not a word, being perhaps underwitted and incapable
of prattle. But it smiled up in his face—a sort of woeful gleam was that smile,
through the sickly blotches that covered its features—and found means to express such a perfect confidence that it was going to be fondled and made much of,
that there was no possibility in a human heart of balking its expectation. It was as
if God had promised the poor child this favor on behalf of that individual, and he
was bound to fulfil the contract, or else no longer call himself a man among men"
(*CE*, 5:300).

It may be difficult to read this passage without judging it to be a piece of overt sentimentality, a Dickensian moment of middle-class redemption in the embrace of the wretched poor. But two important elements alter the conventional tone. First, there is the very serious claim of human otherness, embodied in this case by a child whose alienating features Hawthorne clearly emphasizes. There is, in other words, a face—silent, smiling, but, most importantly—looking at another face. This look, which does nothing to minimize Hawthorne's revulsion, does produce a remarkably candid moment for this notably cagey writer: "Nevertheless, it could be no easy thing for him to do, he being a person burthened with more than an Englishman's customary reserve, shy of actual contact with human beings, afflicted with a peculiar distaste for whatever was ugly, and, furthermore, accustomed to that habit of observation from an insulated stand-point which is said (but, I hope, erroneously) to have the tendency of putting ice into the blood" (*CE*, 5:300–301).

This stark self-portrait, though lightly disguised, undercuts the surge of sentimentality that might otherwise overtake this episode. It is a remarkable moment. Hawthorne is telling us not only that he understands the limitations of his own personality but that in the face of a particular human demand, the disengagement of the shy observer must yield, even if it is never fully relinquished. Whatever ideas may be in place prior to this demand simply do not function. The "struggle" Hawthorne describes before he picks up "the loathesome child" can only be emotional or, at any rate, nonintellectual, to be symbolized and rationalized in retrospect but not at the moment of decision: "No doubt, the child's mission in reference to our friend was to remind him that he was responsible, in his degree, for all the sufferings and misdemeanors of the world in which he lived, and was not entitled to look upon a particle of its dark calamity as if it were none of his concern; the offspring of a brother's iniquity being his own blood-relation, and the guilt, likewise, a burthen on him, unless he expiated it by better deeds" (*CE*, 5:301).

Readers of *The House of the Seven Gables* will recognize Hawthorne's attitude to historical guilt, the transference of responsibility from one generation to the next. But just as important is the conjunction of basic human responsibility with the question of individual "concern." For all of Hawthorne's heightened sense of privacy, for all his interest in the limitations and sanctity of the individual self, he here describes the self as both detached and engaged, inherently separate *and* inherently connected, free to make choices, yes, but bound by "blood-relation" to respond, to answer.

Part III / Shyness and History

"What have you to do here?" said Alice. "Your lot is in another land. You have seen the birthplace of your forefathers, and have gratified your natural yearning for it; now return, and cast in your lot with your own people, let it be what it will. I fully believe that it is such a lot as the world has never yet seen, and that the faults, the weaknesses, the errors of your countrymen will vanish away, like morning-mists before the rising sun. You can do nothing better than to go back."

— HAWTHORNE, *The Ancestral Footstep*

The conversation of what I call the genre of remarriage is . . . of a sort that leads to acknowledgement; to the reconciliation of a genuine forgiveness; a reconciliation so profound as to require the metamorphosis of death and revival, the achievement of a new perspective on existence; a perspective that presents itself as a place, one removed from the city of confusion and divorce. — CAVELL, *Pursuits of Happiness*

CHAPTER SIX

Forgetting the Secret

> But what I wish to suggest above all is that Hawthorne's serious literary
> inventions are never free from the pressures of history; and that, in the
> finest of his early tales, characters like Young Goodman Brown suffer the
> psychological consequences of the moral assumptions peculiar to their own
> historic world.　　　　　— COLACURCIO, *The Province of Piety*

As we turn from politics to Hawthorne's conception of history, we might do well
to begin here, with Michael Colacurcio's claim that Hawthorne's fiction is "never
free from the pressures of history." That such a statement seems obvious enough
to us now only measures the extent to which historical criticism has dominated
the years since 1984. In fact, in his "Polemical Introduction" Colacurcio is attempting, with all the force of his peculiarly pungent rhetoric, to legitimize a
thoroughly historical reading of the writer so often thought to be primarily a
psychologist, a formalist, or some other type of equally detached, ahistorical
artist. For Colacurcio, earlier criticism had ignored not only the settings for
many of Hawthorne's tales but, more important, the extent to which the fiction
engaged the intellectual and cultural histories of early America as well. In this
reading Hawthorne was not merely a romantic artist who looked at the dark side
of the human heart; he was a historian, in the broadest sense, investigating the
"moral assumptions peculiar" to other historic worlds.

In demonstrating Hawthorne's engagement with seventeenth-century history, however, *The Province of Piety* may have simply encouraged newer historicists to see Hawthorne as an ideologue using the past to make political capital in

the nineteenth century. If, for instance, "Young Goodman Brown" turns out to be more concerned with the complexities of "spectral evidence" than with nineteenth-century epistemology, and if "The Minister's Black Veil" primarily conflates the careers of three little-known New England ministers, then their author can begin to seem even less a part of his own time, a cold, magisterial eye looking back, mixing and measuring a distant past. Historicists in Colacurcio's wake thus seem more attracted to Hawthorne's ideological embeddedness in the Jacksonian era than to his apparent mastery of early American materials. Their readings have attempted to show how Hawthorne's imaginings of early American conflicts reflected his own generally conservative vision of nineteenth-century cultural and political issues.[1] Colacurcio's historian has thus become Bercovitch's crafty Democrat, writing compromise large over the history of New England.

Tangential to this somewhat limited debate, the work of Emily Miller Budick stands out both for its independence and its remarkable good sense. Herself a student of Colacurcio's, she explains in the preface to *Fiction and Historical Consciousness* that she began to see Hawthorne's conception of history as deeply related to the problems of self-limitation: "I discovered in Hawthorne's historicity that respect for history was itself a key issue. In recreating the past, Hawthorne insisted that his readers take seriously matters completely outside themselves, matters that they might never fully know or understand or control. Meditating on this aspect of Hawthorne's interest in history, I became aware of the close connections between the problem of respecting the other and that of respecting history."[2] In this way Budick introduces an ethical function for what she calls "historical consciousness," itself a salutary check to the limitations of perspective: "Hawthorne looks to the past for a point outside himself by which to judge his own point of view and to establish that the world always exists under a point of view" (127). Without such a distance, the individual is likely to "squint," as Hawthorne reminded his sister-in-law, Elizabeth Peabody, and it is to the dangers of narrowed vision, particularly to those nearest to the individual, that Hawthorne is particularly attuned.

But even historical consciousness can have its limitations. As Hawthorne's political life makes clear, the "hundred years" distance may provide perspective, but it can also place the individual at too great a remove from contemporary life. The choice between the historian's wider vision and action in the world may not be an easy one, for while narrowness of perspective may lead to ethical violations, too much observation and reflection may effectively permit even darker crimes. Hawthorne's solution, though largely intuitive, is to use history both as an escape from the present and as an opening toward its reengagement. If, as Budick argues, historical consciousness breaks individual perspective, it does so in order to make possible a new relationship to the world. One escapes history in order to recover the world obscured by the shadow of the past. The agent for such a rupture is the "loathsome child," that is, the individual other whose specific demand disrupts historical structure, opening a space for a new relation.

The Comedy of Remarriage: *The House of the Seven Gables*

History is worked over by the ruptures of history, in which a judgment is borne upon it. When man truly approaches the Other he is uprooted from history.

— LEVINAS, *Totality and Infinity*

I have at various junctures characterized this forgiving, the condition of remarriage, as the forgoing of revenge.   — CAVELL, *Pursuits of Happiness*

In the endnotes to her own Cavellian reading of *The House of the Seven Gables*, Budick provides a useful starting point for considering just how Hawthorne establishes this process of relinquishment and reengagement: "Since this chapter is already so indebted to the writings of Stanley Cavell I cannot forbear making one further connection with his work. In *Pursuits of Happiness: The Hollywood Comedy of Remarriage* . . . , Cavell describes a series of films, deriving from the tradition of Shakespearean romance, about couples who separate and remarry, as the woman, under the tutelage of the male, becomes an independent self capable of engaging in the conversation of wedded life. It occurs to me that Hawthorne's *Romance* of Holgrave and Phoebe might be the first such American comedy of remarriage."[3] This suggestion is reasonable in more than one way: Cavell outlines a pattern that might be called both generic (a feature of the comedy/romance) and philosophical (a development of the epistemological revolution proposed by Emerson and Thoreau). The formal gestures of his "romance" — the sequence marriage-divorce-remarriage — represent or reduplicate the process by which the romantic self reforms its relation to the world. For Hawthorne, such a "divorce" can imply social withdrawal or, even more significant for *The House of the Seven Gables*, a fracture in the individual's relation to history, which in this novel means Pyncheon history, the legacy of aristocratic pretension, the secret history of guilt and chosenness. It also means revenge, history reduced to a closed, teleological system, a singular narrative all the more powerful for being hidden. Indeed, there is very little structural difference between Holgrave's potential revenge and the

Pyncheon's reclamation of the lost ancestral claim. Each contracts the present to the limits of the secret story. The historical drama of the novel thus hinges upon the capacity of the individual to relinquish a hidden history, to escape its narrowed perspective and reengage the world outside of its limits.[4]

The central image of Pyncheon history is the "Indian deed." Like the story it is meant to confirm, the deed is invisible. Like the historical guilt it implies, it is always present and yet beyond the grasp, the secret that orders the world by means of its secrecy. It is simultaneously an image of greed, arrogance, and antidemocratic selfishness:

> This impalpable claim, therefore, resulted in nothing more solid than to cherish, from generation to generation, an absurd delusion of family importance, which all along characterized the Pyncheons. It caused the poorest member of the race to feel as if he inherited a kind of nobility, and might yet come into the possession of princely wealth to support it. In the better specimens of the breed, this peculiarity threw an ideal grace over the hard material of human life, without stealing away any truly valuable quality. In the baser sort, its effect was to increase the liability to sluggishness and dependence, and induce the victim of a shadowy hope to remit all self-effort, while awaiting the realization of his dreams. Years and years after their claim had passed out of the public memory, the Pyncheons were accustomed to consult the Colonel's ancient map, which had been projected while Waldo County was still an unbroken wilderness. Where the old land-surveyor had put down woods, lakes, and rivers, they marked out the cleared spaces, and dotted the villages and towns, and calculated the progressively increasing value of the territory, as if there were yet a prospect of its ultimately forming a princedom for themselves. (*CE*, 2:19)

The principle power here is deferment, the imagined goal holding life in abeyance. But just as important for Hawthorne's rhetorical aims is the sense that such deferment issues not only from a posited reward, a sort of earthly heaven, but also from a notably aristocratic and antidemocratic aspiration. As he will continue to do in the *American Claimant* manuscripts, Hawthorne is condemning this sort of pretension as both historically out of step and ethically threatening. If the family can see itself reaching through history, he implies, so can the individual, and such overextension would necessarily include the failure to acknowledge the existence of those outside the individual's drama.[5] In this sense the early Pyncheons' special claim to history folds into the aristocratic social vision of theocrats like John Winthrop, each condemned as a form of greed with negative epistemological and ethical effects.

Judge Pyncheon is the obvious inheritor of this ambition. No longer a Puritan, but still the heir to a history of greed and exclusion, the judge seems to embody the weight of moneyed tradition, the corpulent claim of a powerful but morally defunct social theory. In at least one respect, he is the gabled house walking, though the years of familial decay remain masked in him by the vitality of avarice: "He himself, in a very different style, was as well worth looking at as the house. No better model need be sought, nor could have been found, of a very high order of respectability, which by some indescribable magic, not merely expressed itself in his looks and gestures, but even governed the fashion of his garments, and rendered them all proper and essential to the man. . . . One perceived him to be a personage of mark, influence, and authority; and, especially, you could feel just as certain that he was opulent, as if he had exhibited his bank account—or as if you had seen him touching the twigs of the Pyncheon-elm, and, Midas-like, transmuting them to gold" (*CE*, 2:56–57). The allusion to Midas is not an idle one for Hawthorne, who liked the story well enough to rewrite it in *A Wonderbook* a short time later. In that version Midas is isolated by his desire, turning everything to useless gold, even his food and, eventually, his daughter. The emphasis falls on a failed humanity: Midas reduces all around him to a single substance meant to suggest both excessive appetite and the narrowness of thought brought on by obsession. The judge, like the Pyncheons, in general, lives within his own, extremely limited story line, a narrative as closed and predetermined as the Calvinist conception of history. The only possible end to such a story is the one predestined by the secret history. Finding the deed would thus be the nineteenth-century equivalent of salvation for the Pyncheons, leading them to the terrestrial paradise that has been lost *only* so that it may be recovered at time's end.

Lacking the judge's fierce energies, the other inheritors of this historical "squint," chiefly Hepzibah and Clifford, merely exemplify the debilitating effects of narrowed vision. Hepzibah's nearsightedness acts both as the symbol of Pyncheon self-interest and as the consequence of historical hubris. The squinting itself causes her "forbidding scowl" (*CE*, 2:34), the sign by which she keeps the world away despite its partial misrepresentation of her feelings. For though "her heart never frowned" (*CE*, 2:34), Hepzibah has nevertheless trapped herself inside the life of the house, which is to say, inside the historical vision the house represents. Even on the train, trailing after Clifford in his futile attempt to escape, she sees nothing but the location of her "fixed ideas": "If a fixed idea be madness, she was perhaps not remote from it. Fast and far as they had rattled and clattered along the iron track, they might just as well, as regarded Hepzibah's mental images, have been passing up and down Pyncheon-street. . . . This one great house was everywhere! It transported its great, lumbering bulk, with more than railroad speed, and set itself phlegmatically down on whatever spot she glanced at" (*CE*, 2:258).

Similarly, her concentration on a "single series of ideas" (*CE*, 2:174) has so limited her perception of reality that daily life has been deprived of both substance and structure. We see this in her first attempt to open the cent shop, her crumbling of the "gingerbread elephant" (*CE*, 2:37) with nervous fingers, her sense that she was "walking in a dream," that "all outward occurrences [were] unsubstantial" (*CE*, 2:66). When confronted with the appetites of Ned Higgins — that vigorous, nineteenth-century American consumer — Hepzibah can do little more than marvel: as weak and degenerated as the Pyncheon chickens, she has hardly enough substance herself to comprehend the explosive desires of this new generation of a new nation. Only Phoebe, infused with a heartier strain of New England farm stock, seems solid enough to face the world outside of Hepzibah's historical enclosure. Phoebe, after all, is "real! Holding her hand, you felt something; a tender something; a substance, and a warm one; and so long as you should feel its grasp, soft as it was, you might be certain that your place was good in the whole sympathetic chain of human nature. The world was no longer a delusion" (*CE*, 2:141). A Pyncheon yet outside of Pyncheon history, Phoebe serves several rhetorical functions: as idealized, democratic household angel, as redeemer of both men and time, and as harbinger of the projected success and dominance of middle-class culture. Just as important, however, she cuts through the fragile fabric of Pyncheon history as an embodiment of the "Actual" (*CE*, 2:140), a human presence who exceeds the reductions of the secret story. And it is only by remaining outside that story, ungraspable by its mechanisms, that she can serve to bring substance and reality back to Hepzibah's delusional world.

Clifford understands this better than anyone. Himself reduced to a phantom of the Pyncheon narrative, he alternates between desperate attempts to recover the actual and childish retreats into aesthetisized dreams. He pricks his fingers with rose thorns just to experience the reality of pain. He nearly leaps from his arched window into a passing "political procession" to join "the surging stream of human sympathies" (*CE*, 2:165). And when such desperate measures fail, he blows soap bubbles that burst at the touch of the palpable world in the street below. But he never lacks the consciousness of his position, the understanding that he and Hepzibah are both the victims and the accomplices of a history too narrow to permit an alternate reality. " 'It cannot be, Hepzibah! — it is too late,' said Clifford with deep sadness. — 'We are ghosts! We have no right among human beings — no right anywhere, but in this old house, which has a curse on it, and which therefore we are doomed to haunt' " (*CE*, 2:169). Unable to step across the threshold, even to go to church, the pair are subject to the containment of their own ideas, the image of themselves as inhabitants of an exclusive existence. "At the threshold, they felt his pitiless gripe upon them. For, what other dungeon is so dark as one's own heart! What jailor so inexorable as one's self!" (*CE*, 2:169)

It is appropriate that Clifford speak of the family curse, though it is not clear whether he means the curse of Matthew Maule or the burden of the Pyncheons' own self-conception. To be cursed implies the forcible inclusion in a history created by someone else, but it is debatable whether or not Maule's curse creates Pyncheon history or is merely a part of the story they themselves have fashioned out of a sense of chosenness and aristocratic ambition. The distinction is actually thinner than it appears since both forms of "cursedness" require a basic faith in the power of language to control the minds, or at least measure the mental horizons, of those under its sway. Again like the Calvinist conception of guilt, the curse becomes a version of Christian teleological history, forecasting its own potential dissolution through grace or love. Its specific drama depends upon the possibility of escape within the likelihood of continued damnation. And in true Christian fashion, the key to escape is not action but passivity or, rather, the refusal to repeat the action prescribed by the curse itself.

The choice rests between forgiveness and revenge, and it is to Holgrave that this particular historical challenge appears most directly. As the inheritor of Matthew Maule's vengeance, Holgrave finds himself in a position not so different from that of Clifford and Hepzibah. Like the current Pyncheons, he has been inscribed into a narrative not entirely of his own making and is subject to the logic of its progression, at least for as long as he continues to believe in it.[6] Revenge history is thus structurally no different from the history of the Pyncheon deed; both function as secret stories, as controlling forms beneath the surface of daily life. Both are teleological, both all-consuming, dangerously reductive, and willfully blind. As equal parts mesmerist and photographer, Holgrave represents this particular form of "near sightedness," or focus. That is, he uses his eyes to control others, but his personal mastery is simply the expression of the way revenge masters him.

The isolation this vision demands produces a sense of fragmentation and loss of substance similar to Hepzibah's. It is Holgrave, after all, who tells her that he finds "nothing so singular in life, as that everything appears to lose its substance, the instant one actually grapples with it" (*CE*, 2:44). It is a dissolution of form directly related to Holgrave's mesmeric tendencies, particularly his ambition for total knowledge of others. Like Chillingworth's, Holgrave's vengeance is part and parcel of his passion for totality, his desire to fathom "Clifford to the full depth of my plummet-line!" (*CE*, 2:178). There is a sense in which even his daguer-reotypes are both mesmeric and invasive, images of others that are ultimately too penetrating and reductive. Phoebe, infallible in her feelings, registers the objection: " 'A daguerreotype likeness, do you mean?' asked Phoebe, with less reserve; for, in spite of prejudice, her own youthfulness sprang forward to meet his. 'I don't much like pictures of that sort — they are so hard and stern; besides dodging away from the eye, and trying to escape altogether. They are conscious of looking very unamiable, I suppose, and therefore hate to be seen' " (*CE*, 2:91). The hardness she dislikes is the response to intrusion and to the photographer's pre-tension to truth. Her reaction evokes the question that supports this discussion: Is the truth of another person to be thought of as on or below the surface? Hawthorne's mesmerists and revengers typically conceive of human truth as secret, buried, a thing to be exposed or, for Holgrave, caught. But Phoebe's objection suggests that the truth about others may be just as available in how they present themselves to the world, in how they choose to be seen rather than in what they choose to hide.

The distinction may hinge, of course, upon the character of the person, specif-ically, on whether or not the individual is subject to secret history. In the case of the judge, for instance, the daguerreotype seems not only appropriate but par-ticularly suited to his deceptive character: " 'Now, the remarkable point is, that the original wears, to the world's eye — and, for aught I know, to his most intimate friends — an exceedingly pleasant countenance, indicative of benevolence, open-ness of heart, sunny good humor, and other praiseworthy qualities of that cast. The sun, as you see, tells quite another story, and will not be coaxed out of it, after half-a-dozen patient attempts on my part. Here we have the man, sly, subtle, hard, imperious, and, withal, cold as ice' " (*CE*, 2:92). Because Judge Pyncheon lives within secrecy, the mesmeric camera finds what it seeks. That is, Hol-grave's camera participates in the structure of thinking that presupposes a hidden truth beneath a false surface. As operated by the revenger, it is even more likely to represent the intrusive ambitions of those like the Judge and Holgrave.[7] It becomes an instrument of silent interrogation, of torture even, if we believe

Phoebe, whose reluctance to pry is offered as antidote to the daguerreotype's subtle aggression.

But of course Holgrave is not Chillingworth, nor is he bound to history quite so thoroughly as is Judge Pyncheon. As the voice for radical democratic change, Holgrave contradicts his hidden purpose, offering not so much a deceptive argument for revolution as a sincere plea for escape from his own familial past: " 'Shall we never, never get rid of this Past!' cried he, keeping up the earnest tone of his preceding conversation. — 'It lies upon the Present like a giant's dead body! In fact, the case is just as if a young giant were compelled to waste all his strength in carrying about the corpse of the old giant, his grandfather, who died a long while ago, and only needs to be decently buried' " (*CE*, 2:182–83). There is little doubt that this idea was attractive to Hawthorne. It appears with even greater intensity and frequency in several of his later works and is the driving force behind *The American Claimant* project, in particular. In essence it is a plea for a democratic future, a kind of Thoreauvian liberation in which familial property is not merely a burden to consciousness but also a sign of a lifeless tradition. Even so, the sort of revolution Holgrave envisions takes place on too large a scale for Hawthorne. It is at the level of the individual, specifically in the face-to-face encounter between two individuals, that Hawthorne finds the only realistic potential for change:

> As to the main point — may we never live to doubt it! — as to the better centuries that are coming, the artist was surely right. His error lay, in supposing that this age, more than any past or future one, is destined to see the tattered garments of Antiquity exchanged for a new suit, instead of gradually renewing themselves by patchwork; in applying his own little life-span as the measure of an interminable achievement; and, more than all, in fancying that it mattered anything to the great end in view, whether he himself should contend for it or against it. Yet it was well for him to think so. This enthusiasm, infusing itself through the calmness of his character, and thus taking an aspect of settled thought and wisdom, would serve to keep his youth pure, and make his aspirations high. And when, with the years settling down more weightily upon him, his early faith should be modified by inevitable experience, it would be with no harsh and sudden revolution of his sentiments. He would still have faith in man's brightening destiny, and perhaps love him all the better, as he should recognize his helplessness in his own behalf; and the haughty faith, with which he began life, would be well bartered for a far humbler one, at its close, in discerning that man's best-directed effort accomplishes a kind of dream, while God is the sole worker of realities. (*CE*, 2:180)

As in *The Scarlet Letter*, the choice here is between large-scale reform and individual humility. To many readers, the passage amounts to little more than a plea for acceptance, for the chastened conformity of the failed reformer. Faith in progress is offered as a bromide to soothe the passion for change, and time serves to reduce revolutionary energies. But if we take into account the novel's overall action, we can see that the narrator is offering us less a prescription for stasis than an argument for the effective power of self-limitation. After all, what does it mean to say that "God is the sole worker of realities," that "man" should "recognize his helplessness in his own behalf," that history proceeds by "patchwork"? It means that history is moved by the uncertain, unpredictable interactions of individuals, not by the ideas and "haughty faith" of reformers.[8] This is how society progresses, not through the dominating vision of a single person but through each individual allowing the other to live beyond the reach of any one person's ideas. In this sense Hawthorne is offering not acceptance but a form of radical humility, a recognition that the self cannot impose itself on others, that as individuals we are in this sense "helpless." And it is through this awareness of limitation that an *unpredictable* progress is possible. This is the "faith in man's brightening destiny," for it must be a faith, given the inability of any one person to control history through the application of a single set of ideas.

It is worth stepping aside a moment to set this passage beside Levinas's description of history in *Totality and Infinity*:

> Between a philosophy of transcendence that situates elsewhere the true life to which man, escaping from here, would gain access in the privileged moments of liturgical, mystical elevation, or in dying — and a philosophy of immanence in which we would truly come into possession of being when every "other" (cause for war), encompassed by the same, would vanish at the end of history — we propose to describe, within the unfolding of terrestrial existence, of economic existence (as we shall call it), a relationship with the other that does not result in a divine or human totality, that is not a totalization of history but the idea of infinity. Such a relationship is metaphysics itself. History would not be the privileged plane where Being disengaged from the particularism of points of view (with which reflection would still be affected) is manifested. If it claims to integrate myself and the other within an impersonal spirit this alleged integration is cruelty and injustice, that is, ignores the Other. History as a relationship between men ignores a position of the I before the other in which the other remains transcendent with respect to me. Though of myself I am not exterior to history, I do find in the Other a point that is absolute

with regard to history — not by amalgamating with the Other, but in speaking with him. History is worked over by the ruptures of history, in which a judgment is borne upon it. When man truly approaches the Other he is uprooted from history. (52)

Again, Hawthorne's lack of faith in reform can be taken, as it has been, as a settled conservatism or as an expression of a skepticism toward totality that shares ground with Levinas's distrust of the "impersonal spirit" of historical theory. Acknowledging the individual's placement within the historical, Levinas nevertheless locates the moment of historical rupture in the approach to and conversation with the uncontainable. As Colin Davis explains, the rupture in history occurs because there is no precedence for the ethical encounter. It is wholly unpredictable: "This is because the encounter with the Other lies at the origin of the separateness of the self; only by discovering the irreducibility of the alterity of the Other can I understand that I am neither solipsistically alone in the world nor part of a totality to which all others also belong. This encounter is, Levinas insists, ethical; and the ethical bond with the Other is the most fundamental subject for philosophical reflection because there is nothing that precedes it or has priority over it."[9] It is in this sense that the break within history reflects Cavell's understanding of remarriage as a sequence in which the fundamental "divorce" with time arises through an encounter that serves as the nonfoundational beginning of a new relationship with the world.

The House of the Seven Gables' most important scene, and indeed its entire action, depends upon this point. It begins with Holgrave's story about the mesmeric Matthew Maule and his victim, Alice Pyncheon. Like several of Hawthorne's earlier tales, the story of Alice Pyncheon relies upon the implicit condemnation of "possession," in particular, the possession of one individual by another.[10] Its conclusion, in which Alice's "delicate soul" is taken into the "rude gripe" of Matthew Maule, confirms the romantic argument for the independent self even as it underscores the historical reductions of revenge. It also resonates with the imagery of the preface, where the "iron rod" of the moral skewers the butterfly of romantic truth. In fact, it seems to embody all of Hawthorne's deepest concerns, from the weight of teleological history to the damaging effects of a self-extension that violates ethical distance. Matthew Maule is a willful mesmerist who forces the bewitched Alice to abase herself and so lose "all the dignity of life" (*CE*, 2:209). Because she has no self-control and because there is no space, no identifying difference, between his and her self, she has ceased to exist and is now as much the product of history (as revenge) as she is the slave of Maule's perversity. Here is the weight of time in its ability to determine an individual's existence and to imprison both the obsessed Maule and the entire Pyncheon family, for whom Alice is merely the sacrifice.

The narrative is then replayed in the subsequent scene with Holgrave and Phoebe. As Maule's descendent, Holgrave has inherited mesmeric abilities that are now channeled through his talent as a storyteller. By the end of the tale of Alice Pyncheon, Phoebe, Alice's antitype, has been partially entranced by Holgrave's imitation of his ancestor's "mystic gesticulations" (*CE*, 2:211): "With the lids drooping over her eyes — now lifted, for an instant, and drawn down again, as with leaden weights — she leaned slightly towards him, and seemed almost to regulate her breath by his. Holgrave gazed at her, as he rolled up his manuscript, and recognized an incipient stage of that curious psychological condition, which, as he had himself told Phoebe, he possessed more than an ordinary faculty of producing. A veil was beginning to be muffled about her, in which she could behold only him, and live only in his thoughts and emotions" (*CE*, 2:211). This exclusive control, in which even the bodies assume identical rhythms, marks the crucial moment in the structure of revenge history. In the terms introduced by Cavell, Holgrave now has a choice between repeating history or "divorcing" himself from it.[11] That is, he can reenact Maule's violence or he can simply refuse the opportunity: "I have at various junctures characterized this forgiving, the condition of remarriage, as the forgoing of revenge. [Earlier] I took the experience of the end of a romantic comedy as a matter of a kind of forgetting, one that requires the passage, as it were, from one world (of imagination) to another, as from dreaming to waking. . . . Emerson and Thoreau call the passage to this experience, I take it, dawn."[12] And what better way to describe Holgrave's decision than as one of "forgetting," moving "from dreaming to waking"? "To a disposition like Holgrave's, at once speculative and active, there is no temptation so great as the opportunity of acquiring empire over the human spirit; nor any idea more seductive to a young man, than to become the arbiter of a young girl's destiny. Let us, therefore — whatever his defects of nature and education, and in spite of his scorn for creeds and institutions — concede to the Daguerreotypist the rare and high quality of reverence for another's individuality. Let us allow him integrity, also, forever after to be confided in; since he forbade himself to twine that one link more, which might have rendered his spell over Phoebe indissoluble" (*CE*, 2:212).

This passage is remarkable enough in its combination of censure and praise to deserve a closer look. After all, Hawthorne is crediting Holgrave not merely with being passive but also with heroic resistance to his own genetic and mental tendencies. Holgrave is an idealist, and it is all the more noteworthy that he finds the ability to relinquish that idealism in a moment that is both historically and sexually tempting.[13] In other words, he must sacrifice his own ideas to do something that transcends ideas, to admit a space between Phoebe and his conception of her as the object of revenge.[14] In this way he allows her *her own* existence as a human being and so becomes worthy of confidence, of dialogue, what Levinas names the "astonishment" of conversation: "The face brings a notion of truth which, in contradistinction to contemporary ontology, is not the disclosure of an impersonal Neuter, but *expression:* the existent breaks through all the enveloping and generalities of Being to spread out in its 'form' the totality of its 'content,' finally abolishing the distinction between form and content. This is not achieved by some sort of modification of the knowledge that thematizes, but precisely by 'thematization' turning into conversation. . . . To approach the Other in conversation is to welcome his expression, in which at each instant he overflows the idea a thought would carry away from it."[15] For Cavell this welcoming of the other is best expressed through the metaphor of a remarriage that incorporates the fundamental divorce or separation of individuals. What Levinas calls "thematization" Cavell describes as a narcissistic or incestuous intimacy that must be replaced by "an intimacy of difference or reciprocity."[16] Levinas's "conversation" thus suggests more than simple talk, more even than a dialogue between equals; it represents a complete revision of understanding through a rupture of the "thematized" history. Given distance, the other breaks through, astonishes, liberating perception, scattering "freshness . . . on a human heart" (*CE*, 2:213).[17]

The moment recalls a celebrated passage from *Walden*, in which Thoreau speculates on the likely consequences of revision, of *reseeing* what is before him:

> Let us settle ourselves, and work and wedge our feet downward through the mud and slush of opinion, and prejudice, and tradition, and delusion, and appearance, that alluvion which covers the globe, through Paris and London, through New York and Boston and Concord, through church and state, through poetry and philosophy and religion, till we come to a hard bottom and rocks in place, which we can call *reality*, and say, This is, and no mistake; and then begin, having a *point d'appui*, below freshet and frost and fire, a place where you might found a wall or a state, or set a lamp-post safely, or perhaps a gauge, not a Nilometer, but a Realometer, that future ages might know how deep a freshet of shams and appearances had gathered from time to time. If you stand right fronting and face to face to a fact, you will see the sun glimmer on both its surfaces, as if it were a cimeter, and feel its sweet

edge dividing you through the heart and marrow, and so you will happily conclude your mortal career. Be it life or death, we crave only reality. If we are really dying, let us hear the rattle in our throats and feel cold in the extremities; if we are alive, let us go about our business.[18]

It is hard to imagine Hawthorne writing such sentences, and yet the two Concord neighbors and friends are not that far apart in their interests. The romantic attempt to recover perception here finds a considerably more ironic and skeptical voice, less practical than Wordsworth's or Coleridge's, shrewder than that of Keats. For all Thoreau's sometimes prophetic tone, it is never without the proper leaven of evasive irony, a playful skepticism designed not to undermine the radical suggestion but to place it in a more practical light than its predecessors'. Rather like Hawthorne's, Thoreau's tone is seductive and smiling, offering a vision of truth that his own skepticism finds unlikely but worth looking for just the same.

We can take Thoreau's speculative question to be this: Were it possible to escape history — to throw off custom, sham, appearance — how would human relationships change? How would we see one another and all the world that extends beyond the reach of established conception? *The House of the Seven Gables* might be said to pose the same question, answering it, in part, with its much maligned happy ending.[19] This denouement commences with the death of Judge Pyncheon, himself the victim not so much of revenge (historical, genetic) as of his devotion to the secret. Having written himself into Pyncheon history, it is only fitting that the judge become the telos, caught in the repetition he craved. Clifford and Hepzibah, on the other hand, with Phoebe and Holgrave, move to the judge's "elegant country-seat" (*CE*, 2:314), taking with them the suddenly fertile Pyncheon hens. Even the excessively picturesque Uncle Venner hobbles along to keep Clifford company with his eternal optimism. At the same time, the worthless parchment is discovered, freeing house and family from the ancient curse and opening the way for the union of Phoebe and the newly "conservative" Holgrave (*CE*, 2:315).

This sentimental tableau can be faulted on several levels, most directly for its sudden shift of tone and its incongruity with the book's earlier voice. A sort of narrative giddiness possesses it to such an extent that it reads like little more than a rush for the exit. The automatic machinery we might accept from a stage comedy, the shift from confusion to convention, fails to live up to the complexities of the novelistic surface, even in a self-described romance. And yet what

Hawthorne seems to imagine here is precisely the sort of symbolic rearrange-
ment that drama, especially comedy, is said to offer. Like Thoreau's speculative
"facing" of the real, this is a moment of fantasy meant to express a symbolic
revolution in perception. What are the rewards of "re-marriage," of new sight?
Wealth, a new home, fresh eggs? Not exactly, but each of these tangible bene-
fits represents the return to substance so long prevented by Pyncheon history.
Things are real again; this appears to be the larger message.[20] The isolation that
had deprived the exterior world of form and coherence has ended, and the new
perception that has taken its place has all the stunning magic of Thoreau's sweet-
edged cimeter.[21]

The ending is best understood in counterpoint to two of the book's most famous and widely discussed scenes. The first gives us Hawthorne at his most historically pessimistic: "The Italian turned a crank; and, behold! every one of these
small individuals started into the most curious vivacity. The cobbler wrought
upon a shoe; the blacksmith hammered his iron; the soldier waved his glittering
blade; the lady raised a tiny breeze with her fan; the jolly toper swigged lustily at
his bottle; a scholar opened his book, with eager thirst for knowledge, and turned
his head to-and-fro along the page; the milk-maid energetically drained her cow;
and a miser counted gold into his strong-box; — all at the same turning of a crank.
Yes; and moved by the self-same impulse, a lover saluted his mistress on her lips!"
(*CE*, 2:163). A cynical determinism seems mounting here, but its attractions pale
against the prospect of playful self-criticism:

> Possibly, some cynic, at once merry and bitter, had desired to signify, in this pan-
> tomimic scene, that we mortals, whatever our business or amusement — however
> serious, however trifling — all dance to one identical tune, and, in spite of our
> ridiculous activity, bring nothing finally to pass. For the most remarkable aspect of
> the affair was, that, at the cessation of the music, everybody was petrified at once,
> from the most extravagant life into a dead torpor. . . . All were precisely in the same
> condition as before they made themselves so ridiculous by their haste to toil, to
> enjoy, to accumulate gold, and to become wise. Saddest of all, moreover, the lover
> was none the happier for the maiden's granted kiss! But, rather than swallow this last
> too acrid ingredient, we reject the whole moral of the show. (*CE*, 2:163)

By now we should we ready for such maneuvers, but familiarity fails to steady
this shifting voice. The little allegory comes alive, its message not so different
from Hawthorne's own skeptical take on history and progress. In this case, however, there is no progress at all; the figures may show a blind faith in the future,

but seen from outside, nothing in their small world concludes, nothing satisfies. Skepticism is tipped to the bitter edge, as though to establish a range of thought. At one end, this question: What is the emotional impact of Pyncheon history? The answer: this panorama, a hollow puppet show. The world works toward a goal that is not there, that by definition cannot be there, so that the organ grinder becomes Judge Pyncheon and Matthew Maule in one, becomes New England history, the Calvinist god, invisible and yet somehow strongly related to the avaricious monkey with the "enormous," indecent tail. Sex, money, inordinate desire — these are the inheritances of the Pyncheon past. And Hawthorne cannot resist telling us how likely and how hopeless such a history really is — unless, of course, we follow the narrator's example and reject it.

Placed against the book's other moment of historical theory, the organ grinder episode seems the dark voice in an internal debate. Clifford's frenetic, desperately joyful lecture on the "ascending spiral curve" hopes to provide an alternative but cannot escape its own dependence on abstraction. What Clifford actually says, of course, is once again not so different from Hawthorne's historical theories, but by giving such thoughts to the desiccated victim of the Pyncheon past, Hawthorne effectively presents them and criticizes them at the same time: "You are aware, my dear Sir — you must have observed it, in your own experience — that all human progress is in a circle; or, to use a more accurate and beautiful figure, in an ascending spiral curve. While we fancy ourselves going straight forward, and attaining, at every step, an entirely new position of affairs, we do actually return to something long ago tried and abandoned, but which we now find etherialized, refined, and perfected to its ideal" (*CE*, 2:259). The mysterious process by which events are "etherialized" is never spelled out by either Clifford or Hawthorne, but it is safe to say that it corresponds roughly to Hawthorne's reliance on progress.

If this is a vision of human perfectibility, however, why give so important a set of ideas to so ravaged and easily dismissed a character? And, even more important, why demonstrate Clifford's failure to carry such ideas into the world at large? Why reiterate his entrapment by means of his flirtation with Hawthorneian historical theories? The answer lies in the contrast between this rather hollow repetition of abstract concepts and the tangibility of the book's conclusion. For if we place the comic restoration of order that is the ending against these half-serious moments of historical summation, we see that the difference between them is the presence or absence of love. The organ grinder has mocked it, and Clifford, by age and impotence, is excluded from it, but Holgrave and Phoebe embody it, not only as middle-class types — domestic symbols of democratic vitality—but as ethical agents in a bond based on separateness. Clifford's theories, though potentially accurate, lack the human element; they convert strangeness to system and thereby repeat the reductions carried out by earlier versions of Pyncheon history. Against system, then, whether theoretical or allegorical, Hawthorne places uncertainty. It is a way of recovering the world, including others, by letting it go.[22]

Self-Reliance: *The American Claimant*

The Pyncheons' failure to relinquish the past marks them, in Hawthorne's terms, as anti-"American," which is to say opposed to the development of individuality and democracy.[23] It was an argument dear to him from the time of "My Kinsman, Major Molineux," if not earlier. *The House of the Seven Gables* gives it its largest scope, offering a family so enamored of its ties to Europe (or at least to aristocratic ideas inherited from Europe) that it simply falls out of history, only to be rescued by country cousins (Yankee stock) and a dose of commercial humility. It may not have been a surprise, then, that six years later the consul to Liverpool found his office frequented by Pyncheons of one stripe or another:

> A knot of characters may be introduced as gathering round Middleton, comprising expatriated Americans of all sorts; the wandering printer who came to me so often at the Consulate, who said that he was a native of Philadelphia, and could not go home, in the thirty years that he had been trying to do so, for lack of the money to pay his passage. The large banker; the consul of Leeds; the woman asserting her claims to half Liverpool; the gifted literary lady, maddened by Shakspeare &c, &c. The Yankee, who had been driven insane by the Queen's notice, slight as it was, of the photographs of his two children which he had sent her. (*CE*, 12:58)

> Now, as to the arrangement of the Romance;—it begins, as an integral and essential part, with my introduction, giving a pleasant and familiar summary of my life in the Consulate at Liverpool; the strange species of Americans, with strange purposes in England, whom I used to meet there; and, especially, how my countrymen used to be put out of their senses by the idea of inheritances of English property. (*CE*, 12:87)

Within the notes and drafts that make up the *American Claimant Manuscripts* Hawthorne seems first of all intent upon addressing what he sees as an unnecessary and unhealthy reverence for English culture and power in displaced "Yankees." His goal is to write a novel that acknowledges the ties between the two countries but concludes with a principled rejection of "English property" in favor of the dynamic future of American self-reliance. The earliest versions of the tale center upon a character named Middleton or Etheridge, an American politician, formerly a member of Congress, on what appears to be a leisurely tour of the English countryside. He is the claimant in question, and he has come to "those rich portions of England" searching for links to his ancestral past. As Hawthorne labors to build the narrative, he once again turns to the secret history, its invisibility, entrapment, futility:

> And yet there has always been one queer thing about this generally very common-place family. It is that each father, on his death-bed, has had an interview with his son, at which he has imparted some secret that has evidently had an influence on the character and after life of the son, making him ever after a discontented man, aspiring for something he has never been able to find. Now the American, I am told, pretends that he has the clue which has always been needed to make this secret available; the key whereby the lock may be opened; the something that the lost son of the family carried away with him, and by which through three centuries he has impeded the prosperity of his race. And, wild as the story seems, he does certainly seem to bring something that looks very like proof of what he says. (*CE*, 12:16–17)

Instead of the Pyncheon map, we now have a key, in some versions to a hidden chest thought to have held documents that proved succession to a family title. The chest or cabinet is empty or contains something unexpected, which will demonstrate the futility of the search. Lost at times in a sea of fictional devices, Hawthorne never settles on the specifics, but the fundamental goal remains the same: devotion to a hidden history poisons the present, threatening an American, democratic future.

As with Phoebe and Holgrave, Hawthorne is intent on presenting Middleton/Etheridge as the exemplar of American vitality and democratic self-sufficiency. His most important act, therefore, will not be an act at all but a refusal, the expression of a preference: "In the traditions that he brought over, there was a key to some family secrets that were still unsolved, and that controlled the descents of estates and titles. His influence upon these matters involves him in divers strange and perilous adventures; and at last it turns out that he himself is the rightful heir to the title and estate, that had passed into another name, within the last half-century. But he rejects both, feeling that it is better to take a virgin soil, than to try to make the old name grow in a soil that had been darkened with so much blood and misfortune as this" (*CE*, 12:11). English history is the "bloody footstep," a stain said to be visible on the threshold of the family estate. It is the history of guilt, certainly, but guilt associated with inheritance and property, with the hubris of genetic and political extension over time. America is the "virgin soil" of history, relatively speaking, a new Eden in which Middleton and his projected wife will become "the Adam and Eve of a new epoch, and the fitting missionaries of a new social faith" (*CE*, 12:58). In this way hidden history is relinquished to yield democratic promise; the American escapes a European past by giving up his claim so that he can reenter and reengage a new pluralism.

Once again revenge plays a role. In those drafts collected as "Etheredge" and "Grimshawe," Hawthorne tried to construct a background for his principle character's later career. In these sections Middleton, now called Etheredge, begins life as an orphan adopted by a gruff, embittered old "doctor" who drinks too much and studies spider webs. Hawthorne apparently hoped to make the boy into an overt symbol for America's anxiety over and escape from Old World history: "In a dim, uncertain way, the boy's unaccountable legends shall be half-shown, about the Bloody Footstep, &c &. And, without pretensions as he is, an alms-house child, he shall have great sensitiveness to the pride of birth; his imagination dwelling on it so much the more because he has all the world, all possibilities to choose his ancestry from. He shall have imaginative and poetic tendencies; but yet young America shall show a promising blossom in him — there shall be a freedom of thought, a carelessness of old forms of things, which shall sometimes shock the Doctor, and contrast oddly with his imaginative conservatism in other respects" (*CE*, 12:123). This is the process by which nobility, tied to property and title, is replaced by the nobility of imagination and potential. The orphan represents the romantic distinction of self-sufficiency, his low birth "giving additional value and merit to every honorable effort and success that he had thus far made" (*CE*, 12:136). Hawthorne even goes so far as to claim that to be "deprived of all kindred" leaves one "in a truly American condition" (*CE*, 12:233), and just in case we fail to understand, he has given his quintessential American a "father" who represents the contrasting restrictions of European conservatism.

Among the doctor's limitations is his obsession with historical vengeance, the same reductive secret that grips Holgrave. Though his role varies throughout the drafts, the doctor's primary function is to gather the symbolic remnants of European culture; his intense study of cobwebs, for instance, suggests both the alchemical overreaching of Chillingworth and the decay of Old World ideas. "There were cobwebs in his own brain" (*CE*, 12:111), Hawthorne tells us, that led to a lot of "cobwebby old hereditary nonsense" (*CE*, 12:127), one element of which is his fascination with an "enormous spider, the biggest and ugliest ever seen, the pride of the grim Doctor's heart, his treasure, his glory, the pearl of his soul, and, as many people said, the demon to whom he had sold his salvation" (*CE*, 12:350). The demonic bargain presumably allows him access not only to medicinal secrets but to the webs' metaphorical reflection of his vengeful plotting, as well. The doctor is the spider, and the spider is nothing more than the distillation of historical arrogance, the doctor's desire to control events through his own wounded vanity.

To make this clear, Hawthorne reminds us that Dr. Grim is fundamentally the product of aristocratic social structure: "It was the feeling of a man lowly born, when he contracts a hostility to his hereditary superior; in one way, being of a powerful, passionate nature, gifted with forces and ability far superior to that of the aristocrat, he might scorn him and feel able to trample on him; in another, he had the same awe as a simple country boy feels of the magnate who flings him a sixpence, or shakes his horsewhip at him. Had the grim Doctor been an American, he might have had the vast antipathy to rank, without the sense of awe that made it so much more malignant; it required the low-born Englishman to feel the two together" (*CE*, 12:368). In other words, the doctor is *not* an American, in Hawthorne's terms. Though he lives in the nation, he thinks in a way that Hawthorne wishes to characterize as outmoded and dangerous, the result of an unnatural system of heredity that produces a perverse combination of loyalty and resentment. His desire for vengeance is therefore a product of the system, but so too is the very structure of revenge thought, whereby others become little more than players in the singular story of one man's social shame.

The agent of the doctor's revenge, at certain points in the manuscripts, will be Etheredge, the orphan Ned. Dr. Grim plants the story of his own past in the boy's mind, hinting that Ned is the rightful and displaced heir while providing what may be the means to claim both title and property. Hawthorne emphasizes the essentially destructive nature of this historical conception, its backward focus and its self-consuming, involuted energy: "The grim Doctor's face looked fierce with the earnestness with which he said these words. You would have said that he was taking an oath to overthrow, and annihilate a race, rather than to build one up, by bringing forward the infant heir out of obscurity, and making plain the links, the filaments, which connected that feeble childish life, in a far country, with the great tide of a noble life, embracing great strands of kindred, which had come down like a chain from antiquity, in old England" (*CE*, 12:359). The destructive potential hinges upon the willingness of Etheredge to assume the doctor's vision, to become something other than an American not only by giving up his own desires but also by supplanting a faith in democracy with a reverence for property and rank. This of course Hawthorne will not allow, because Etheredge is his representative democrat, orphan from a nation of orphans, whose chief function is to surrender the claim, to choose equal opportunity over inherited wealth and station:

> The great gist of the story ought to be the natural hatred of men . . . to an Aristocracy; at the same time doing a good degree of justice to the aristocratic system by depicting its grand, beautiful, and noble characteristics. At last, I think, the American must have it in his power to put an end to the nobility of the race; and shall do so, not without reluctance and pain. He shall have proof of something, long ago, that shall have given him this power. . . . The end must be the ruin of the nobleman, at all events, the absorption of his property, the cancelment of his title. (*CE*, 12:475–76)

> Etheredge, on the other hand, must have a series of seeming proofs, contrived by the Doctor, for the purposes of revenge; they should seem to strengthen at every step, and become indubitable; but, at the very last moment, most unexpectedly, they should crumble into nothings. Etheredge must discover, by means of Elsie, that the Doctor had contrived this plan. He had revealed this on his death-bed, and given her a paper, signed and witnessed, which she was to produce on occasion; but he could not bring himself to blacken his memory with Etheredge, whom he loved so well, by revealing it sooner. He was in hopes that Etheredge would never really take up the claim. At the last moment, Elsie delivers the paper, of which she herself does not know the contents. It produces a violent effect on Etheredge, but he honorably resolves (when the prize seems actually within his grasp) to relinquish it. (*CE*, 12:263–64)

> He shall be the rightful heir, but still the gist of the story shall be not to install him in possession of the property. (*CE*, 12:480)

Relinquishment—this is the key. The true "American" gives up what he has a right to claim as part of the reenactment of emigration and democratic choice. Even the doctor seems converted to this vision in the end, hoping on his death-bed to vacate his vengeful plot and release Etheredge from the false history he has created. Even so, it is ultimately Etheredge's own values, stated repeatedly in conversation with English friends, that persuade him to choose American democracy over the attractive and revered institutions of an aristocratic society.

As in *The House of the Seven Gables*, reengagement follows relinquishment, in this case through the necessity of return and the rejection of exile. It is a note, more anxious than patriotic, that sounds with increasing frequency during Hawthorne's European years. America is the future; place is requisite to being: " 'What have you to do here?' said Alice. 'Your lot is in another land. You have seen the birthplace of your forefathers, and have gratified your natural yearning for it; now return, and cast in your lot with your own people, let it be what it will. I fully believe that it is such a lot as the world has never yet seen, and that the faults, the weaknesses, the errors of your countrymen will vanish away, like morning-mists before the rising sun. You can do nothing better than to go back' " (*CE*, 12:56). This is a worrying voice, as though from inside. It gives vent to a native discomfort while leaning upon a faith that history — for Hawthorne if not for the world — rests with the development of democracy. To be in history or outside of it, to watch from a distance or engage close at hand through strategies of distance — these are the anxieties of Hawthorne the writer as much as of Hawthorne the politician. England made that clear enough, and if he was not entirely sure, there was always Rome.

CHAPTER SEVEN

Exiled by History

The Marble Faun

By 1860, the ironies and anxieties of exile were familiar topics to the author of "Wakefield." At the very least, this brilliant early tale (1835) registers the perils rather than the advantages of distance. The pettily selfish Wakefield deliberately steps out of his own life in order to watch it, to measure his own absence by observing his wife. Another parody of Hawthorne's artistic strategies, Wakefield playfully puts a distance between himself and the world, as though to calculate his importance to it, to see it crumble without him. To his horror, it does nothing of the sort. Neither his wife nor the larger life of London seems greatly affected by his disappearance. As though observing the space of his own death, Wakefield learns that the world outside the self is independent, other, neither the product of his imagination nor subject to his decisions. Even more, he comes to understand that his own existence depends upon acknowledgment by others, that he must in some basic sense be seen and known and given a place as someone recognizable. Self-reliance may be essential, but the world does not exist by permission of the self. Whether we know it or not, we rely upon others for placement, absent which we risk social and historical invisibility.

No doubt similar thoughts were occurring to the older Nathaniel Hawthorne as he made his way across Europe in the late 1850s. His fifth published novel, *The Marble Faun*, as well as *The Italian Notebooks* upon which it is based, takes up the question of exile in its broadest sense, from fundamental estrangement, the entrance into consciousness, to the more personal condition of the American removed from America. What does it mean to enter history, to engage the real from a position of exile? And if America is the new reality, the site of historical development, as Hawthorne argued, what does it mean to be an American caught in the ruins of Rome? On one level, with the story of Donatello, Hawthorne seems interested in the process that occupies "Wakefield" — the establishment of the self as an ethical agent. On another, with Kenyon and Hilda, he worries more about the fate of Americans at too great a distance from the seat of their cultural and political identity. Their excessive concern with aesthetics signals, at least for the skeptical Hawthorne, a potential disconnection from the development of democratic history. They risk losing their American identity not through claims to aristocratic titles but through an overly intense devotion to Old World art.

Discussions of *The Marble Faun* typically begin with the theme of the fortunate fall.[1] The venerable theological debate over the beneficial results of sin — self-consciousness, responsibility, civilization, salvation — translates into the romantic interest in the nobility of the uncivilized, in this case the pastoral "savage," Donatello. Animalistic enough to be compared to the faun of Praxiteles, Donatello is presented as prelapsarian man, without consciousness or guilt, without history: " 'You cannot conceive how this fantasy takes hold of me,' responded Miriam, between jest and earnest. 'Imagine, now, a real being, similar to this mythic Faun; how happy, how genial, how satisfactory would be his life, enjoying the warm, sensuous, earthy side of Nature; revelling in the merriment of woods and streams; living as our four-footed kindred do — as mankind did in its innocent childhood, before sin, sorrow, or morality itself, had ever been thought of! Ah, Kenyon, if Hilda, and you, and I — if I, at least — had pointed ears! For I suppose the Faun had no conscience, no remorse, no burthen on the heart, no troublesome recollections of any sort; no dark future neither' " (*CE*, 4: 13–14). "Between jest and earnest" though this fantasy is, it is the ideal against which we are to measure the more real but no less innocent Donatello, a man who has "nothing to do with time" (*CE*, 4:15). It might be said more accurately that Donatello has yet to enter time, that he is exiled in his own way from the "more real life" of consciousness and suffering. His portion of the narrative, therefore, will be devoted to his inevitable engagement with time through a process of estrangement and (re)engagement.

This development begins, of course, in the emotional wake of murder. Bound by their mutual crime, Miriam and Donatello find themselves in a "new sphere" (*CE*, 4:174), cut off from human sympathy and yet ecstatic in their "sense of freedom" (*CE*, 4:176). They feel free because they have broken the law, certainly, but also because their mutual guilt, their new responsibility, is the basis for whatever freedom they will eventually earn. The fall is fortunate because it makes clear the relationship between choice and responsibility, between freedom and guilt. Donatello has made his first true choice, his first conscious transgression, and he has done so by looking his victim in the face:

> "Ah, that terrible face!" said Donatello, pressing his hands over his eyes. "Do you call that unreal?"
>
> "Yes; for you beheld it with dreaming eyes," replied Miriam. "It was unreal; and, that you may feel it so, it is requisite that you see this face of mine no more. Once, you may have thought it beautiful; now, it has lost its charm. Yet it would still retain a miserable potency to bring back the past illusion, and, in its train, the remorse and anguish that would darken all your life. Leave me, therefore, and forget me!"
>
> "Forget you, Miriam!" said Donatello, roused somewhat from his apathy of despair. "If I could remember you, and behold you, apart from that frightful visage which stares at me over your shoulder — that were a consolation, at least, if not a joy." (*CE*, 4:200)

Miriam's attempts to free Donatello from the haunting "visage" seem little more than evidence of a desperate self-delusion. The face is not merely an illusive sign of guilt; it is self-consciousness in its purest form, the recognition of the self's isolation *and* its dependence on others. Donatello is remorseful, to be sure, but he is more profoundly horrified by the irruption of otherness into his dreamlike preconsciousness. He has discovered the power of the stranger's face, its accusation, its fundamental challenge to his oneness with nature. As a result he is cast out, estranged from nature as from his own reflection:

> "The difficulty will drive me mad, I verily believe!" cried the sculptor nervously. "Look at that wretched piece of work yourself, my dear friend, and tell me whether you recognize any manner of likeness to your inner man!"
>
> "None," replied Donatello, speaking the simple truth. "It is like looking a stranger in the face." (*CE*, 4:271)

Though doubtless a comment on the limits of Kenyon's talent, Donatello's admission summarizes his condition: the world that was once singular, a unity, is now fractured. The pastoral is broken by the intrusion of the stranger; the animals of his childhood no longer recognize Donatello because distance has become integral to identity. He is now ready, in other words, to engage time, to enter history as an individual fundamentally isolated and yet, through that isolation, inevitably dependent upon "other minds" for recognition and acknowledgment.

This entrance into history will come through Donatello's reunion with Miriam. If Donatello is outside history at the book's beginning, Miriam is trapped in a history of guilt that bears a strong resemblance, once again, to the structure of Calvinism. Already implicated in a secret past as the book begins, Miriam seems to represent fallenness, as though her "model," the monk who shadows her, is as much the figure for "total depravity" as for the "bloody footstep" of European, Catholic history. Like the devout predestinarian, Miriam is trapped by an inescapable burden that must also remain unspoken, depriving the world of substance. Like Holgrave, she alternates between periods of darkness and desperate pleas for an escape from so limited and limiting a history:

> The chasm was merely one of the orifices of that pit of blackness that lies beneath us, everywhere. The firmest substance of human happiness is but a thin crust spread over it, with just reality enough to bear up the illusive stage-scenery amid which we tread. It needs no earthquake to open the chasm. A footstep, a little heavier than ordinary, will serve; and we must step very daintily, not to break through the crust, at any moment. By-and-by, we inevitably sink! (*CE*, 4:161–62)

> Methinks, too, it will be a fresher and better world, when it flings off this great burthen of stony memories, which the ages have deemed it a piety to heap upon its back! (*CE*, 4:119)

The echo of Jonathan Edwards's "Sinners in the Hand of an Angry God" is no accident here; Miriam has absorbed the imagery as well as the emotive power of the Calvinist condition.[2] Against it, as with so many of Hawthorne's displaced romantics, she projects a radical escape, not expiation, which would only complete the pattern, but a thorough rupture of history altogether, a way out of the structure of guilt and redemption that orders her world.

As with Elizabeth in "The Minister's Black Veil," the projected savior is friendship, the ideal of the sympathetic ear. But the sort of self-erasure Hawthorne posits as a necessary condition for sympathy is difficult, if not impossible, to find, particularly among the broken columns of European civilization: " 'Oh, my friend,' cried she, with sudden passion, 'will you be my friend indeed? I am lonely, lonely, lonely! There is a secret in my heart that burns me! — that tortures me! Sometimes, I fear to go mad of it! Sometimes, I hope to die of it! But neither of the two happens. Ah, if I could but whisper it to only one human soul! And you — you see far into womanhood! You receive it widely into your large view! Perhaps — perhaps — but Heaven only knows — you might understand me! Oh, let me speak!' " (*CE*, 4:128). Miriam requires a listener, but Kenyon, the American losing his national character, cannot oblige. It is as though Rome will not permit such an exchange, as though the weight of the past forbids the sort of sympathy Hawthorne projects as part of the newly democratic experience. Europe is the confessional, and as we learn from Hilda's experience, its apparent attractions are mitigated by its implication in the structure of Catholic secrecy. It becomes a trap rather than a force for liberation, certainly not the sort of infinite openness Hawthorne projects as the ideal of personal relationships.

A similar limitation applies to the book's handling of revenge. Like Holgrave's in *The House of the Seven Gables,* Miriam's secret history cannot avoid implication in the patterns of retribution. Her paintings dwell upon it, caught in an endless repetition: "Over and over again, there was the idea of woman, acting the part of a revengeful mischief towards man. It was, indeed, very singular to see how the artist's imagination seemed to run on these stories of bloodshed, in which woman's hand was crimsoned by the stain" (*CE*, 4:44). The pattern has become so ingrained, so much a part of her identity, that relinquishment is out of the question. In its place we get maturity through suffering, the sort of hard lesson put forth in *The Scarlet Letter,* for in each the cultural setting makes no place for democratic reverence. Donatello enters history as a fully responsible individual, aware of distance, but without the ideal liberation of Hawthorne's American who has cast off the stone of the past. Place matters, Hawthorne seems pained to say, given that place carries with it cultural and political possibilities.

For Kenyon and Hilda place will matter even more. If Donatello begins the book outside of history, Kenyon comes to understand that an American abroad is similarly removed from reality, exiled within a past that, for Hawthorne at least, has no immediate connection to the democratic present. From this perspective Roman history does little more than drain the world of its substance: "It is a vague sense of ponderous remembrances; a perception of such weight and density in a by-gone life, of which this spot was the centre, that the present moment is pressed down or crowded out, and our individual affairs and interests are but half as real, here, as elsewhere" (*CE*, 4:6). This is a problem, clearly, for the American artist who has come to Europe for greater cultivation but finds himself caught in a lifeless repetition of Old World models. For Hawthorne this exchange of isolation for aesthetic community was understandable but unfortunate. The American abroad risked losing the one advantage he carried with him — the awkward freshness and energy of the New World: "Nevertheless, in spite of all these professional grudges, artists are conscious of a social warmth from each other's presence and contiguity. They shiver at the remembrance of their lonely studios in the unsympathizing cities of their native land. For the sake of such brotherhood as they can find, more than for any good that they get from galleries, they linger year after year in Italy; while their originality dies out of them, or is polished away as a barbarism" (*CE*, 4:132).

It was Hawthorne's observation of the expatriate art scene in Rome that led him to such conclusions and to his expanding theory of the power of place. His comments on the various artist-exiles he encountered in Rome and Florence suggest that he saw little real advantage to their displacement. Some, like the sculptor Joseph Mozier, retained their provincial lack of taste despite the supposedly edifying air of old world culture.[3] Others, like Hiram Powers, had "lost [their] native country without finding another" (*CE*, 14:280) and risked losing their national identity for little more than the prospect of abundant marble. Each of these expatriate artists seemed to Hawthorne to have sacrificed something irreplaceable, their national character, for the dilettante's second-hand acquisition of a pseudo-European sophistication.

This criticism rests upon a theory of "originality," in its most literal sense. It can be seen most forcefully in the chapter of *The Marble Faun* devoted to Donatello's ancestral wine, the "Sunshine" of Monte Beni. This "pale golden" liquor is the product of Donatello's pastoral family estate, but its "deliciousness" depends upon its location. According to tradition, its flavor will not travel: "The wine, Signor, is so fond of its native home, that a transportation of even a few miles turns it quite sour" (*CE*, 4:224). Originality of taste, in other words, depends upon origin, and the displaced have a tendency to lose the subtleties of local flavor that result from the strict cultivation of origin. This is as much a personal caution as a criticism of Americans abroad. Attractive though it may be, Italian art and culture could only defer or misdirect the New Englander's native talents. Hawthorne had no desire to spend his remaining days as a cultural copyist, no matter how alluring the subjects.

The Americans in *The Marble Faun* are copyists, however. Kenyon, a sculptor unable to carve his own stone, reflects the anxiety and distraction of his real-life model, the American sculptor William Wetmore Story: "It may be, that he feels his strength, in any one direction, not quite adequate to his perception, his purpose, and his longing desire; he would rather have one great diamond, than a larger bulk and weight divided among many brilliants. The great difficulty with him, I think, is a too facile power; he would do better things, if it were more difficult for him to do merely good ones" (*CE*, 14:448). Hawthorne liked Story but saw him as unfulfilled and frustrated by his own various but shallow talents. For Story and for Kenyon the cultural treasures of Europe seem little more than distractions, spreading American artists too thin and confusing their priorities. This scattering of force extends even to the choice of medium. As a sculptor, a "man of marble," Kenyon is associated with stone and ruin. He works in a medium that, within the book's cultural argument, seems notably un-American, associated with the past, with the weight of history, and with a symbolic blood-lessness, the failure of sympathy:

> "Methinks, too, it will be a fresher and better world, when it flings off this great burthen of stony memories, which the ages have deemed it a piety to keep upon its back!"
>
> "What you say," remarked Kenyon, "goes against my whole art. Sculpture, and the delight which men naturally take in it, appear to me a proof that it is good to work with all time before our view."
>
> "Well, well," answered Miriam, "I must not quarrel with you for flinging your heavy stones at poor Posterity; and, to say the truth, I think you are as likely to hit the mark as anybody. These busts, now, much as I seem to scorn them, make me feel as if you were a magician. You turn feverish men into cool, quiet marble. What a blessed change for them! Would you could do as much for me!" (*CE*, 4:119)

Here are the poles of Hawthorne's internal debate yet again: throw off the past, yes, but use it just the same to take the long view, the "hundred years" vision. The deciding blow in this conversation, however, comes with Miriam's final criticism, not so subtly disguised as a compliment. Sculpture fails the sympathy test just as Kenyon fails to listen to Miriam. Flesh can become stone, but to make that transformation requires a level of disdain for the human, both present and future, that Hawthorne seems unwilling to venture.

In artistic terms, Hilda is Kenyon's similar opposite, the emotional equivalent of stone, a "virgin" painter who has sacrificed her own ambitions to the worship of European art. Like Phoebe Pyncheon she is a "New England girl" (*CE*, 4:327), but the influence of Rome's Catholic iconography has taken away her native warmth. Removed from the everyday in a fashion similar to Wakefield's, Hilda suggests the pitfalls of artistic distance, especially when taken to its cloistral extreme. In her tower, her "maiden elevation" (*CE*, 4:53), she finds an atmosphere purer than the "evil scents of Rome," but she loses contact with the lives of others. Her elevation is the symbolic equivalent of her devotion to the old masters and her transition from potential American original to saintly copyist. There may be a nobility in this sort of self-sacrifice, but the intense connoisseurship she represents ultimately reinforces her emotional frigidity, her distance from love and friendship.[4] Even Kenyon, in love with her from a distance, can do little better than "steal" her hand in marble rather than take it in the flesh:

> "There is but one right hand, on earth, that could have supplied the model," answered Miriam; "so small and slender, so perfectly symmetrical, and yet with a character of delicate energy! I have watched it, a hundred times, at its work. But I did not dream that you had won Hilda so far! How have you persuaded that shy maiden to let you take her hand in marble?"
>
> "Never! She never knew it!" hastily replied Kenyon, anxious to vindicate his mistress's maidenly reserve — "I stole it from her. The hand is a reminiscence. After gazing at it so often — and even holding it once, for an instant, when Hilda was not thinking of me — I should be a bungler indeed, if I could not now reproduce it to something like the life." (*CE*, 4:120–21)

This is what has become of the union of Holgrave and Phoebe: the touch of stone rather than flesh, stolen affection deferred through the substitute of art. The Americans in exile represent more than geographic displacement; they demonstrate their own irrelevance through their removal from the American present, the only cultural location that will permit immediacy of human contact. Art, or aesthetic devotion, though attractive and valuable, plays a major role in preventing the sort of democratic renewal Hawthorne envisions for his symbolically youthful, New England democrats.

If the sculptured hand is a substitute for the real, then it is possible too that under art's influence people will be seen more readily as objects rather than as resistant others. This is the likely significance of Hilda's "fall," as witness to murder and as symbolically deflowered virgin. Her disillusionment recalls that of Robin Goodfellow in "My Kinsman, Major Molineux": She undergoes a fundamental estrangement, the sudden awareness that the world outside the self is indeed outside, beyond control, though not separate. And like Robin, her estrangement is not a simple disconnection but, paradoxically, a sign of her fundamental ties to others, her responsibility: "Never before had this young, energetic, active spirit, known what it is to be despondent. It was the unreality of the world that made her so. Her dearest friend, whose heart seemed the most solid and richest of Hilda's possessions, had no existence for her any more; and in that dreary void, out of which Miriam had disappeared, the substance, the truth, the integrity of life, the motives of effort, the joy of success, had departed along with her" (*CE*, 4:205–6). The Miriam who has disappeared is the construct of Hilda's restricted imagination, a projected fantasy of her own imagined purity. In her place is the stranger, Miriam transformed into a disturbance, an irruption into Hilda's "virgin" consciousness. And the demand that Miriam makes — for sympathy, for listening — cannot be reduced to the terms of Hilda's former thinking. Miriam is now an excess, uncontainable, and Hilda can do little more than turn away, implicating herself, already guilty, through the very structure of friendship.

Hilda is now doubly an exile, the displaced American removed from her own self-made allegory. The solution for her, Hawthorne seems ready enough to say, is a return to origin, a recovery of American democracy, the reentrance into history.[5] It is also love, the sympathy of Kenyon, his listening ear and attuned spirit:

> And now, for the first time in her lengthened absence, comprising so many years of her young life, she began to be acquainted with the exile's pain. . . . How she pined under this crumbly magnificence, as if it were piled all upon her human heart! How she yearned for that native homeliness, those familiar sights, those faces which she had known always. . . .
>
> We ought not to betray Hilda's secret; but it is the truth, that being so sad, and so utterly alone, and in such great need of sympathy, her thoughts sometimes recurred to the sculptor. Had she met him now, her heart, indeed, might not have been won, but her confidence would have flown to him like a bird to its nest. One summer-afternoon, especially, Hilda leaned upon the battlements of her tower, and looked over Rome, towards the distant mountains, whither Kenyon had told her that he was going.
>
> "Oh, that he were here!" she sighed. "I perish under this terrible secret; and he might help me to endure it. Oh, that he were here!"
>
> That very afternoon, as the reader may remember, Kenyon felt Hilda's hand pulling at the silken cord that was connected with his heart-strings, as he stood looking towards Rome from the battlements of Monte Beni. (*CE*, 4:342–43)

This romantic telepathy suggests more than a simple union of souls. Within Hawthorne's rhetorical framework, it repeats Hilda's homesickness, her desire for native soil doubled by her need for an "American" sympathy. We see this notion reinforced by Hilda's subsequent experience with the Catholic confessional, an institution attractive to Hawthorne, though ultimately too much a part of Old World history to escape its conspiratorial limits.[6] Trapped by the casuistry of the American priest—an exile who has no doubt lost his national tone—she "falls" as though into European history, vanishing for a time like the captive John Williams beset by the Jesuits of "Quebeck."

Hilda's fall precipitates Kenyon's similar estrangement from European art and culture. We see this most clearly on the Roman campagna, when the sculptor in his brooding comes across "a marble woman" half-buried in the ruins of a "suburban villa" (*CE*, 4:423). The discovery of yet another ancient treasure cannot substitute for the missing Hilda: "But, in reality, he found it difficult to fix his mind upon the subject. He could hardly, we fear, be reckoned a consummate artist, because there was something dearer to him than his art; and, by the greater strength of a human affection, the divine statue seemed to fall asunder again, and become only a heap of worthless fragments" (*CE*, 4:424). The "man of marble" prefers a woman of flesh; or rather, in his exile, he sees the lack of "human affection" that characterizes his remove from history, in the fragments of a past that no longer seems relevant to the democratic future.

What remains for the fallen Americans, divorced from the continental past, is the ripening trope of return, reengagement of what for Hawthorne was the timely, the real:

> So, Kenyon won the gentle Hilda's shy affection, and her consent to be his bride. Another hand must henceforth trim the lamp before the Virgin's shrine; for Hilda was coming down from her old tower, to be herself enshrined and worshiped as a household Saint, in the light of her husband's fireside. And, now that life had so much human promise in it, they resolved to go back to their own land; because the years, after all, have a kind of emptiness, when we spend too many of them on a foreign shore. We defer the reality of life, in such cases, until a future moment, when we shall again breathe our native air; but, by-and-by, there are no future moments; or, if we do return, we find that the native air has lost its invigorating quality, and that life has shifted its reality to the spot where we have deemed ourselves only temporary residents. (*CE*, 4:461)

This passage is drawn, almost verbatim, from Hawthorne's notebooks. It summarizes what *The Marble Faun* has already taken pains to say, that Hawthorne's sense of reality was inseparable from his sense of place. Absent the connection between origin and substance, we risk the fate of Wakefield, an inhabitant of no place. Even more important, it tells us that the world cannot easily be remade through the dramatic extension of the self across space or time. We are dependent upon places for recognition and identity as much as place is dependent upon us. The world outside the self is not infinitely malleable: the self must take its place within time and within its community to find the "more real life" that Hester Prynne reenters in Salem.

The Elixir of Life

To have known him, to have loved him
  After loneness long;
And then to be estranged in life,
  And neither in the wrong;
And now for death to set his seal; —
  Ease me a little ease, my song!

By wintry hills his hermit-mound
  The sheeted snow-drifts drape,
And houseless there the snow-bird flits
  Beneath the fir-trees' crape:
Glazed now with ice the cloistral vine
  That hid the shyest grape.   — MELVILLE, "Monody"

May 24, 1864
  Yesterday, 23 May, we buried Hawthorne in Sleepy Hollow, in a pomp of
sunshine & verdure, & gentle winds. James F. Clarke read the service in the
Church & at the grave. Longfellow, Lowell, Holmes, Agassiz, Hoar,
Dwight, Whipple, Norton, Alcott, Hillard, Fields, Judge Thomas, & I,
attended the hearse as pall bearers. Franklin Pierce was with the family. The
church was copiously decorated with white flowers delicately arranged. The
corpse was unwillingly shown — only a few moments to this company of his
friends. But it was noble & serene in its aspect — nothing amiss — a calm &
powerful head. A large company filled the church, & the grounds of the
cemetery. All was so bright & quiet, that pain or mourning was hardly suggested, & Holmes said to me, that it looked like a happy meeting.
                                          — EMERSON, *Journals*

There is little doubt that Hawthorne's death was a signal event in the history of
American letters. The list of pallbearers alone is a striking example of his importance to the cultural scene of the mid-nineteenth century. But for many, Melville
and Emerson among them, he remained in death as elusive and frustrating a
figure as he had been in life. If he was the "shyest grape" to Melville, to Emerson

he was an attractive but difficult acquaintance, always on the verge of intimacy, it seemed, without ever actually granting it:

> Moreover I have felt sure of him in his neighborhood, & in his necessities of sympathy & intelligence, that I could well wait his time — his unwillingness & caprice — and might one day conquer a friendship. It would have been a happiness, doubtless to both of us, to have come into habits of unreserved intercourse. It was easy to talk with him — there were no barriers — only, he said so little, that I talked too much, & stopped only because — as he gave no indications — I feared to exceed. He showed no egotism or self-assertion, rather a humility, &, at one time, a fear that he had written himself out. One day, when I found him on the top of his hill, in the woods, he paced back the path to his house, & said, "*this path is the only remembrance of me that will remain.*" Now it appears that I waited too long.[1]

It might be said that Emerson's puzzlement and Melville's resigned regret are typical reactions to Hawthorne's oblique relation to the world. His "sociable silence" plays at the edge of revelation, offering closeness while stepping away. Surely this must have been, at times, a "painful solitude," as Emerson describes it. And yet, out of whatever discomfort his natural personality may have given him he made for himself a finer understanding of the possibilities and limits of friendship. Pain, in others words, became less an unfortunate departure from an imaginary norm than a part of the fundamental condition of those attuned enough to feel it. Isolation was not the absence of intimacy but a positive reality for all individuals, as real and as basic as the need for community.

What was important about his personal shyness was the way it clarified his sense of ethical restraint, the way all relationships came to represent the difficulty of knowing others and the even greater challenge of admitting his own lack of knowledge. Call it a skeptical ethics of friendship, delicate and sometimes dangerous when the world refused to allow for such refinement. It had the effect, of course, of making him silent, enigmatic, an attractive walking partner, a good listener — not in spite of his shyness but *because* of it, not to counter distance but to *express* it. Maddening, it must have been, to Melville, who wondered by the time he wrote *Clarel* whether there was as much behind the silence as there seemed.[2] But revelation was Melville's mode, while Hawthorne's was to expose the dangers of revolutionary thinking.

Distance was as necessary, in other words, as death, without which the world would be forced down by the weight of time. How else can actions matter, he asked in his final years, unless made meaningful by limit? How else can there be acknowledgment of others without the realization of one's own boundaries, without a consciousness that the self and the world are not one in the same but separate, estranged? The questions posed in *The Elixir of Life* manuscripts extend the pro-American, democratic arguments of *The House of the Seven Gables* and *The Marble Faun*. They revolve around a character named Septimius, who has no use for death, viewing it as an ignoble check on the powers of the self: "And how I hate the thought and anticipation of that contemptuous sort of appreciation of a man, after his death. Every living man triumphs over every dead one, as he lies, poor and helpless, under his mound; a pinch of dust, a heap of bones, an evil odor! I hate the thought! I shall not be so!" (*CE*, 13:15). Hawthorne's emphasis is less on the shame of death than on the ethical dangers of its absence, which would be, above all, antidemocratic. It might be said, for instance, that the Pyncheons try to eliminate death, that aristocratic history seeks to overcome the natural limits of individuals. Part of Hawthorne's plan was to make his deathless character a symbolic burden, a history that cannot be escaped: "Make this legend grotesque, and express the weariness of the tribe at the intolerable control the Undying One had of them, his always bringing up precepts from his own experience, his habits hardening into him, his assuming to himself all wisdom, — his intolerable wisdom — and depriving everybody of his rights to successive command" (*CE*, 13:85).

Septimius eventually isolates himself in an effort to understand the elixir of life from a recipe that has unexpectedly come into his hands. In fact, the regimen requires isolation and asceticism, trading love and happiness for self-extension. Again, there is more than the hint of ironic self-criticism here, Hawthorne pushing his own artistic solitude and distance to extremes: "But, even while he spoke, there was something that dragged upon his tongue; for he felt that the solitary pursuit in which he was engaged carried him apart from the sympathy of which he spoke, and that he was concentrating his efforts and interest entirely upon himself, and that the more he succeeded, the more remotely he should be carried away, and that his final triumph would be the complete seclusion of himself from all that breathed — the converting him, from an interested actor, into a cold and disconnected spectator of all mankind's warm and sympathetic life" (*CE*, 13:65).

Like his thoughts on exile, this is a type of self-warning. After all, distance can only function within a context of nearness; complete isolation, as Hawthorne tells us time and again, leads to nothing but a harmful failure to see others, to acknowledge the world. And the world in this case is Concord, Massachusetts, at the start of the Revolutionary War. The situation parallels Hawthorne's own: for him the Civil War was beginning, and like Septimius, he was less than enthusiastic about its purpose or his role in the world it projects. Nevertheless, the war comes to Septimius in the form of a brash English officer who challenges him to a duel. The Englishman's death is presented movingly, emphasizing the proximity of violence and intimacy: " 'I thank you, my enemy that was, my friend that is,' " said he, faintly smiling. 'Methinks, next to the father and mother that give us birth, the next most intimate relation must be with the man that slays us — that introduces us to the mysterious world to which this is but the portal. You and I are strangely connected, doubt it not, in the scenes of the unknown world' " (*CE*, 13:28).

"Strangely connected" — the phrase might be the summation of Hawthorne's thoughts on human relationships. And it is fitting that this distant union arises out of killing, itself the darkest form of self-extension. In the typical Hawthorneian vocabulary, this moment creates guilt, but it is less the historical guilt of the Calvinist inheritance than a fundamental recognition, an awareness of where the self begins and ends and how violence comes to another. It is similarly a moment of divorce, of rupture, which, in Hawthorne's more hopeful tales, leads to re-engagement, a return to the world through estrangement. In the case of Septimius, however, there is no return. His isolation only increases, and he becomes another tragic character who takes self-concern too far.

Notes

PROLOGUE: The Whipple Daguerreotype, 1848

1. Rita K. Gollin, *Portraits of Nathaniel Hawthorne: An Iconography* (1983), 26–27.
2. Quoted in Leon Edel, *Henry James: The Untried Years* (1953), 23.

CHAPTER 1: The Ethical Subject

1. Alfred Kazin, *Writing Was Everything* (1995), 18, 20.
2. Ibid., 10–11.
3. Kazin, *A Lifetime Burning in Every Moment* (1996), 5.
4. A few works that show what can be done in American literary and cultural studies without special pleading and political reduction are Richard Brodhead's *The School of Hawthorne* (1986), his *Cultures of Letters: Scenes of Reading and Writing in Nineteenth-Century America* (1993), David Reynolds's *Walt Whitman's America: A Cultural Biography* (1995), and Richard Millington's *Practicing Romance: Narrative Form and Cultural Engagement in Hawthorne's Fiction* (1992).
5. As Frank Kermode reminds us, "Many of these types of criticism profess to engage in a critique of power structures, yet it is obvious that their authors are replicating those structures within the world of academic criticism, struggling for visibility, keeping an eye open for passing bandwagons, looking for the valuable mutation, the new set of tricks that will ensure success or at any rate survival." *An Appetite for Poetry* (1989), 41. More recently, Mark Krupnick has noticed that "baby-boom and younger academics in English often project a sanctimony about their secular political-cultural convictions. . . . Their moralism strikes me as being at odds with their obsession with intradepartmental power plays and their rapt attention to new fashions in criticism and whatever will advance their careers." "Why Are English Departments Still Fighting the Culture Wars?" *Chronicle of Higher Education*, Sept. 20, 2002.
6. For a careful account of just how inaccurate such attacks can be, see G. R. Thompson and Eric Carl, *Neutral Ground: New Traditionalism and the American Romance Controversy* (1999).
7. According to Eric Cheyfitz, for instance, "some truths seem politically or ideologically evident at this moment, among which is the truth that all truth is partial, that is, political." "The Irresistibleness of Great Literature: Reconstructing Hawthorne's Politics," *American Literary History* 6, no. 3 (1994): 540.
8. Morris Dickstein, "Literary Theory and Historical Understanding," *Chronicle of Higher Education*, May 23, 2003, B7. Dickstein goes on to argue that many recent "histor-

icist readings too often seem idiosyncratic, empirically tenuous, or merely suggestive. In addition, they are often all too predictable in their political sympathies. Eager to weigh in on the side of the insulted and the injured, they seem determined by their well-meaning political agendas."

9. Louis Althusser, "Ideology and the State," in *Lenin and Philosophy and Other Essays* (1971), 162.

10. Jacques Rancière, "On the Theory of Ideology — Althusser's Politics," in *Ideology*, ed. Terry Eagleton (1994), 147.

11. Raymond Williams, *Marxism and Literature* (1977), 64.

12. Myra Jehlen and Sacvan Bercovitch, eds., *Ideology and Classic American Literature*, (1986), "Introduction," 15.

13. The exceptions include Gerald Graff's "American Criticism Left and Right" and Henry Nash Smith's "Symbol and Idea in *Virgin Land*," though these can hardly be called ideological self-analyses. (Smith's seems forced on him by changes in the field rather than by some new historical delight in his own contingency.) Other critics in the volume certainly discuss definitions of ideology but not their own probable biases. Jane Tompkins, whose "Sentimental Power: *Uncle Tom's Cabin*" appears in her later *Sensational Designs: The Cultural Work of American Fiction, 1790–1860* (1986), may be the true exception, given that her radical reader-response approach throws out all pretension to analysis beyond the limits of her own private interests.

14. Pease, "Melville and Cultural Persuasion," in Jehlen and Bercovitch, *Ideology*, 388.

15. For Jeffrey Wallen, many current literary critics "hardly ever state what possible changes are presumed, desired, or envisioned in their criticism; it is implied that we already know what should change (and we must therefore raise people's consciousness to the existence of the problem), so that there really is no subject here for political debate. . . . The supposed work of destabilizing and assailing 'ideological formations' is achieved by refusing to put one's own 'formations' or framework into play and shielding them from examination and contestation by those whose consciousness has not yet been properly elevated." *Closed Encounters: Literary Politics and Public Culture* (1998), 126. See as well Melvyn New's introduction to *In Proximity: Emmanuel Levinas and the Eighteenth Century* (2001), xii.

16. Pease, "New Americanists: Revisionist Interventions into the Canon," *boundary 2*, 17, no. 1 (Spring 1990): 8.

17. Reed Way Dasenbrock, *Truth and Consequences: Intentions, Conventions, and the New Thematics* (2001), 195. My debt to Dasenbrock's superb study will be evident in what follows.

18. For Mark Bauerlein, "The presumptuousness of [ideological analysis] lies in the imputations of unconscious control that ideology exercises upon those experiencing it. People watch movies and take in their ideology without realizing it. People read history without sensing the ideology enacted in it." *Literary Criticism: An Autopsy* (1997), 71.

19. As Melvyn New notes in *In Proximity*, "we have developed an aesthetics of reading that does seem at times to bury the past in 'sameness,' a charge of universal culpability for not being as ethical, liberal, right-thinking as we are; and, indeed, by reducing literature to the boredom of sameness, we have also turned against the concept of an interesting text, a better text" (xvii).

20. Graff, "American Criticism Left and Right," in Jehlen and Bercovitch, *Ideology*, 91.

21. Eagleton, *Ideology*, 11.

22. One positive example from Hawthorne studies is Joel Pfister's 1991 study, *The Production of Personal Life: Class, Gender, and the Psychological in Hawthorne's Fiction*. But what was an innovative way of looking at domestic ideology in the early nineties has in recent years become something of an orthodox set of assumptions for many critics who are generally less successful than Pfister at offering subtle and complex descriptions of the relationship between author and context. A more measured and welcome adjustment of this type of reading can be found in Brook Thomas's essay "Citizen Hester: *The Scarlet Letter* as Civic Myth," *American Literary History* 13, no. 2 (2001): 181–211. It is notable that Thomas has moved away from the term "ideology" to a (renewed) version of "myth":

> In noting that many of Hawthorne's critics remain as much within the myth of Puritan origins of US citizenship as he does, I am not implying that I somehow can stand outside of and above myth to expose it as an ideological distortion. Whereas I fully recognize that *The Scarlet Letter*, as a work of fiction, does not give us a historically accurate account of seventeenth-century Puritan society and political thought, to dismiss is as mere ideology does not get us very far. On the contrary, since according to today's critical commonplace we are always within ideology, it is not enough to expose persistent national myths as ideological, which is how the present generation of critics of American literature has generally distinguished itself from the myth and symbol school. What we need to do as well is to evaluate the effect of various myths in terms of what Kenneth Burke called 'equipment for living.' Such work on/with myth might help to generate a revitalized political criticism that once again, like Aristotle, sees politics as the art of the possible. (204)

23. The other commonly used term for such a method is "social constructionism." According to Graham Good, "constructionism is a theory of how works of art (or 'texts') originate (or 'are produced'): they are socially constructed rather than individually created. They are (perhaps in indirect and complex ways) 'effects' of ideological imperatives to which they remain blind. . . . As ideology is a higher order of knowledge than that of creative art, the theorist implicitly knows more than the artist, though this claim is usually concealed." *Humanism Betrayed: Theory, Ideology, and Culture in the Contemporary University* (2001), 53.

24. Isaiah Berlin, "Two Concepts of Liberty," in *Isaiah Berlin: The Proper Study of Mankind* (1998), 208.

25. For instance, Pease, in "New Americanists," argues that "New Americanists have a responsibility to make these absent subjects representable in their field's past and present" (31). And yet, the only way to make such a responsibility meaningful is to imagine a realm outside of ideology in which individuals have some choice between repression and liberation. Pease clearly imagines that the New Americanists have made such a choice, though in order to do so, they must exist outside whatever political unconscious may be in operation in their own ideological framework.

26. Dasenbrock, *Truth and Consequences*, 170.

27. Wendell V. Harris offers a similar approach: "The very process of reconstructing authorial meaning demands a process of excluding what the author could not have intended to express, which in turn implies the possibility, in fact unavoidability, of interest in what the author and audience could have shared. Stated another way, in seeking the author's intention the mind works centripetally, moving as far into the context presumably anticipated by the author as possible while jettisoning as much as possible of what we know

could not belong to that context." *Literary Meaning: Reclaiming the Study of Literature* (1996), 142.

28. Kenneth Dauber, "Ordinary Language Criticism: A Manifesto," *Arizona Quarterly* 53 (1997): 133–34.

29. This approach is obviously similar to what Daniel R. Schwarz describes as the "humanistic revival" of ethical criticism. He outlines what he sees as the shared concepts of such readers:

> 1. The form of a literary text—its style, structure, and narrative technique—expresses its value system. Put another way, form discovers the meaning of content.
>
> 2. A literary text is a creative gesture of the author. Understanding the process of imitating the external world gives us insight into the artistry and meaning of the text.
>
> 3. A literary text imitates a world that precedes the text, and the critic should recapture that world primarily by formal analysis of the text, although knowledge of the historical context and author is often important.
>
> 4. A literary text has an original meaning, a center, that can be approached, albeit perhaps not reached, by perceptive reading. The goal is to discover what the author said to the intended audience, as well as what the author says to us now. Acts of interpretation at their best—subtle, lucid, inclusive, perceptive—can bring that goal into sight, even while allowing for unintended meanings in what is now called the subtext.
>
> 5. Human behavior is central to most literary texts and should be a major concern of analysis. Although modes of characterization differ, the psychology and morality of characters must be understood as if the characters were metaphors for real people, for understanding others helps us to understand ourselves.
>
> 6. The inclusiveness, the depth, and the range of the literary text's vision is a measure of that text's quality.

"A Humanistic Ethics of Reading," in *Mapping the Ethical Turn: A Reader in Ethics, Culture, and Literary Theory* (2001), 3–4.

30. Cavell distinguishes acknowledgment from "empathic projection": "Isn't the wish for such a concept really a persistence of the idea that the other is 'like' oneself, that whatever one can know about the other one first has to find in oneself and then read *into* the other (by analogy): whereas the essence of acknowledgement is that one conceive the other from the other's point of view." "Between Acknowledgement and Avoidance," in *The Claim to Reason: Wittgenstein, Skepticism, Morality, and Tragedy* (1979), 440–41.

31. Russell Goodman, *American Philosophy and the Romantic Tradition* (1990), 28.

32. The conjunction of Cavell and Levinas may be surprising given their basic placement in two commonly opposed philosophical traditions. However, Cavell's career has to an extent been built upon his readings of Continental philosophers (Nietzsche and Heidegger, in particular) from within the framework of his own Anglo-American allegiances to the philosophy of ordinary language. I therefore agree with Gerald Bruns when he explains that he sees "in recent Anglo-American philosophy an acceptance of particularity—of singularity, even—that is closer to a Levinasian ethics of proximity, alterity, and responsibility than to the traditions of logic and empiricism, Kantian morality and British utilitarianism, in which this philosophy has its roots. What is more, this philosophy sees—or is close to seeing—literature as a place in which to engage this particularity conceptually and concretely, whether in the interests of language, practical reasoning, or ethical

theory (or, as in the case of Cavell, all three together)." *Tragic Thoughts at the End of Philosophy: Language, Literature, and Ethical Theory* (1999), 18.

33. Emmanuel Levinas, "Ethics as First Philosophy," in *The Levinas Reader*, ed. Seán Hand (1989), 82.

34. Levinas, *Totality and Infinity: An Essay on Exteriority*, trans. Alphonso Lingis (1969), 50–51.

35. Krzysztof Ziarek, *Inflected Language: Toward a Hermeneutics of Nearness: Heidegger, Levinas, Stevens, Celan* (1994), 68.

36. Levinas, *Totality and Infinity*, 43.

37. Ziarek, *Inflected Language*, 70.

38. Levinas, *Totality and Infinity*, 62.

39. Dasenbrock, *Truth and Consequences*, 99.

40. Jill Robbins, *Altered Reading: Levinas and Literature* (1999), 78.

41. Such a collection as Melvyn New's *In Proximity* demonstrates the increasing attractiveness of wider applications of Levinas to literature. The essays in this volume include readings of Behn, Defoe, Sterne, de Laclos, Goethe, and Wordsworth, demonstrating, in New's words, "the diversity of uses to which readers may employ Levinasian insights to read major literary texts" (xiii).

42. Elaine Scary, *On Beauty and Being Just* (1999), 111–12.

43. It also argues for a heightened attention that resonates with Martha Nussbaum's claim that a "finer responsiveness to the concrete," as found in James's novels, is itself an ethical awareness. See *Love's Knowledge: Essays on Philosophy and Literature* (1990), 37.

44. Alexander Nehamas, "An Essay on Beauty and Judgement," *Threepenny Review* (Winter 2000). I would add to this Melvyn New's similar description of reading: "Succintly, as readers we are not called on simply to disturb the text, but to be disturbed by it as well. Reading breaks our repose by confronting us with an infinite, obsessive challenge to our self-interests and our certainties. Teaching others to read well is not radically or solely a defining of lapses in the text; rather, prior to all understanding, we demonstrate responsibility to the text by welcoming the disturbance, displacement, and disorientation of ourselves in *response* to the text. This mode of responsiveness is rarely reflected in present-day critical reading — not even in deconstructive reading, wherein we find suprising insistence in many practitioners that the disorienting indeterminacy of meaning in other texts simply does not occur in their own" (xvi–xvii).

45. Gerald Bruns, *Heidegger's Estrangements: Language, Truth, and Poetry in the Later Writings* (1989), 33.

CHAPTER 2 : Romantic Truth

1. Sophia Hawthorne to Elizabeth Peabody, quoted in Hershel Parker, *Herman Melville: A Biography*, vol. 1, *1819–1851* (1996), 776. The erratic punctuation is reproduced in Parker's text.

2. "Self-Reliance," in *Selections from Ralph Waldo Emerson*, ed. Stephen E. Whicher (1960), 160.

3. It is important to note that Melville's ideas progressed quickly from 1845, when he was writing *Typee*, to 1850–51, when he produced *Moby-Dick*, to 1857, when *The Confidence-Man* concluded his career as a publishing fiction writer. Accordingly, it is difficult, not to say inadvisable, to reduce his entire body of work to the theoretical statements of any one period. The author who created the pointedly fictive, insubstantial world of *The*

Confidence-Man clearly conceived the shape and potential of human relationships differently than did the creator of Tommo or Ishmael. Likewise, it is perfectly feasible to argue that Melville's conception of truth underwent significant modifications from his early fact-based narratives to his encyclopedic romances and further through the more pessimistic, despairing short fiction, poetry, and other late materials. Thus, any investigation of Melville's relation to Hawthorne in the early 1850s entails some disservice to Melville's lifelong complexity. What follows is therefore based on the ideas and statements in the "Mosses" essay and the letters to Hawthorne rather than on the more complex fictional presentations in Melville's work as a whole.

4. Herman Melville, "Hawthorne and His Mosses," in *The Piazza Tales and Other Prose Pieces, 1839–1860*, vol. 9, *The Writings of Herman Melville*, ed. Harrison Hayford, Hershel Parker, and G. Thomas Tanselle (1987), 240. For examples of critical attention to the erotic resonances in Melville's review, see Edwin Haviland Miller, *Melville* (1975), 32; Parker, *Herman Melville*, 760; and James R. Mellow, *Nathaniel Hawthorne in His Times* (1980), 335. For a more general discussion and overview of the topic, see the special issue of *ESQ: A Journal of the American Renaissance* 46 (2000), ed. Robert K. Martin and Leland S. Person.

5. For a particularly valuable discussion of Melville's "misreading" of Hawthorne as a literary exemplar, see Richard Brodhead, "Hawthorne, Melville, and the Fiction of Prophecy," in *Nathaniel Hawthorne: New Critical Essays*, ed. A. Robert Lee (1982), 229–50. See as well Seymour L. Gross, "Hawthorne versus Melville," *Bucknell Review* 14, no. 3 (1966): 89–109.

6. As Edgar A. Dryden and others have pointed out, this truth, a "white doe," is also destructive, a "sane madness" paradoxically dark in meaning. *Melville's Thematics of Form: The Great Art of Telling the Truth* (1968), 26.

7. John D. Seelye argues that the essay's "structure adheres closely to the quest pattern." "The Structure of Encounter: Melville's Review of Hawthorne's *Mosses*," in *Melville and Hawthorne in the Berkshires: A Symposium*, ed. Howard P. Vincent (1968), 65.

8. Melville, "Hawthorne and His Mosses," 250.

9. See, for example, Brodhead, "Fiction of Prophecy," 233–34; Dryden, *Melville's Thematics of Form*, 117–48; and R. W. B. Lewis, *Trials of the Word: Essays in American Literature and the Humanistic Tradition* (1965), 36–76.

10. See Mellow, *Nathaniel Hawthorne*, 204–5, 366–67, 379.

11. Richard Millington describes this anxiety well: "There are, moreover, several reasons to conclude that Hawthorne found the acts of self-presentation and reception involved in writing and reading genuinely unsettling. A strong conviction of the unreliability of linguistic representation, especially attempts to represent intimate emotion to others, runs through his love letters; and a remarkably intense vision of the dangerous permeability of one self to the power and influence of another emerges from a famous letter half-warning and half-begging Sophia not to try the services of a mesmerist." *Practicing Romance: Narrative Form and Cultural Engagement in Hawthorne's Fiction* (1992), 4.

12. As John Carlos Rowe reminds us, "studies in Romantic thought and expression generally seem to have difficulty in establishing clear distinctions between 'poetic' and 'philosophical' modes of representation, because Romanticism itself seems always to be characterized by the desire both for philosophical truth and figurative energy." "The Internal Conflict of Romantic Narrative: Hegel's *Phenomenology* and Hawthorne's *The Scarlet Letter*," *Modern Language Notes* 95 (1980): 1205.

13. I disagree in general with those readers who take Hawthorne literally when he offers his moral. Evan Carton, for instance, claims that Hawthorne offers the moral to counteract the romantic definition of legend, yet Carton offers no explanation for the subsequent sentences, which seriously qualify the availability of such a moral within the fabric of romance. See *The Rhetoric of American Romance: Dialectic and Identity in Emerson, Dickinson, Poe, and Hawthorne* (1985), 163.

14. In his letters Melville describes *the* secret about Nathaniel Hawthorne (*C*, 186), a conviction he held, according to Julian Hawthorne, into his later years; he divulged to Hawthorne the "secret motto" of *Moby-Dick* (*C*, 196); and he at various times in his career seemed convinced that he himself either possessed or would never possess the truth he sought (never surrendering the necessary notion that truth exists in a definable, expressible form). For accounts of Melville's interview with Julian Hawthorne, see Turner, *Nathaniel Hawthorne*, 308; and Jay Leyda, *The Melville Log: A Documentary Life of Herman Melville, 1819–1891* (1969), 2:782–83.

15. As Peter J. Bellis has argued, for "Hawthorne . . . the romance's historical and rhetorical self-consciousness works in just this way—to resist co-optation by any hegemonic discourse or totalizing representation." *Writing Revolution: Aesthetics and Politics in Hawthorne, Whitman, and Thoreau* (2003), 7.

16. Samuel Taylor Coleridge, *Biographia Literaria; or, Biographical Sketches of My Literary Life and Opinions*, ed. James Engell and W. Jackson Bate, vol. 7, pt. 2, of *The Collected Works of Samuel Taylor Coleridge* (1983), 6–7.

17. John Keats to George and Thomas Keats, Hampstead, Dec. 21, 1817, *The Letters (1815–1818)*, vol. 6 of *Poetical Works* (1970), 104.

18. Walter Jackson Bate, *John Keats* (1963), 249.

19. Paul DeMan, "Introduction," in *Selected Poetry of John Keats*, ed. Paul de Man (1966), xiv.

20. Edgar A. Dryden notes that both Hawthorne's "daughter and son remark on his ability to make 'himself all things to men.'" See Dryden, *Nathaniel Hawthorne* (1977), 28; quoting from *The Complete Works of Nathaniel Hawthorne* (Cambridge, MA: Houghton Mifflin, 1882), 11:469.

21. Keats to Richard Woodhouse, Hampstead, Oct. 27, 1818, *Letters (1818–1819)*, vol. 7 of *Poetical Works*, 129–30.

22. Keats to John Hamilton Reynolds, Hampstead, Feb. 19, 1818, *Letters (1815–1818)*, vol. 6 of *Poetical Works* (1970), 149.

23. Kenneth Dauber explains Hawthorne's "craftiness" through what he calls "outsidedness, which is the freedom of being at a distance from what he writes, committed to what he writes nevertheless." See "Hawthorne and the Responsibility of Outsidedness," in *The Idea of Authorship: Democratic Poetics from Franklin to Melville* (1990), 176–77.

24. Gerald L. Bruns, *Heidegger's Estrangements: Language, Truth, and Poetry in the Later Writings* (1989), xx. My reliance on Bruns's excellent reading of the later Heidegger will be apparent in what follows. It should be noted that Heidegger's comments are based upon readings of German romantic poets, particularly Hölderlin.

25. Hawthorne's language in this respect resembles "Socratic irony" as Schlegel describes it: "For Schlegel (Critical Fragment 108), Socratic irony is 'the only involuntary and yet completely deliberate dissimulation. It is equally impossible to feign it or to divulge it. . . . It originates in the union of *savoir vivre* and scientific spirit, in the conjunction of a perfectly instinctive and a perfectly conscious philosophy. It contains and arouses

a feeling of indissoluble antagonism between the absolute and the relative, between the impossibility and the necessity of complete communication.'" See Piotr Parlej, *The Romantic Theory of the Novel: Genre and Reflection in Cervantes, Melville, Flaubert, Joyce, and Kafka* (1997), 37; quoting from *Friedrich Schlegel's "Lucinde" and the Fragments*, trans. Peter Firchow (Minneapolis: University of Minnesota Press, 1971), 155–56.

26. Emily Miller Budick, "Sacvan Bercovitch, Stanley Cavell, and the Romance Theory of American Fiction," *PMLA* 107 (1992): 78–91. I am indebted to this article for its conjunction of Cavell and Hawthorne in terms of the romance.

27. Stanley Cavell, *The Senses of Walden: An Expanded Edition* (1981), 49, 105.

28. See Henry David Thoreau, *Walden*, ed. J. Lyndon Shanley, in *The Writings of Henry D. Thoreau* (1971), 3; and Emerson, *Selections*, 160.

29. Stanley Cavell, "Aversive Thinking: Emersonian Representations in Heidegger and Nietzsche," in *Conditions Handsome and Unhandsome: The Constitution of Emersonian Perfectionism* (1989), 59.

30. Bruns, *Heidegger's Estrangements*, 22.

31. Cavell, "Aversive Thinking," 39. And from Levinas: "To know amounts to grasping being out of nothing or reducing it to nothing, removing it from its alterity" (*Totality and Infinity*, 44).

32. Shoshona Felman, "Turning the Screw of Interpretation," in *Literature and Psychoanalysis: The Question of Reading — Otherwise* (1977; 1982), 167–68.

33. Dryden describes the romance in similar terms: "Romance for Hawthorne offers a mode of communication that maintains a tension between the hidden and the shown, thereby insuring that something will always remain in reserve, either as an unformulated thought shaded by language or in the form of a veiled figure whose meaning is not explicitly signified." "Through a Glass Darkly: 'The Minister's Black Veil' as a Parable," in *New Essays on Hawthorne's Major Tales*, ed. Millicent Bell (1993), 146.

34. Martin Heidegger, "The Origin of the Work of Art," in *Poetry, Language, Thought*, trans. Albert Hofstadter (1971), 60.

35. Bruns, *Heidegger's Estrangements*, 34, 33.

CHAPTER 3 : Ethics and the Face: Hawthorne and Levinas

1. See "The Politics of *The Scarlet Letter*," in *Ideology and Classic American Literature*, ed. Myra Jehlen and Sacvan Bercovitch (1986), 58. See also Bercovitch "Hawthorne's A-morality of Compromise," *Representations* 24 (Fall 1988): 37.

2. A similar point is made by Jean Fagin Yellin: "The studied ambiguity of these works, generally understood to be the result of deliberate artistic decisions, must also be considered as a strategy of avoidance and denial. Hawthorne, it appears, could not acknowledge the necessary engagement of politics and art, of life and letters — the engagement that Emerson demanded of his generation and of all generations." "Hawthorne and the Slavery Question," in *A Historical Guide to Nathaniel Hawthorne*, ed. Larry J. Reynolds (2001), 157. My contention, as will be evident in what follows, is that such a reading presumes a fairly simplistic notion of engagement, which Hawthorne's work both questions and significantly elaborates.

3. Emily Miller Budick, "Sacvan Bercovitch, Stanley Cavell, and the Romance Theory of American Fiction," *PMLA* 107 (1992): 85.

4. Kenneth Dauber, "Hawthorne and the Responsibility of Outsidedness," in *The Idea of Authorship: Democratic Poetics from Franklin to Melville* (1990), 164.

5. Colin Davis, *Levinas: An Introduction* (1996), 49.

6. For a useful comparison of Levinas's thought to that of Hegel and Kant, see Adriann Peperzak, "Some Remarks on Hegel, Kant, and Levinas," in *Face to Face with Levinas*, ed. Richard A. Cohen (1986), 205–17. It is Levinas's distrust of totalization that brings him closer than Hegel to Hawthorne's epistemological resistances: "Whereas Hegel regards the individual, the moral subject, and the perspective of morality as mere moments of a concept that triumphs in the concrete universality of the state, Levinas interprets the state as an essentially violent system of equality and justice, intermediate — and in a sense mediating — between goodness and war. The difference between their perspectives explains why Levinas holds that true peace cannot come from the state and that the dialectics of violence must be oriented by a voice that 'comes from the outside, "through the door" (*thurathen*), whereas Hegel — from his 'totalitarian' perspective — must defend the state as the highest expression and guarantee of peace, above which no *practical* reconciliation is possible" (ibid., 215).

7. See Michael Colacurcio, *The Province of Piety: Moral History in Hawthorne's Early Tales* (1984), and J. Hillis Miller, *Hawthorne and History: Defacing It* (1991). For a partial survey of the many responses to the story, see Lea Bertani Vozar Newman, "One-Hundred-Fifty Years of Looking At, Into, Through, Behind, Beyond, and Around 'The Minister's Black Veil,' " *Nathaniel Hawthorne Review* 13, no. 2 (1987): 5–12.

8. Colacurcio, *Province of Piety*, 384–85. Original emphasis.

9. James, *Pragmatism*, 84. Original emphasis.

10. Miller, *Hawthorne and History*, 89.

11. For an extension of Miller's reading, see Dryden, who explores Hawthorne's use of the figural method of parable to dramatize "a collision between literal reference and illustrative significance." "Through a Glass Darkly: 'The Minister's Black Veil' as a Parable," in *New Essays on Hawthorne's Major Tales*, ed. Millicent Bell (1933), 138.

12. As Budick puts it, "At the center of Hawthornean romance, and the historical romances that succeed it, is the basic problem of the skeptical dilemma, of determining whether or not elements of the dualism, the self and the world, exist at all." *Fiction and Historical Consciousness: The American Romance Tradition* (1989), 84.

13. As Richard Millington explains, "Hooper exposes as fiction the premise that we can be known to each other, which is the ground upon which speech, love, art, community all rest; yet what he fails to understand is that this fiction when shared — and when it remains unnamed — makes possible a provisional but significant speech, love, and art in the community that accepts it." *Practicing Romance*, 30.

14. Emmanuel Levinas, *Totality and Infinity: An Essay on Exteriority*, trans. Alphonso Lingis (1969), 34.

15. Davis, *Levinas*, 135.

16. As John Carlos Rowe argues, for Hegelian romanticism (and for Hawthorne), "ethical fictions and inaccessible divine 'laws' must be replaced by the willful acts of a 'conscience' certain of itself as Spirit manifesting itself in the world. Such an attitude seems generally characteristic of the ethics of Romanticism. Romantic moral truths generally depend on the manifestation of their universality in and through the particular acts of human experience in their temporal environment. Unrecognized by individual acts of self-consciousness, moral universals remain unrealized abstractions." "The Internal Conflict of Romantic Narrative: Hegel's *Phenomenology* and Hawthorne's *The Scarlet Letter*," *Modern Language Notes* 95 (1980): 1213.

17. I address the specifically political implications of this self-positioning, particu-

larly in light of Sacvan Bercovitch's reading of the novel in *The Office of Scarlet Letter,* in Part Two.

18. See Richard Chase, *The American Novel and Its Tradition* (1957), 74; Leland S. Person Jr., *"The Scarlet Letter* and the Myth of the Divine Child," *ATQ* 44 (Fall 1979): 303; Darrel Abel, *The Moral Picturesque: Studies in Hawthorne's Fiction* (1988), 190–93; and Elizabeth Aycock Hoffman, "Political Power in *The Scarlet Letter,"* in *The Critical Response to Nathaniel Hawthorne's The Scarlet Letter,* ed. Gary Scharnhorst (1992), 217.

19. Rowe follows a similar line of thinking: "Hester's recognition of her alienation from social law is thus followed by an acknowledgement of her only real ties to the world: Pearl and Hester's responsibility for her education. Pearl is no longer merely another sign of Hester's own external representation of Puritan justice, but she does remain something of an abstract, general 'child' to be educated," "The Internal Conflict," 1213.

20. Mary Rowlandson, "The Sovereignty and Goodness of God," in *Puritans among the Indians: Accounts of Captivity and Redemption: 1676–1724,* ed. Alden T. Vaughn and Edward W. Clark (1981), 38.

21. Brook Thomas argues in a similar way that for Hawthorne "sin is not so much — as it would have been for Winthrop — a sin against God's law as it is a sin against the intersubjective agreements that human beings make with one another." "Citizen Hester: *The Scarlet Letter* as Civic Myth," *American Literary History* 13.2 (Summer 2001): 181–211.

22. See Sacvan Bercovitch, *The Office of The Scarlet Letter* (1991), 7.

23. As Levinas states in "Ideology and Idealism," "Yet the invincible concern for the other man in his destitution and his homelessness — in his nakedness — in his condition or noncondition of a proletarian, this concern escapes the suspect finality of ideologies; the *search* for the other man who is still far away is already the *relationship* with this other man, a relationship in all its rectitude — a trope specific to the approach of the neighbor, which is already proximity. Here we see something coming that is other than the complacency in ideas agreeing with the particularism of a group and its interests." "Ideology and Idealism," in *Of God Who Comes to Mind,* trans. Bettina Bergo (1998), 9.

24. Jill Robbins, *Altered Reading: Levinas and Literature* (1999), 49, 50.

25. See T. Walter Herbert, *Dearest Beloved: The Hawthornes and the Making of the Middle-Class Family* (1993), 201. Joel Pfister makes essentially the same point though with a bit more allowance for intention, arguing that "the fundamental ideological project of *The Scarlet Letter* seems contradictory but self-consciously so: Hawthorne reinforces *and* problematizes the middle-class ideology that domesticity 'humanizes.'" *The Production of Personal Life: Class, Gender, and the Psychological in Hawthorne's Fiction* (1991), 142.

26. James, *Pragmatism,* 77.

27. Or, as John Carlos Rowe puts it, "Hawthorne's 'Unpardonable Sin' is not merely excessive pride in one's knowledge, but a denial of the charity (or 'grace') that springs from one's recognition of self in the fallibility of others." "The Internal Conflict," 1219.

CHAPTER 4: Ethics and Politics: The Question of Engagement

1. These include, most notably, Sacvan Bercovitch, *The Office of "The Scarlet Letter"* (1991); Larry J. Reynolds, *"The Scarlet Letter* and Revolutions Abroad," *American Literature* 77 (1985): 44–67; Jonathan Arac, "The Politics of *The Scarlet Letter,"* in *Ideology and Classic American Literature,* ed. Myra Jehlen and Sacvan Bercovitch (1986), 247–66; and Jane Tompkins, *Sensational Designs: The Cultural Work of American Fiction, 1790–1860*

(1985). See as well Milton R. Stern, *Contexts for Hawthorne: The Marble Faun and the Politics of Openness and Closure in American Literature* (1991).

2. Bercovitch's well-known argument, developed through several important studies, need not be summarized here. For an overview see *The Rites of Assent* (1992).

3. Richard Millington, *"The Office of The Scarlet Letter:* An 'Inside Narrative'?" *Nathaniel Hawthorne Review* 22, no. 1 (1996): 4. See as well Robert Milder, *"The Scarlet Letter* and Its Discontents," *Nathaniel Hawthorne Review* 22, no. 1 (1996): 9–25; Paul K. Johnston, "Killing the Spirit: Anne Hutchinson and the Office of the Scarlet Letter," *Nathaniel Hawthorne Review* 22, no. 1 (1996): 26–35; Charles Swann, *Nathaniel Hawthorne: Tradition and Revolution* (1991), 94, and Robert Daly, " 'We Really Have No Country at All': Hawthorne's Reoccupations of History," *Arachne* 3, no. 1 (1996): 69.

4. Millington, "Inside Narrative," 4. Brook Thomas reinforces this concern: "But Hester . . . is defined much more by her commitment to interpersonal relations that by her individualism, which is not to say that Hawthorne does not value the independence that she displays in contrast to the 'childlike loyalty' of other Puritan subjects. But that independence for Hawthorne is not a product of a naturally self-sufficient self; it is instead bred and cultivated in the associational activities of an independent civil society." "Citizen Hester: *The Scarlet Letter* as Civic Myth," *American Literary History* 13, no. 2 (2001): 199. In his *Practicing Romance*, Millington summarizes his critique of reductive ideological readings: "I pause upon this point because of the tendency of some 'rehistoricizing' accounts of his work to narrow Hawthorne as badly as the moralizing or psychologizing criticism of old. The readings I have in mind displace Hawthorne too easily from the position of the analyst. Because they do not read him closely enough, they reduce him to a site through which ideology plays or deprive him of the intellectual acuity and ideological maneuverability that we think we possess." *Practicing Romance: Narrative Form and Cultural Engagement in Hawthorne's Fiction* (1992), 8.

5. Bercovitch, *Office*, 8.

6. In his perceptive critique of Bercovitch's ideological reading, Peter J. Bellis explains that "Bercovitch is required to make a second move, to project the existence of a non-ideological realm outside liberal discourse, a space from which viable action or critique can emerge. In his autobiographical introduction to *The Rites of Assent*, he claims just such an outsider's position for himself, as a Canadian, a Socialist, and a Jew, whose work takes the form of an external intervention, a 'border-crossing.' . . . Bercovitch offers his critique from within the American academy, of course, and his opposition between American reformist discourse and European revolutionary action is itself an ideological and discursive construct." "Representing Dissent: Hawthorne and the Drama of Revolt," *ESQ: A Journal of the American Renaissance* 41, no. 2 (1995): 98. See as well Bellis, *Writing Revolution: Aesthetics and Politics in Hawthorne, Whitman, and Thoreau* (2003). Similarly, Eric Cheyfitz describes *The Office of the Scarlet Letter* as "a lament for any form of collective dissent" in America. "The Irresistibleness of Great Literature: Reconstructing Hawthorne's Politics," *American Literary History* 6, no. 3 (1994): 543.

7. For an overview of this question see Carol Colatrella, "Bercovitch's Paradox: Critical Dissent, Marginality, and the Example of Melville," in *Cohesion an Dissent in America*, ed. Carol Colatrella and Joseph Alkana (1994), 229–50.

8. Sacvan Bercovitch, "Emerson, Individualism, and the Ambiguities of Dissent," in *Ralph Waldo Emerson: A Collection of Critical Essays*, ed. Laurence Buell (1993), 124.

9. Bercovitch, *Office*, xii.

10. Brook Thomas argues for just such a position for Hester: "The power of *The Scarlet Letter* as civic myth has to do with its dramatization of the difference that a preference for freedom of choice can make and how important the existence of an independent civil society is for its cultivation. That difference is most poignantly dramatized in Hester's decision to return to Boston at the end of the book. . . . With her lover and husband dead and her child apparently married and in another country, she returns as a woman, a woman devoted, nonetheless, not to individual fulfillment but to the interpersonal relations of civil society." "Citizen Hester," 196.

11. Bercovitch, *Office*, 3, 5.

12. Swann argues that "Hester expects a lot: the Second Coming. To be without sin, shame and sorrow is to be more than human." *Nathaniel Hawthorne*, 94.

13. Ibid., 8. See also Swann's discussion of Hawthorne's preference for a "nineteenth century tradition in which tragedy and history were consciously connected" (13–14).

14. Bellis similarly claims that "this may well be a moment of initiation and transition for Robin, but it is also a nightmare image of the Revolution as a parricidal disorder; the way the crowd carries the major along in 'an uncovered cart' suggests not only a Boston popular festival but also a Parisian mob bringing a victim to the guillotine." "Representing Dissent," 107.

15. F. O. Matthiessen, *American Renaissance: Art and Expression in the Age of Emerson and Whitman* (1941), 317, 318–19.

16. Bellis argues, for instance, that for Bercovitch "the literary and the political are continuous and inseparable. . . . Literature thus cannot be said to transcend the realm of propaganda because 'its imaginative forms incorporate the complexity of beliefs implicit in any single-minded doctrine we commonly associate with propaganda.'" "Representing Dissent," 101.

17. Matthiessen, *American Renaissance*, 318.

18. Jehlen and Bercovitch, *Ideology*, 9–10. Indeed, were the tables turned, the ideology of such criticism might be called a sort of conspiratorial political idealism, in which surfaces inevitably mask a self-righteously detected truth available only through a retrospective application of late twentieth-century political debates.

19. Bellis, "Representing Dissent," 102. Bellis also concludes that Bercovitch's ideological critique is itself ideological: "My point is not that Bercovitch's analysis is 'really' a Marxist one, but that the European 'history' he places outside or against American ideology can itself be grasped only from a particular ideological perspective" (102).

20. Emily Miller Budick, *Fiction and Historical Consciousness: The American Romance Tradition* (1989), 97.

21. Thomas Carl Wall, *Radical Passivity: Levinas, Blanchot, and Agamben* (1999), 50–51.

22. Simon Critchley, *Ethics, Politics, Subjectivity: Essays on Derrida, Levinas, and Contemporary French Thought* (1999), 275–76.

23. Levinas's "Ideology and Idealism" is particularly helpful here:

As though the other man were sought, or approached, within an alterity where no administration could ever reach him; as though, through justice, there should open in the other man a dimension that bureaucracy, even if it had a revolutionary origin, blocks up by its very universality, by the entry of the singularity of the other into a concept that universally comprises, and as though *in the form* of a relationship with the other stripped of all essence—with an *other*, who is thus irreducible to the individual of a genus, or to the individual of the human race—there opened up the *beyond* of essence or, in some idealism, *dis-interestedness* in the strong sense of the term, or in the sense of a suspension of essence. . . . Is this an idealism of suspect ideology? Yet it is a movement so little ideological—so little similar to resting in an established situation, to self-satisfaction—that it is the putting into question of the self, posing itself directly as de-posed, as for the other.

Of God Who Comes to Mind, trans. Bettina Bergo (1998), 9–10.

24. According to Gerald Bruns, the Levinasian position would likewise say "that the claims of the other are in advance of reason, and that our beliefs, values, and rules often obstruct the workings of these claims, as if it were as much a function of our beliefs and values to protect us from the ethical as to bring us in line with it. For the point would be that the ethical is not a rule or measure or standard that one could get in line with. It is something much more difficult to live with than a set of principles." *Tragic Thoughts,* 108.

25. Critchley, *Ethics, Politics, Subjectivity,* 113, 115.

26. If we follow Gerald Bruns's explanation, it becomes clear that Hawthorne and Levinas share an essentially tragic vision: "Levinasian ethics presupposes catastrophe as an ontological condition, even as it presupposes skepticism as an unsatisfiable questioning that takes us out of the mode of self-sufficiency and control, as if the ethical were something hardly to be borne, like begin human." *Tragic Thoughts,* 111. It is from within this tragic vision that I understand Hawthorne's comment to Elizabeth Peabody that "the good of others, like our own happiness, is not to be attained by direct effort, but incidentally. . . . I am really too humble to think of doing good; if I have been impertinent enough to aim at it, I am ashamed." Hawthorne to Elizabeth Peabody, Oct. 8, 1857. Quoted in Brenda Wineapple, *Hawthorne: A Life* (2003), 331.

27. See the discussion of "War-Matters" below for a more complete consideration of the debate over the purpose of the editorial footnotes.

28. Cheyfitz is clearly one such reader. He objects to Matthiessen's separation of literature and propaganda because "pamphleteering, in both the strict and broad senses of the term, comprises a crucial part of the discourses 'we' might refer to as American or, more precisely, US literature" ("Irresistibleness of Great Literature," 546). Replacing Matthiessen's distinction with "strict and broad" sorts of propaganda, Cheyfitz then collapses the Pierce biography into "War-Matters": "I think it would be difficult to argue that any of the above-mentioned 'pamphlets' does not deal with 'complex actuality'— something I think Hawthorne evades in both the Pierce biography and 'Chiefly about War-Matters,' which, in a manner characteristic of the passages we have been considering, is equivocal about virtually all of the political subjects it takes up" (547). Because for Cheyfitz "all truth is partial, that is, political" (540), this equivocality must be understood as a dishonest, mystifying complexity that avoids action. And yet, while accusing Bercovitch of celebrating this complexity (a dubious charge in itself), he readmits the basic distinction between art and politics: "While this equivocal politics may produce 'complex' fictions and criticism, it can also produce a deadly simple politics of paralysis" (548).

29. Richard Brodhead explains it in similar terms: "I do not pretend to know how to resolve the contradictions in Hawthorne's politics. But I think that it gives at least a preliminary kind of help with the problem of Hawthorne's politics to recognize that it is an affair of contradictions. For Hawthorne, the political is a mode of engagement that generates plural and incompatible outlooks, each with the power, at certain moments, to compel

understanding and to motivate action, and each with the power to make the others appear delusory. . . . Hawthorne is finally skeptical of the political; yet his skepticism is not a fixed or stable stand, but a position constantly re-generated out of a play with its opposite." "Hawthorne and the Fate of Politics," *Essays in Literature* 11, no. 1 (1984): 95–96. This interesting if slight article offers a useful starting point for discussing the complexities of Hawthorne's political positions without special ideological pleading. Though I see Hawthorne's skepticism as more enabling than Brodhead does, I agree with his conclusion that Hawthorne feels "equally strongly, and in full awareness of their contradiction, two things: on the one hand, that the political is a sphere of delusion, an arena in which men and women act on other motives than they admit to for other ends than they forsee; and on the other, that to fail to be politically engaged is to sacrifice a dimension, to rob the self and its world of the fullest form of their reality" (102).

30. Arac, "The Politics of *The Scarlet Letter,*" 262, 263.

31. This is clearly the position of Scott E. Casper, who notes that "the trick here, of course, was that Hawthorne — anything but 'so little of a politician' — merely claimed to offer a new form of mediation, even as he presented an utterly conventional portrait." "The Two Lives of Franklin Pierce: Hawthorne, Political Culture, and the Literary Market," *American Literary History* 5, no. 2 (1993): 224.

32. Casper, for instance, paints Hawthorne as an apparently undisturbed, manipulative office seeker whose only concern was to secure a lucrative diplomatic post for his efforts. "For Hawthorne's biography to succeed in the political marketplace, both the candidate's 'authoring' (the assistance he provided the biographer) and the author's 'politicking' had to remain covert. Pierce was the author of his own fortunes but could not seem the author of his own biography. Hawthorne, the former custom-house official, had to declare political biography 'remote from his customary occupations'" ("Two Lives," 225). The strategies implied here may well have been in operation, but such a conspiratorial reading must ignore the fact that Hawthorne was not accustomed to writing political biographies, despite his patronage career. It is likewise difficult to see how the biography could be thought to "succeed" if, as Casper himself argues, it was both predictable in its politics and understood by its audience to be strictly partisan.

33. A passage in *The House of the Seven Gables* seems apropos: "So also, as regards the Judge Pyncheon of to-day, neither clergyman, nor legal critic, nor inscriber of tombstones, nor historian of general or local politics, would venture a word against this eminent person's sincerity as a christian, or respectability as a man, or integrity as a judge, or courage and faithfulness as the often-tried representative of his political party. But, besides these cold, formal, and empty words of the chisel that inscribes, the voice that speaks, and the pen that writes for the public eye and for distant time — and which inevitably lose much of their truth and freedom by the fatal consciousness of so doing — there were traditions about the ancestor, and private diurnal gossip about the Judge, remarkably accordant in their testimony" (122). See also Casper, "Two Lives," for a description of the partisan responses to the biography (213).

34. Casper, "Two Lives," 205.

35. Arlin Turner, *Hawthorne: A Biography* (1980), 372.

36. Quoted in ibid.

37. "You do not in the least shake me by telling me that I shall be supposed to disapprove of the war; for I always thought that it should have been avoided, although, since it

has broken out, I have longed for military success as much as any man or woman of the North. I agree with your friend Gen¹ Hitchcock, who thinks . . . that the war will only effect by a horrible convulsion the self-same end that might and would have been brought about by a gradual and peaceful change. . . . The best thing possible, as far as I can see, would be to effect a separation of the Union, giving us the West bank of the Mississippi, and a boundary line affording as much Southern soil as we can hope to digest into freedom in another century" (*CE*, 18:590–91).

38. According to Casper, "The candidate must have been pleased when he read his friend's biography in August, for contrary to the assertions of recent scholars, Hawthorne wrote an extremely traditional Democratic life that could offend nobody except abolitionists, who were unlikely to support Pierce anyway" ("Two Lives," 221).

39. "If recent revaluation has shown that *Uncle Tom's Cabin* is also art, may it not be equally important to show that *The Scarlet Letter* is also propaganda — *not* to change your life? I at once draw back from the extremity of this last suggestion." Arac, "The Politics of *The Scarlet Letter*," 251.

40. Turner, *Hawthorne*, 352.

41. Ibid., 687.

42. In his recasting of Hawthorne's "complexity" as a disguise for quietism, Cheyfitz inevitably dismisses these fictional devices as meaningless distractions from Hawthorne's "typical laissez-faire attitude toward social action" ("Irresistibleness of Great Literature," 546). To read the essay this way Cheyfitz is required not only to dismiss the obvious self-parody in the characterization of the "Peaceable Man" but also to see the editorial notes as no more than a cynical attack on the critics of the fictionalized narrator. Grace E. Smith does both, arguing that Hawthorne used the "Swiftian satirical technique" of the footnotes to attack Lincoln. " 'Chiefly About War-Matters': Hawthorne's Swift Judgment of Lincoln," *American Transcendental Quarterly* 15, no. 2 (2001): 150–61. Smith in particular argues that because Hawthorne was pressured by James T. Fields to remove passages critical of Lincoln, he could only have intended the footnotes (written subsequently) as an extension of what she sees as the Peaceable Man's pro-Democratic satire. I find that this reading oversimplifies the devices at work in the essay, ignoring the complex relationship between the Peaceable Man and Hawthorne while reducing the multivocal texture to the partisanship it playfully undermines.

43. Hawthorne to James T. Fields, May 23, 1862. Quoted in Turner, *Hawthorne*, 689.

44. Brodhead describes the incursion of fantasy into the essay: "What happens in 'Chiefly About War Matters' is that fantasy, a power at first thought to operate in isolation from historical reality, begins to work within and upon that reality. In consequence fantasy begins to serve as a means to historical vision, as an agent of historical prophecy." "Hawthorne and the Fate of Politics," 98.

CHAPTER 5 : Chiefly about Coverdale: *The Blithedale Romance*

1. Beverly Hume, "Restructuring the Case against Hawthorne's Coverdale," *Nineteenth-Century Fiction* 40, no. 4 (1986): 399.

2. Harvey L. Gable Jr., "Inappeasable Longings: Hawthorne, Romance, and the Disintegration of Coverdale's Self in *The Blithedale Romance*," *New England Quarterly* 67, no. 2 (1994): 258.

3. Richard Brodhead, *Hawthorne, Melville, and the Novel* (1976), 100.

4. Irving Howe, *Politics and the Novel* (1957), 170 and Edgar A. Dryden, *Nathaniel Hawthorne: The Poetics of Enchantment* (1977), 106.

5. Brodhead, *Hawthorne*, 108, and Charles Swann, *Nathaniel Hawthorne: Tradition and Revolution* (1991), 239.

6. I disagree in this respect with Kenneth Marc Harris, who argues that "Coverdale is neither a hypocrite nor a self-deceiver at the time he is actually telling his story, although he may now regard himself as having been either or both at the time of the events he is describing." *Hypocrisy and Self-Deception in Hawthorne's Fiction* (1988), 129.

7. See the discussion of Hilda from *The Marble Faun* in Part 3.

8. One precedent might have been his treatment of the equally eccentric Jones Very: "Hawthorne received it [Very's 'mission'] in the loveliest manner — with the same abandonment with which it was given — for he has that confidence in truth — which delivers him from all mean fears — and it was curious to see the respect of Very for *him* — and the reverence with which he treated his genius. There is a petulance about Hawthorne generally — when truth is taken out of the forms of nature . . . though the happiest and healthiest physical nature tempers it — so that it only expresses itself on that one occasion. But in this instance he repressed it and talked with him beautifully." Elizabeth Peabody to Emerson, December 3, 1838, quoted in Edwin Gittelman, *Jones Very: The Effective Years 1833–1840* (1967), 282–83.

9. Brenda Wineapple suggests that Bacon is less of a threat to Hawthorne than other women writers because she wrote nonfiction. *Hawthorne: A Life* (2003), 290. The example of Margaret Fuller might suggest otherwise. Indeed, Hawthorne's complex relationship with Fuller provides a balance of sorts both to his infamous attacks on "scribbling women" and to his more tolerant encounter with Bacon. Fuller clearly provoked equal measures of intimate sympathy and vengeful misreading. She is perhaps the one person with respect to whom Hawthorne had difficulty maintaining his own ethical distance. See Thomas Mitchell, *Hawthorne's Fuller Mystery* (1998).

10. Isaiah Berlin, *The Roots of Romanticism* (1999), 140.

11. "Hawthorne would neither cast Bacon off nor take credit when he secured a publishing contract [for her] from Parker and Son. Nor would he balk at assuming financial responsibility for her book, which Parker required as a condition. (To cover his investment, Hawthorne demanded that Ticknor bring out half the agreed-on copies — five hundred in all — doubtless hoping to offset inevitable losses.) He also consented to write a preface for the book, another crucial item for the negotiations with Parker." Wineapple, *Hawthorne*, 292–93.

CHAPTER 6: Forgetting the Secret

1. See Part Two for an extended discussion of this particular strain of Hawthorne criticism. Colacurcio explains: "A firm believer in 'intentionality,' I do not happen to believe that the thematic ambition of 'Young Goodman Brown' is more clearly revealed in the sayings of *Grandfather's Chair* than in the speculative drama of the tale itself. And if I have been guided 'backwards' in some of my expositions by the example of Miller — or, as our own historical plot has unfolded itself, of Edmund Morgan, or Bernard Bailyn, or Sacvan Bercovitch — the fact is that I have merely been emboldened by such modern commentary to notice that the texts Hawthorne read really do have the most fascinating

social and psychological implications, and that it is not at all absurd, therefore, to imagine Hawthorne as entering into significant dialogue with them." *The Province of Piety: Moral History in Hawthorne's Early Tales* (1984), 3.

2. Emily Miller Budick, *Fiction and Historical Consciousness: The American Romance Tradition* (1989), xii.

3. Ibid., 231.

4. I will touch on the potential resonances with Levinas's well-known "escape from history" below. While Hawthorne's notion of relinquishment might very well be less stringently organized by twentieth-century philosophical disputes, it shares a similar concern with the way totality (history as a closed system) obscures and eventually eliminates the romantic search for substance.

5. This is similarly true of *The Elixir of Life* manuscripts, which suggest that pretensions to aristocratic heritage are similar to, if not the same as, the attempt to prolong one's life unnaturally.

6. To Alan Trachtenberg, Holgrave "has nothing to hide, only something hidden within himself he needs to ferret out and overcome. The process of coming to himself, a process enacted in the historical time of the narrative, requires that he exorcize the ghost haunting the house, a ghost in the form of that very typological system that prophesies Maule to be Maule and Pyncheon Pyncheon and by which Holgrave-Maule must expose and exorcize the corrupt Judge." "Seeing and Believing: Hawthorne's Reflections on the Daguerreotype in *The House of the Seven Gables*," *American Literary History* 9, no. 3 (1997): 476.

7. Trachtenberg suggests something similar when he argues that "what the sun reveals through Holgrave's failed daguerreotype, then, is not that Judge's ineptitude in maintaining an affable facade before the camera but his alienation from his own 'character.' What the sun reveals, in short, is not just something to be glimpsed beneath a facade, something merely visible, but something to be interpreted. A visibility incomplete in itself, the daguerrean image Holgrave offers to Phoebe's eyes is in search of an explanatory narrative." "Seeing and Believing," 468.

8. For Trachtenberg, the patched Uncle Venner "is a walking theory of social change as slow accretion rather than sudden irruption or the imposition of rationalist utopia." "Seeing and Believing," 478.

9. Colin Davis, *Levinas: An Introduction* (1996), 48.

10. This particular theme has been discussed at length in Hawthorne criticism. See, for instance, "The Birthmark" and "Rappaccini's Daughter." What separates *The House of the Seven Gables* from these earlier works is Hawthorne's willingness to imagine a positive outcome to what is typically, for him, a tragic scenario.

11. For Susan L. Mizruchi, "History seems to vanish in the love scene of Phoebe and Holgrave. And the community as a whole leaves the memory of Judge Pyncheon to future historians." *The Power of Historical Knowledge: Narrating the Past in Hawthorne, James, and Dreiser* (1988), 101. In a similar vein, Michael Davitt Bell, while noting Hawthorne's general skepticism of progress, explains that "the emphasis [in the novel] is on change rather than repetition. . . . Instead of destroying Phoebe, Holgrave finally marries her. This marriage is clearly intended to be contrasted with the abortive relationship of Alice Pyncheon and Matthew Maule, one hundred years before. In this case, it would appear, progress is possible; the past *can be* escaped." *Hawthorne and the Historical Romance of New England* (1971), 216.

12. Stanley Cavell, *Pursuits of Happiness: The Hollywood Comedy of Remarriage* (1981), 261.

13. I disagree with T. Walter Herbert's characterization of Holgrave as a "fortune hunter" who deceives Phoebe into a relationship that will strip her of her property. In this reading, Holgrave's scene of relinquishment becomes a part of his larger strategy to display "the virtue that establishes his right to a fortune only in his relation to the woman from whom he filches it, and her love for him cleanses away the stain of his having dispossessed her." Of course, at the time of the scene in question, Holgrave has no reason to believe that marrying Phoebe would produce anything more than the historical irony of a Maule joining a Pyncheon. Unless we ascribe supernatural powers to Holgrave the mesmerist, he cannot have known that the Pyncheon heir would die at sea, leaving the estate to Hepzibah and Clifford. Herbert is correct in arguing that the domestic arrangements of the period ultimately grant Holgrave control of Phoebe's sudden wealth, and the book's ending does place their relationship within the reassuring patterns of nineteenth-century domestic bliss. This may reaffirm the existing order, but it does so only *after* the transformative, symbolic relinquishment of revenge. *Dearest Beloved: The Hawthornes and the Making of the Middle-Class Family* (1993), 102, 104.

14. This moment also recalls the scene between Elizabeth and the Reverend Mr. Hooper in "The Minister's Black Veil." There Hooper is incapable of the sort of surrender, the positive passivity, of Holgrave and proceeds instead with his own, Calvinist version of the secret history.

15. Emmanuel Levinas, *Totality and Infinity: An Essay on Exteriority*, trans. Alphonso Lingis (1969), 51.

16. Cavell, *Pursuits*, 103.

17. Richard Millington similarly claims that "the narrator's acknowledgment of Holgrave's integrity, by moving him from the margins of culture to its center, establishes 'reverence for another's individuality' — the obverse of the Pyncheon habit of treating people as property — as the ethical ground of community and the basis for demarcating a legitimate form of democratic authority. Holgrave's refusal to appropriate Phoebe breaks the relation between Maule and Pyncheon out of the determinism of gothic legend and reveals it to be part of a transformable history of human choices. And implicit in Holgrave's act is an ethics of private relationship that understands the violability of the self as the condition of human connection." *Practicing Romance: Narrative Form and Cultural Engagement in Hawthorne's Fiction* (1992), 140.

18. Henry David Thoreau, *Walden* (New York: Norton, 1992).

19. A typical reaction to the much-discussed conclusion might be Kenneth Marc Harris's notation of the novel's "escape from seriousness." See *Hypocrisy and Self-Deception in Hawthorne's Fiction* (1988), 140. Of those less directly critical of the conclusion, Charles Swann argues that Holgrave's sudden "conservatism" does not "mean that Hawthorne's historical narrative is itself conservative: rather it places Holgrave by interrogating the conventions of the 'happy ending.'" *Nathaniel Hawthorne: Tradition and Revolution* (1991), 116. And Susan Mizruchi claims that "the novel's final image of Alice Pyncheon's ascension, leaving the weight of past sins behind in the ancient mansion, signifies the victory of myth over history" (101).

20. As Budick argues, "The marriage of Phoebe and Holgrave is not a transcendental event redeeming the world and renewing Eden. It is simply the ceremony that ensures 'keeping house,' not the way the patriarchal and avaricious Judge or the spinster and

bachelor Pyncheons kept it, but the way it was meant to be kept, by a commitment to the process of life and death." *Fiction and Historical Consciousness,* 141. In a similar vein, Richard Brodhead argues that "the marriage at the end marks the healing of this split as well, so that when the survivors inherit Jaffrey's house and wealth they are not just expropriating the expropriators but truly coming into their own, into the wealth of whole selfhood." *Hawthorne, Melville, and the Novel* (1976), 87.

21. Herbert's charge that Hawthorne was engaged in a "confidence game . . . more insidious than a marketing strategy" that falsely represented the domestic relation misses the point. The question is not, as Herbert asks, what sort of life the "Maule household" will lead; it is to what extent the rupture in historical continuity can lead to a new understanding of the middle-class marriage. See *Dearest Beloved,* 106.

22. For Budick, "Holgrave and Phoebe are the heroes of Hawthorne's romance because they wed the past to present, moral responsibility to guilt, and Puritanism to Transcendentalism, not through some kind of ineffable process but through their own rigorous commitment to history and the world. The triumph they prophesy is not, as has often been assumed, a change in the course of history, erasing the perpetuity of evil announced at the beginning of the book. Rather, perceiving the intermingling of past and present as itself proffering a version of noble doubt, they ride the perpetuity of evil into a vision of an Eden in a fallen world." *Fiction and Historical Consciousness,* 135–36.

23. I am somewhat forced, in what follows, to use the words *American* and *European* in a widely generalized way to represent Hawthorne's own cultural and political oppositions. It should be understood that in so doing I am describing Hawthorne's attempt to define and clarify the opposition between democracy and what he took to be the political forms it opposed.

CHAPTER 7 : Exiled by History: *The Marble Faun*

1. See, for instance, David Howard, "The Fortunate Fall and Hawthorne's *The Marble Faun,*" in *Romantic Mythologies,* ed. Angus Fletcher (1967), 97–136. As Evan Carton explains, "Readers of *The Marble Faun,* from its first appearance, have most frequently understood it be an allegory of the Fall of Man." *The Marble Faun: Hawthorne's Transformations* (1992), 28.

2. "Unconverted men walk over the pit of hell on a rotten covering, and there are innumerable places in this covering so weak that they won't bear their weight, and these place are not seen." Jonathan Edwards, "Sinners in the Hands of an Angry God," in *A Jonathan Edwards Reader,* ed. John E. Smith, Harry S. Stout, and Kenneth P. Minkema (1995), 93. Blythe Ann Tellefsen has also commented on this allusion. See "'The Case with My Dear Native Land': Nathaniel Hawthorne's Vision of American in *The Marble Faun,*" *Nineteenth-Century Literature* 54, no. 4 (March 2000): 455–79.

3. "Mr. Mozier has now been seventeen years in Italy; and, after all this time, he is still intensely American in everything but the most external surfaces of his manners; scarcely Europeanized, or much modified, even in that. He is a native of Ohio, but had his early breeding in New York, and might — for any polish or refinement that I can discern in him — still be a country shopkeeper in the interior of New York or New England. How strange! For one expects to find the polish, the close grain, and white purity of marble, in the artist who works in that noble material; but, after all, he handles clay, and judging from the specimens I have seen here, is apt to be clay, not of the finest, himself" (*CE,* 14:154).

4. As Joel Porte notes, "Although Hawthorne is here praising Hilda's humility, he might with deeper justification have complimented her instinctive shrewdness in choosing a métier which excuses her from putting herself forward in a far more important sense. Original art, as in Miriam's case, demands as exposure of the secret self that Hilda is not prepared to make." *The Romance in America: Studies in Cooper, Poe, Hawthorne, Melville, and James* (1969), 142.

5. In this respect I agree with Charles Swann: "And the very form that Hawthorne's development of the Fortunate Fall story takes necessarily commits him to a positive valuation of it. This is to argue against what seem to have been common critical attitudes." *Nathaniel Hawthorne: Tradition and Revolution* (1991), 199.

6. "If I had had a murder on my conscience or any other great sin, I think I should have been inclined to kneel down there, and pour it into the safe secrecy of the confessional. What an institution it is! Man needs it so, that it seems as if God must have ordained it. This popish religion certainly does apply itself most closely and comfortably to human occasions; and I cannot but think that a great many people find their spiritual advantage in it, who would find none at all in our formless mode of worship" (*CE*, 14:59–60).

EPILOGUE: *The Elixir of Life*

1. Ralph Waldo Emerson, *Emerson in His Journals* (1982), 522.

2. See Clark Davis, *After the Whale: Melville in the Wake of Moby-Dick* (1995), 146. Assuming the accuracy of the traditional association of Hawthorne with *Clarel*'s Vine, we can begin to hear a critical edge emerging in Melville's attitude toward Hawthorne: "In fact, it is precisely this sort of teasing irony that finally characterizes Vine, for though he refuses dialectical definition, he does so from an apparent hopelessness that considers any statement or action ultimately useless. . . . Ultimately incapable of self-investigation, Vine is constructed solely of attitudes and strategies that no member of the traveling party can apparently penetrate."

Bibliography

Abel, Darrel. *The Moral Picturesque: Studies in Hawthorne's Fiction.* West Lafayette, IN: Purdue University Press, 1988.

Althusser, Louis. *Lenin and Philosophy and Other Essays.* Trans. Ben Brewster. London: New Left Books, 1971.

Arac, Jonathan. "The Politics of *The Scarlet Letter.*" In *Ideology and Classic American Literature,* edited by Myra Jehlen and Sacvan Bercovitch, 247–66. Cambridge: Cambridge University Press, 1986.

Bate, Walter Jackson. *John Keats.* Cambridge: Harvard University Press, 1963.

Bauerlein, Mark. *Literary Criticism: An Autopsy.* Philadelphia: University of Pennsylvania Press, 1997.

Bell, Michael Davitt. *Hawthorne and the Historical Romance of New England.* Princeton, NJ: Princeton University Press, 1971.

Bellis, Peter J. "Representing Dissent: Hawthorne and the Drama of Revolt." *ESQ: A Journal of the American Renaissance* 41, no. 2 (1995): 97–119.

———. *Writing Revolution: Aesthetics and Politics in Hawthorne, Whitman, and Thoreau.* Athens: University of Georgia Press, 2003.

Bercovitch, Sacvan. "Emerson, Individualism, and the Ambiguities of Dissent." In *Ralph Waldo Emerson: A Collection of Critical Essays,* edited by Laurence Buell, 101–29. Englewood Cliffs, NJ: Prentice-Hall, 1993.

———. "Hawthorne's A-morality of Compromise." *Representations* 24 (Fall 1988): 1–27.

———. *The Office of "The Scarlet Letter."* Baltimore: Johns Hopkins University Press, 1991.

———. *The Rites of Assent.* London: Routledge, 1992.

Berlin, Isaiah. *Isaiah Berlin: The Proper Study of Mankind.* New York: Farrar, Straus & Giroux, 1998.

———. *The Roots of Romanticism.* Princeton, NJ: Princeton University Press, 1999.

Brodhead, Richard. *Cultures of Letters: Scenes of Reading and Writing in Nineteenth-Century America.* Chicago: University of Chicago Press, 1993.

———. "Hawthorne and the Fate of Politics." *Essays in Literature* 11, no. 1 (Spring 1984): 95–103.

———. *Hawthorne, Melville, and the Novel.* Chicago: University of Chicago Press, 1976.

———. *The School of Hawthorne.* New York: Oxford University Press, 1986.

Bruns, Gerald. *Heidegger's Estrangements: Language, Truth, and Poetry in the Later Writings.* New Haven, CT: Yale University Press, 1989.

———. *Tragic Thoughts at the End of Philosophy: Language, Literature, and Ethical Theory.* Evanston, IL: Northwestern University Press, 1999.

Budick, Emily Miller. *Fiction and Historical Consciousness: The American Romance Tradition.* New Haven, CT: Yale University Press, 1989.

———. "Sacvan Bercovitch, Stanley Cavell, and the Romance Theory of American Fiction." *PMLA* 107 (1992): 78–91.

Carton, Evan. *The Marble Faun: Hawthorne's Transformations.* New York: Twayne, 1992.

———. *The Rhetoric of American Romance: Dialectic and Identity in Emerson, Dickinson, Poe, and Hawthorne.* Baltimore: Johns Hopkins University Press, 1985.

Casper, Scott E. "The Two Lives of Franklin Pierce: Hawthorne, Political Culture, and the Literary Market." *American Literary History* 5, no. 2 (1993): 203–30.

Cavell, Stanley. *The Claim to Reason: Wittgenstein, Skepticism, Morality, and Tragedy.* New York: Oxford University Press, 1979.

———. *Conditions Handsome and Unhandsome: The Constitution of Emersonian Perfectionism.* Chicago: University of Chicago Press, 1989.

———. *Pursuits of Happiness: The Hollywood Comedy of Remarriage.* Cambridge: Harvard University Press, 1981.

———. *The Senses of Walden: An Expanded Edition.* San Francisco: North Point Press, 1981.

Chase, Richard. *The American Novel and Its Tradition.* New York: Doubleday, 1957.

Cheyfitz, Eric. "The Irresistibleness of Great Literature: Reconstructing Hawthorne's Politics." *American Literary History* 6, no. 3 (Fall 1994): 539–58.

Colacurcio, Michael. *The Province of Piety: Moral History in Hawthorne's Early Tales.* Cambridge: Harvard University Press, 1984.

Colatrella, Carol. "Bercovitch's Paradox: Critical Dissent, Marginality, and the Example of Melville." In *Cohesion and Dissent in America,* edited by Carol Colatrella and Joseph Alkana, 229–50. Albany: State University of New York Press, 1994.

Coleridge, Samuel Taylor. *The Collected Works of Samuel Taylor Coleridge.* Princeton, NJ: Princeton University Press, 1983.

Critchley, Simon. *Ethics, Politics, Subjectivity: Essays on Derrida, Levinas, and Contemporary French Thought.* London: Verso, 1999.

Daly, Robert. " 'We Really Have No Country at All': Hawthorne's Reoccupations of History." *Arachne* 3, no. 1 (1996): 66–88.

Dasenbrock, Reed Way. *Truth and Consequences: Intentions, Conventions, and the New Thematics.* University Park: Pennsylvania State University Press, 2001.

Dauber, Kenneth. *The Idea of Authorship in America: Democratic Poetics from Franklin to Melville.* Madison: University of Wisconsin Press, 1990.

———. "Ordinary Language Criticism: A Manifesto." *Arizona Quarterly* 53 (1997): 123–39.

Davis, Clark. *After the Whale: Melville in the Wake of Moby-Dick.* Tuscaloosa: University of Alabama Press, 1995.

Davis, Colin. *Levinas: An Introduction.* South Bend, IN: Notre Dame University Press, 1996.

Davis, Todd F. and Kenneth Womack. *Mapping the Ethical Turn: A Reader in Ethics, Culture, and Literary Theory.* Charlottesville: University Press of Virginia, 2001.

DeMan, Paul. "Introduction." In *Selected Poetry of John Keats,* edited by Paul DeMan. New York: Signet, 1966.

Dickstein, Morris. "Literary Theory and Historical Understanding." *Chronicle of Higher Education,* May 23, 2003.

Dryden, Edgar A. *Melville's Thematics of Form: The Great Art of Telling the Truth*. Baltimore: Johns Hopkins University Press, 1968.

———. *Nathaniel Hawthorne: The Poetics of Enchantment*. Ithaca, NY: Cornell University Press, 1977.

———. "Through a Glass Darkly: 'The Minister's Black Veil' as a Parable." In *New Essays on Hawthorne's Major Tales*, edited by Millicent Bell, 133–51. New York: Cambridge University Press, 1933.

Eagleton, Terry. *Ideology: An Introduction*. London: Verso, 1991.

Edel, Leon. *Henry James: The Untried Years*. New York: Lippincott, 1953.

Edwards, Jonathan. *A Jonathan Edwards Reader*. Ed. John E. Smith, Harry S. Stout, and Kenneth P. Minkema. New Haven, CT: Yale University Press, 1995.

Emerson, Ralph Waldo. *Emerson in His Journals*. Cambridge: Harvard University Press, 1982.

———. *Selections from Ralph Waldo Emerson*. Ed. Stephen E. Whicher. Boston: Houghton Mifflin, 1960.

Felman, Shoshona. *Literature and Psychoanalysis: The Question of Reading — Otherwise*. Baltimore: Johns Hopkins University Press, 1982.

Gable, Harvey L., Jr. "Inappeasable Longings: Hawthorne, Romance, and the Disintegration of Coverdale's Self in *The Blithedale Romance*." *New England Quarterly* 67, no. 2 (1994): 257–77.

Gittelman, Edwin. *Jones Very: The Effective Years, 1833–1840*. New York: Columbia University Press, 1967.

Gollin, Rita K. *Portraits of Nathaniel Hawthorne: An Iconography*. DeKalb: Northern Illinois University Press, 1983.

Good, Graham. *Humanism Betrayed: Theory, Ideology, and Culture in the Contemporary University*. Montreal: McGill-Queen's University Press, 2001.

Goodman, Russell. *American Philosophy and the Romantic Tradition*. Cambridge: Cambridge University Press, 1990.

Graff, Gerald. "American Criticism Left and Right." In Jehlen and Bercovitch, *Ideology*, 91–121.

Gross, Seymour L. "Hawthorne versus Melville." *Bucknell Review* 14, no. 3 (Dec. 1966): 89–109.

Harris, Kenneth Marc. *Hypocrisy and Self-Deception in Hawthorne's Fiction*. Charlottesville: University Press of Virginia, 1988.

Harris, Wendell V. *Literary Meaning: Reclaiming the Study of Literature*. New York: New York University Press, 1996.

Hawthorne, Nathaniel. *The Centenary Edition of the Works of Nathaniel Hawthorne*. Ed. William Charvat, Roy Harvey Pearce, and Claude M. Simpson. 23 vols. Columbus: Ohio State University Press, 1962–.

Heidegger, Martin. *Poetry, Language, Thought*. Trans. Albert Hofstadter. New York: Harper & Row, 1971.

Herbert, T. Walter. *Dearest Beloved: The Hawthornes and the Making of the Middle-Class Family*. Berkeley: University of California Press, 1993.

Hoffman, Elizabeth Aycock. "Political Power in *The Scarlet Letter*." In *The Critical Response to Nathaniel Hawthorne's The Scarlet Letter*, edited by Gary Scharnhorst, 202–19. New York: Greenwood Press, 1992.

Howard, David. "The Fortunate Fall and Hawthorne's *The Marble Faun*." In *Romantic Mythologies*, edited by Angus Fletcher, 97–136. New York: Barnes & Noble, 1967.

Howe, Irving. *Politics and the Novel*. New York: Horizon Press, 1957.

Hume, Beverly. "Restructuring the Case against Hawthorne's Coverdale." *Nineteenth-Century Fiction* 40, no. 4 (1986): 387–99.

James, William. *Pragmatism*. 1907; New York: Dover, 1995.

Jehlen, Myra, and Sacvan Bercovitch, eds. *Ideology and Classic American Literature*. Cambridge: Cambridge University Press, 1986.

Johnston, Paul K. "Killing the Spirit: Anne Hutchinson and the Office of the Scarlet Letter." *Nathaniel Hawthorne Review* 22, no.1 (1996): 26–35.

Kazin, Alfred. *A Lifetime Burning in Every Moment: From the Journals of Alfred Kazin*. New York: HarperCollins, 1996.

———. *Writing Was Everything*. Cambridge: Harvard University Press, 1995.

Keats, John. *The Poetical Works and Other Writings of John Keats*. Ed. H. Buxton Forman. 8 vols. New York: Phaeton, 1970.

Kermode, Frank. *An Appetite for Poetry*. Cambridge: Harvard University Press, 1989.

Krupnick, Mark. "Why Are English Departments Still Fighting the Culture Wars?" *Chronicle of Higher Education*, Sept. 20, 2002.

Lee, A. Robert. *Nathaniel Hawthorne: New Critical Essays*. London: Vision Press, 1982.

Levinas, Emmanuel. *The Levinas Reader*. Ed. Seán Hand. Cambridge: Basil Blackwell, 1989.

———. *Of God Who Comes to Mind*. Trans. Bettina Bergo. Stanford: Stanford University Press, 1998.

———. *Totality and Infinity: An Essay on Exteriority*. Trans. Alphonso Lingis. Pittsburgh: Duquesne University Press, 1969.

Lewis, R. W. B. *Trials of the Word: Essays in American Literature and the Humanistic Tradition*. New Haven, CT: Yale University Press, 1965.

Leyda, Jay. *The Melville Log: A Documentary Life of Herman Melville, 1819–1891*. New York: Gordian Press, 1969.

Matthiessen, F. O. *American Renaissance: Art and Expression in the Age of Emerson and Whitman*. Oxford: Oxford University Press, 1941.

Mellow, James R. *Nathaniel Hawthorne in His Times*. Baltimore: Johns Hopkins University Press, 1993.

Melville, Herman. *The Writings of Herman Melville*. Vol. 14, *Correspondence*. Ed. Harrison Hayford, Hershel Parker, and G. Thomas Tanselle. Evanston, IL: Northwestern University Press; Chicago: Newberry Library, 1993.

———. "Hawthorne and His Mosses." In *The Writings of Herman Melville*. Vol. 9, *Piazza Tales and Other Prose Pieces, 1839–1860*. Ed. Harrison Hayford, Hershel Parker, and G. Thomas Tanselle. Evanston, IL: Northwestern University Press; Chicago: Newberry Library, 1987.

Milder, Robert. "*The Scarlet Letter* and Its Discontents." *Nathaniel Hawthorne Review* 22, no.1 (1996): 9–25.

Miller, Edwin Haviland. *Melville*. New York: Braziller, 1975.

Miller, J. Hillis. *Hawthorne and History: Defacing It*. Cambridge: Basil Blackwell, 1991.

Millington, Richard. "*The Office of The Scarlet Letter*: An 'Inside Narrative'?" *Nathaniel Hawthorne Review* 22, no.1 (Spring 1996): 1–8.

————. *Practicing Romance: Narrative Form and Cultural Engagement in Hawthorne's Fiction.* Princeton, NJ: Princeton University Press, 1992.

Mitchell, Thomas R. *Hawthorne's Fuller Mystery.* Amherst: University of Massachusetts Press, 1998.

Mizruchi, Susan L. *The Power of Historical Knowledge: Narrating the Past in Hawthorne, James, and Dreiser.* Princeton, NJ: Princeton University Press, 1988.

Nehamas, Alexander. "An Essay on Beauty and Judgement." *Threepenny Review* 80 (Winter 2000).

New, Melvyn, ed. *In Proximity: Emmanuel Levinas and the Eighteenth Century.* Lubock: Texas Tech University Press, 2001.

Newman, Lea Bertani Vozar. "One-Hundred-Fifty Years of Looking At, Into, Through, Behind, Beyond, and Around 'The Minister's Black Veil.'" *Nathaniel Hawthorne Review* 13, no. 2 (1987): 5–12.

Nussbaum, Martha. *Love's Knowledge: Essays on Philosophy and Literature.* New York: Oxford University Press, 1990.

Parker, Hershel. *Herman Melville: A Biography.* Vol. 1, *1819–1851.* Baltimore: Johns Hopkins University Press, 1996.

Parlej, Piotr. *The Romantic Theory of the Novel: Genre and Reflection in Cervantes, Melville, Flaubert, Joyce, and Kafka.* Baton Rouge: Louisiana State University Press, 1997.

Pease, Donald. "Melville and Cultural Persuasion." In Jehlen and Bercovitch, *Ideology,* 384–417.

————. "New Americanists: Revisionist Interventions into the Canon." *boundary* 2, 17, no. 1 (Spring 1990): 1–37.

Peperzak, Adriann. "Some Remarks on Hegel, Kant, and Levinas." In *Face to Face with Levinas,* edited by Richard A. Cohen, 205–17. Albany: State University of New York Press, 1986.

Person, Leland S., Jr. "*The Scarlet Letter* and the Myth of the Divine Child." *American Transcendental Quarterly* 44 (Fall 1979): 295–309.

Pfister, Joel. *The Production of Personal Life: Class, Gender, and the Psychological in Hawthorne's Fiction.* Stanford: Stanford University Press, 1991.

Porte, Joel. *The Romance in America: Studies in Cooper, Poe, Hawthorne, Melville, and James.* Middletown, CT: Wesleyan University Press, 1969.

Rancière, Jacques. "On the Theory of Ideology — Althusser's Politics." In *Ideology,* edited by Terry Eagleton, 141–61. London: Longman, 1994.

Reynolds, David. *Walt Whitman's America: A Cultural Biography.* New York: Knopf, 1995.

Reynolds, Larry J. "*The Scarlet Letter* and Revolutions Abroad." *American Literature* 77 (1985): 44–67.

————, ed. *A Historical Guide to Nathaniel Hawthorne.* Oxford: Oxford University Press, 2001.

Robbins, Jill. *Altered Reading: Levinas and Literature.* Chicago: University of Chicago Press, 1999.

Rowe, John Carlos. "The Internal Conflict of Romantic Narrative: Hegel's *Phenomenology* and Hawthorne's *The Scarlet Letter.*" *Modern Language Notes* 95 (1980): 1203–31.

Rowlandson, Mary. "The Sovereignty and Goodness of God." In *Puritans among the Indians: Accounts of Captivity and Redemption, 1676–1724,* edited by Alden T. Vaughn and Edward W. Clark, 31–75. Cambridge: Belknap Press of Harvard University Press, 1981.

Scary, Elaine. *On Beauty and Being Just*. Princeton, NJ: Princeton University Press, 1999.

Seelye, John D. "The Structure of Encounter: Melville's Review of Hawthorne's *Mosses.*" In *Melville and Hawthorne in the Berkshires: A Symposium*, edited by Howard P. Vincent, 63–69. Kent: Kent State University Press, 1968.

Smith, Grace E. " 'Chiefly about War-Matters': Hawthorne's Swift Judgment of Lincoln." *American Transcendental Quarterly* 15, no. 2 (June 2001): 150–61.

Smith, Henry Nash. "Symbol and Idea in *Virgin Land.*" In Jehlen and Bercovitch, *Ideology*, 21–35.

Stern, Milton R. *Contexts for Hawthorne: The Marble Faun and the Politics of Openness and Closure in American Literature*. Urbana: University of Illinois Press, 1991.

Swann, Charles. *Nathaniel Hawthorne: Tradition and Revolution*. Cambridge: Cambridge University Press, 1991.

Tellefsen, Blythe Ann. " 'The Case with My Dear Native Land': Nathaniel Hawthorne's Vision of America in *The Marble Faun.*" *Nineteenth-Century Literature* 54, no. 4 (March 2000): 455–79.

Thomas, Brook. "Citizen Hester: *The Scarlet Letter* as Civic Myth." *American Literary History* 13, no. 2 (Summer 2001): 181–211.

———. *Cross-examinations of Law and Literature: Cooper, Hawthorne, Stowe, and Melville*. Cambridge: Cambridge University Press, 1987.

Thompson, G. R., and Eric Carl Link. *Neutral Ground: New Traditionalism and the American Romance Controversy*. Baton Rouge: Louisiana State University Press, 1999.

Thoreau, Henry David. *The Writings of Henry D. Thoreau*. Princeton, NJ: Princeton University Press, 1971.

Tompkins, Jane. *Sensational Designs: The Cultural Work of American Fiction, 1790–1860*. New York: Oxford University Press, 1985.

Trachtenberg, Alan. "Seeing and Believing: Hawthorne's Reflections on the Daguerreotype in *The House of the Seven Gables.*" *American Literary History* 9, no. 3 (Fall 1997): 460–81.

Turner, Arlin. *Nathaniel Hawthorne: A Biography*. New York: Oxford University Press, 1980.

Wall, Thomas Carl. *Radical Passivity: Levinas, Blanchot, and Agamben*. Albany: State University of New York Press, 1999.

Wallen, Jeffrey. *Closed Encounters: Literary Politics and Public Culture*. Minneapolis: University of Minnesota Press, 1998.

Williams, Raymond. *Marxism and Literature*. Oxford: Oxford University Press, 1977.

Wineapple, Brenda. *Hawthorne: A Life*. New York: Alfred A. Knopf, 2003.

Ziarek, Krzysztof. *Inflected Language: Toward a Hermeneutics of Nearness: Heidegger, Levinas, Stevens, Celan*. Albany: State University of New York Press, 1994.

Index